T0290536

GLASS WALLS

GLASS WALLS

Shattering the
Six Gender Bias Barriers
Still Holding Women Back at Work

AMY DIEHL AND LEANNE M. DZUBINSKI

ROWMAN & LITTLEFIELD
Lanham • Boulder • New York • London

Published by Rowman & Littlefield
An imprint of The Rowman & Littlefield Publishing Group, Inc.
4501 Forbes Boulevard, Suite 200, Lanham, Maryland 20706
www.rowman.com

86-90 Paul Street, London EC2A 4NE

British Library Cataloguing in Publication Information Available

Library of Congress Cataloging-in-Publication Data

Names: Diehl, Amy, author. | Dzubinski, Leanne M., author.
Title: Glass walls : shattering the six gender bias barriers still holding
    women back at work / Amy Diehl and Leanne M. Dzubinski.
Description: Lanham, Maryland : Rowman & Littlefield, [2023] | Includes
    bibliographical references and index.
Identifiers: LCCN 2022055843 (print) | LCCN 2022055844 (ebook) | ISBN
    9781538170960 (cloth) | ISBN 9781538170977 (ebook)
Subjects: LCSH: Sex discrimination in employment. | Women—Employment.
    | Sex discrimination against women.
Classification: LCC HD6060 .D54 2023 (print) | LCC HD6060 (ebook) |
    DDC 331.4/133—dc23/eng/20230227
LC record available at https://lccn.loc.gov/2022055843
LC ebook record available at https://lccn.loc.gov/2022055844

♾™ The paper used in this publication meets the minimum requirements of
American National Standard for Information Sciences—Permanence of Paper
for Printed Library Materials, ANSI/NISO Z39.48-1992.

CONTENTS

PREFACE

In May 2014, a year after Amy earned her PhD, she boarded a flight to Utah. She was headed to a three-day conference meant to advance research on women in leadership. Sometime between takeoff and landing, Amy developed laryngitis and lost her voice. On the van ride to the hotel, she strained to communicate instructions to the driver. Upon arriving, she sought out the conference organizer to—as best she could—apologize and explain that she was too sick to attend the night's activities. But the organizer encouraged her to come—this was pre-COVID-19—since the evening session would be foundational for the event. Amy skipped the dinner but came just in time to mime to her working group members that she had lost her voice and to listen to the evening's talk. Hopeful her illness would resolve quickly, Amy drank lots of tea and went to bed. But she woke up to no voice. Deciding to make the best of it, she attended the day's events. Her working group included Dr. Leanne Dzubinski. While the group had a lively discussion of bias impacting women in leadership, Amy could only listen. Wanting to speak up but not being able was frustrating and anxiety invoking. Was this whole conference and this whole chance to move gender bias research forward going to be a waste? She penned an introduction of herself and gave it to a group member to read. That was as much as she accomplished on conference day two.

All during the conference Leanne had been wanting to hear about Amy's research. Leanne was one-year post PhD completion and had just finished her first year as a professor. The little bits Amy was able to communicate, and her nods of interest and agreement as various ideas were discussed in the work group, made Leanne think that further conversations might be interesting. She wanted to hear more and compare notes!

Yet Amy's laryngitis seemed like an impossible obstacle. On the final day, when Amy could finally talk a bit, Leanne was delighted to realize they would be able to compare notes after all. Leaving from the same airport, we had several hours before our respective flights. So, we used that time to catch up on all the things we hadn't been able to discuss during the conference.

While Amy had researched women in the higher education industry, Leanne's dissertation had focused on challenges of women leaders in faith-based nonprofits. Sharing stories from our respective studies, we realized that the participants' challenges were strangely similar. The higher education leaders felt they had to over prepare and work twice as hard as men to succeed. So did the faith-based leaders. Both groups complained of being constrained with when and how they communicated. Some faith-based leaders were placed in roles that had a high risk of failure, as were some higher education leaders. We quickly came to suspect that these challenges weren't specific to the industry or sector. In fact, these two industries couldn't be more different; higher education is thought to be progressive and liberal, while religion is quite conservative. Yet the similarity of the women's challenges was striking. Perhaps what was pertinent wasn't the industry, sector, profession, or specific role. Perhaps these women faced challenges because they were women in leadership.

Amy's bout of laryngitis could have easily prevented her and Leanne's research partnership from happening. Fortunately, it did not. During the past eight years, we have worked to understand the complex and insidious phenomenon of gender bias. Our goal has been to comprehensively identify the aspects of bias impacting women in the workplace and then to develop strategies to root them out. As we came to discover, some biased behaviors didn't have names. When things don't have names, it is as though they don't exist. People have no easy way to talk about them, and searching the Internet for solutions is next to impossible. We coined terms for specific types of bias where none existed. With the help of colleagues, Drs. Amber Stephenson and David Wang, we became the first researchers to identify the structure of gender bias—the six core barriers that form the basis for this book.[1] We've created a tool to measure gender bias, published in journals, book chapters, and mass media, shared our knowledge on social media and as organizational consultants, and spoken about gender bias via presentations, podcasts, and interviews. While we have been successful in getting the message out, the length and depth at which we can share our knowledge in those outlets are necessarily limited. Our goal from the beginning has been to identify the structure and aspects of gender bias thoroughly and comprehensively. This book is the outcome of our work. We detail the six primary gender bias barriers, including their subcomponents, using examples from both prominent and everyday women. We share solutions for organizational leaders and workplace allies to root out bias, and we offer strategies for individual women to navigate it. While we recognize that there may be yet-unknown aspects and manifestations of bias—especially as the world continues to change—this book is the most comprehensive treatise to date on the structure of and solutions for workplace gender bias.

On that day in the airport, we discussed how we both considered ourselves to be *feminists*—believing in women's equality—but felt that the term "feminist" had become demonized in some circles, especially conservative ones. We also held an expansive perspective of equality that included all people. Hence, that day, we coined a new term: *equalist*—the belief that "all human beings regardless of any socially defined identity category are of equal value and deserve equal access, treatment, rights, opportunity, and freedom in all realms of society."[2] As our research thus far has been primarily through the lens of women, women's perceptions and experiences are foregrounded in this book. While we often discuss "women" and "men," we recognize that gender is a socially constructed non-fixed identity category. In addition, every person has other identity categories, such as race, ethnicity, sexual orientation, religion, ability, parental status, and more. As the study of intersectionality informs us, some identity categories carry privilege and others do not.[3] While this book focuses on the gender identity category of women, we recognize that other identity categories intersect with and influence women's experiences. Our goal is to tease out the commonalities of experience within the category of gender, while remaining true to our identification as feminists and equalists, which is that *all people* have equal value.

We discovered the six core gender bias barriers covered in this book using a tool called factor analysis during the development of the Gender Bias Scale for Women Leaders, working with Drs. Stephenson and Wang.[4] The data we present come from several sources: interviews with 38 women leaders from our respective dissertations, open-ended and statistical survey data from 1,606 women professionals gathered during the creation of the Gender Bias Scale (in conjunction with Stephenson), thousands of public social media posts and published articles, and our own stories.[5] Names have been changed in some stories involving nonpublic individuals to protect their privacy. Throughout this book we refer to named individuals with doctorates using their *Dr.* titles, but we refer to ourselves with our first names (Amy and Leanne), even though we each have a PhD. As you will read, omitting professional titles for women when using them for men is a common form of gender bias, known as untitling (a term we coined). We have chosen to use first names for ourselves as we consider you, the reader, to be a colleague and friend.

Whether you are an organizational leader, an ally, or an individual woman, it is our hope that you will learn how to both recognize gender bias and eliminate it. If you are the person experiencing bias, recognize that it is not your responsibility to eliminate this pervasive problem on your own—nor would that be possible. You may have read other books that suggest you lean in, be more confident and assertive, dress a certain way, engage in certain activities with the guys, and other ways that you can succeed in a male-normed workplace. In this book we do not do that. We will not tell you how to act, how to dress, or suggest that you change what is unique about you. Gender bias is a systemic issue embedded in workplace cultures created by men for men to suit men's lifestyles and needs—but not women's. Shattering gender bias requires all of us working together, starting with those responsible for our institutions and including those who work in them. It's not the women who must change, it is the organizational culture.

Drs. Amy Diehl and Leanne Dzubinski
October 2022

THE SIX GENDER BIAS BARRIERS

G ender bias is a pervasive, invisible, and harmful bias that demeans, discourages, and disadvantages women at work. By and large, men have built institutions to serve themselves, with their own needs and life patterns in mind. While organizations often appear to be gender neutral, bias against women is embedded into daily functions. Structures of work, patterns of interaction, and even organizational values reflect male norms.[1] The harms of workplace gender bias to society are huge. Bias prevents women from fully contributing at work and keeps them out of positions of influence. Not only does this limit potential corporate earnings and organizational effectiveness, but it also restricts society's ability to solve its most pressing problems.

Consider the story of biochemist Dr. Katalin Karikó. While Karikó researched messenger RNA (mRNA) for decades, her efforts were repeatedly dismissed and devalued. During one lab meeting, Karikó made a pointed but accurate criticism of a well-funded professor's data and "was asked not to come back."[2] She applied for numerous grants but was rejected; colleagues and bosses doubted her. Venture capitalists initially promised money but then refused to return her phone calls. Since she lacked grant funding, in 1995 the University of Pennsylvania demoted her out of her tenure-track position and gave her a substantial pay cut— a salary that was lower than a technician who worked alongside her.[3] Normally, university faculty who do not receive tenure leave. Karikó stayed, but thought, "Maybe I'm not good enough, not smart enough."[4] Working all the time and having little money for vacations or even childcare, she struggled with balancing family life. Her young daughter learned to "get up, get dressed, and take care of herself."[5] However, Karikó persisted with her research and in 2005 began publishing

1

groundbreaking articles on mRNA therapy.[6] In 2013, she left the university when it refused to reinstate her to a tenure-track position telling her that she "was not of faculty quality."[7] She took a senior vice president role at BioNTech, which later partnered with Pfizer to make the first COVID-19 vaccine based on her breakthrough mRNA technology. When the university released its first promo video about the COVID-19 vaccine in early 2021, it focused on her male research partner, mentioning Karikó only in passing. Karikó's tenacity brought forth a technology that is saving the world from the first large-scale deadly pandemic in more than a hundred years. Yet her employer put up roadblocks to her work and did not give proper credit for her accomplishments.[8]

For every story like Dr. Karikó's, there may be millions of untold stories of women who never made their full potential due to gender bias and discrimination, such as a sixty-six-year-old former scientist. Bias started when this former scientist was a student and persisted throughout her career. Her graduate school interviewer asked what kind of birth control she used, so as not to "waste" a spot on someone who might get pregnant. Through her career as a research scientist, she spoke up in meetings only to be ignored. Then when a man said the same thing, people listened. When her grant proposal was fully funded on the first attempt—an extremely rare achievement—she continued to work in another scientist's lab. Luckily, a women's group formed at her institution and discovered that every man who got a grant—and even one who hadn't—immediately got his own lab. When the women's group made a fuss, this scientist finally got her own lab. But she left the field in 1995, at the same time as research was published showing that the chances of a woman going beyond her level were essentially nil. She went into scientific publishing and then back to school for textile design. As she said, "Got paid less. Enjoyed life more. Until I saw the effect on my social security check." Gender bias led to an early end to her scientific career, forfeiting both research for societal good and her own income. Just think what breakthroughs, what conveniences, what modernizations the world is missing due to organizations devaluing or even prohibiting women's work. We can only imagine. Gender bias harms absolutely everyone in society.

We (Amy and Leanne) have personally experienced gender bias. As a straight-A student, Amy never felt held back in school. When she entered the world of work, however, strange things started happening. As a young IT staffer, her job intersected frequently with her department's administrative assistant, a woman who had been in the role for many years. Amy's goal was to get her work done, but when she asked the administrative assistant for help, she got negative attitudes and roadblocks. The assistant was responsible for purchasing new computers. Amy had the most outdated computer, but the assistant refused to order a new one, while replacing those of her male counterparts. Amy's male colleagues saw the differential treatment, asking, "What did you do to her?" Amy tried to get in the assistant's good graces. She spent hours in the assistant's office talking about the assistant's interests, vacations, and opinions. Anything to make it easier for Amy to get her job done. Though Amy thought the two were on friendly terms, when Amy needed help, she still got resistance from the assistant.

Amy was treated differently in other ways. To learn how to lead, Amy had watched her boss and other male leaders. In meetings when there was no consensus, her boss made the decision, and the group accepted it. Her boss's authoritative approach seemed to add to his level of respect. At one point, Amy was promoted into a new role, in charge of a team that her male boss had previously led. But when Amy, as the new supervisor, tried the same decisive approach, she found she had lost points with the team. They were clearly unhappy with Amy and the decision. But Amy didn't understand why, as her leadership behavior mirrored that of her male boss. She took it personally, thinking she must be at fault.

Amy encountered other diminishing treatment. At work one day, a male colleague she was dating at the time told her that she would *never* be a vice president (a position to which she openly aspired). Similarly, her male boss told her that while she was a "manager," she was not a leader. Later her boss was promoted to a new role, and the organizational structure was changed such that they both reported to her boss's supervisor. Just before the reporting change was made official, Amy mentioned to her boss that they would be peers. He responded, "You'll never be my peer." Why did these men try to keep Amy in a subordinate position? As we will show in the chapters that follow, they valued Amy in a supportive role, consistent with feminine stereotypes, but viewed her as competition in the workplace and tried to keep her in her place.

Leanne has also encountered her share of bias. Like Amy, she was a straight-A student and loved school. But things shifted when she went to seminary where she was frequently the only woman in class. Male students mostly kept their distance from her, and professors did nothing to encourage her academic career. After graduation, she spent years working for a faith-based nonprofit alongside her husband where her work was literally invisible—whatever she did went onto her husband's report. Leadership roles weren't available to her, and she was expected to juggle home and ministry responsibilities all on her own. Leanne made many attempts to advocate for change. She studied women's organizational contributions to present to male leaders. She led workshops for women to increase their leadership skills and confidence. She advocated for women every chance she got. But when she tried to talk with an organizational leader about the need for women's voices in the leadership team, he told her, "I don't need anyone advocating for women." Another time she spoke with a different leader; he referred her to his wife. And so, nothing changed.

While in school to earn a PhD, Leanne learned how such organizations were designed to make women's contributions invisible. Many followed a two-person career structure in which both spouses worked for the organization but were treated as a "unit" with the paycheck going to the husband and the wife's work attributed to him as well. While women were typically required to have the same qualifications as their husbands, organizations assigned the couple to work in places that suited the husband's interests. During one assignment, Leanne and her husband were sent to a location with a church ministry for her husband, but which did not have a teaching role to fit Leanne's expertise. Leanne was expected to just figure it out. In such organizations, women's concerns were sidelined through a "women's ministry" department rather than being handled through human resources or standard procedures. Leanne began to realize that it would take more than her individual advocacy to bring change.

We each wanted to make sense of our personal experiences, understand what was holding us back at work, and learn how to overcome it. To do this, we each embarked on a PhD in which our dissertation research focused on challenges women leaders experienced in our respective industries (higher education for Amy and faith-based nonprofits for Leanne). Through our interviews with women in these industries, we learned that our experiences were not unique. When we first met in 2014, we discovered we had very similar research findings. In these two very different industries, women leaders were running into almost identical obstacles. They were experiencing barriers that were not due to the organization or industry or sector but were due to being a woman in leadership.

To expand our understanding of gender barriers across more industries, in 2017 we conducted a survey of 1,606 women leaders in higher education, faith-based organizations, healthcare, and law across the United States. These four industries have historically been the most resistant to the entrance of women.[9] A majority of the participants (59.4 percent) reported experiencing gender discrimination at work. In addition, 53.6 percent said that the behavior of male colleagues sometimes made them feel uncomfortable, 66.1 percent reported earning less than male counterparts, and 72.1 percent felt challenged balancing their personal and professional lives. Other surveys confirm these results. A 2017 nationally representative Pew survey of 4,914 adults found 42 percent of employed U.S. women say they have faced discrimination in their job due to gender. This survey found women were two to five times more likely than men to say they have experienced aspects of gender discrimination such as salary inequality, being treated as not competent, being passed over for important assignments, and sexual harassment.[10] A 2017–2022 global study of nationally representative data from eighty-eight countries found 35 percent of people believe men make better political leaders than women, 31 percent think men are better business executives, and 32 percent think men have more right to jobs when they are scarce. And more than half of people (51 percent) think that it is a man's job to earn money and a woman's job to take care of home and family.[11] This largely invisible bias is prevalent almost everywhere.

Since today's gender bias is often invisible, we were determined to make it visible. Our first step was to identify and name the components. We started with a list of twenty-seven barriers that women faced when they went to work. This list was derived by combining our research on women executives in higher education and faith-based organizations and was published in the academic journal *Human Resource Development Quarterly*.[12] While we sensed that these barriers would group into a smaller number of categories, we were unable to see the common threads. We next created a survey instrument to measure the bias, the Gender Bias

Scale for Women Leaders, and validated it across four industries.[13] The survey questions were derived from examples of the twenty-seven barriers. We analyzed the survey results using factor analysis, a method that allowed us to discover the underlying themes behind the twenty-seven barriers.[14] We also asked some open-ended questions about other impediments the women had experienced.

What we found was revealing: the six primary barriers that comprise gender bias—male privilege, disproportionate constraints, insufficient support, devaluation, hostility, and acquiescence.[15] These barriers are more than a glass ceiling—they are glass walls surrounding women. No matter which way a woman turns, the ever-present but invisible barriers impede her. See Figure 0.1.

Shattering these walls is the basis for this book. First, we make them visible by revealing all the barriers that women encounter when they go to work. Women's stories from the survey, our prior research, public sources, as well as our own experiences are used throughout this book to illustrate the barriers. We share stories from famous, wealthy, and highly

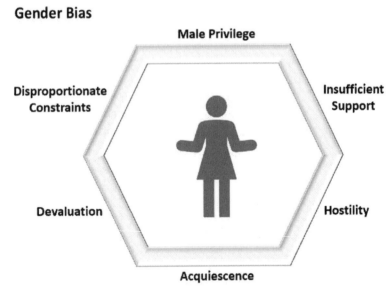

Figure 0.1.   The six walls of gender bias: *male privilege, disproportionate constraints, insufficient support, devaluation, hostility,* and *acquiescence. Image credit:* Amy Diehl

educated women as well as everyday women. While extremely privileged women sometimes have more ability than others to fight back, no woman in the workplace is exempt from gender bias.

Based on our research findings, we show the following:

- How *male privilege*, the bedrock on which gender bias is built, results in a workplace created by men and for men
- How women encounter *disproportionate constraints* in that workplace, being expected to play supportive roles to men
- The surprising ways in which women experience *insufficient support* based on gender
- The concept of *devaluation*, and how it tells women they don't belong at work
- The troubling ways women face *hostility* to keep them in their supposed place, merely because of their gender
- How the combined weight of these barriers leads to *acquiescence*, when women internalize the obstacles and adapt to the limitations

Chapters 1 through 6 are devoted to these six major barriers that limit women at work. In each chapter, we define the barrier and its subcomponents, present learnings from the research, and discuss the consequences—with a variety of fascinating stories from women working in various sectors. Each chapter includes practical actions that organizational leaders, allies, and women can take to shatter these walls and work to eliminate gender bias.

Chapter 7 tackles gender bias holistically to describe the outcomes of frequently encountered combinations of barriers. It spells out their limiting effects on individuals and organizations and provides a roadmap for gender equity and inclusion. And chapter 8 offers practical advice for women impacted by bias—a message of hope with empowering, research-based strategies to navigate adversity, enabling women to take charge of their own success.

In researching this book, we came across many biased behaviors that did not have names. When something doesn't have a name, it's as if it doesn't exist. So we coined new terms that we present throughout these chapters. You will learn how *role incredulity* keeps women from being recognized as leaders or professionals in male-dominated roles. How *gender blindness* keeps people from understanding that gender bias exists and reinforces the status quo. How *diminishment* is used to make women seem less important in the workplace. How *untitling* and *uncredentialing* render women's professional titles and credentials invisible. How women use a *mantermediary* to present their ideas as a workaround to not being heard. How *credibility deficit* leads to women's statements not being believed. And worst, how organizational leaders use *institutional assault* to silence and vilify women who've been abused and to protect abusers within their ranks.

We also apply new labels to other aspects of bias. You will learn how some men use *shunning* by refusing to take orders from or even work with women. How women's work is hidden as *invisible contributions*. How *masculine language* applied to women makes them feel excluded. How *female hostility* including *queen bee* and *mean girl behaviors* is both a symptom and a consequence of the discrimination women experience.[16] How women *self-blame* for problems outside their control because no one tells them any different, and how they *self-silence* to protect themselves. After reading this book, you will understand the structure and composition of gender bias and have a new vocabulary of terms—including those created by us and by others—to apply to the multitude of barriers women face.

Another term we coined is "equalism." We consider ourselves to be *equalists*, meaning "all human beings regardless of any socially defined identity category are of equal value and deserve equal access, treatment, rights, opportunity, and freedom in all realms of society."[17] Although we focus on women in our research and in this book, our underlying value is equality for all people. The goal of this book is to *shatter* gender bias, by comprehensively identifying the barriers and by providing solutions to eliminate them. The costs of gender bias are high in terms of individual, organizational, and societal losses. The gains for eliminating gender bias are also clear, and not just limited to women. Society, organizations, families, and even men benefit when women—and indeed all people—are included and flourishing to their full potential. Just look at Dr. Karikó's mRNA technology and the effect it had on changing the course of the COVID-19 pandemic.

The findings in this book are new. The overarching barriers identified here, and the subcomponents of each, are destined to become the framework for understanding gender bias. *Glass Walls* provides the roadmap to shatter barriers holding women back once and for all.

1

MALE PRIVILEGE

"The young men are groomed by the older men to run the thing. And they're not predisposed to treat a female as anything more than a female, not a business partner."

—Carol Bartz

In the early 2010s, investor Ellen Pao was a junior partner and chief of staff for a managing partner at Kleiner Perkins, then one of the most powerful Silicon Valley venture capital firms. One day Pao was on a private jet with four men—two partners, a tech chief executive officer (CEO), and an investor. During the flight the CEO bragged about meeting porn star Jenna Jameson, detailing her TV show. When Pao replied that she wasn't familiar with the show, the CEO switched topics to sex workers, asking a partner which type of "girls" he liked. In her book, *Reset: My Fight for Inclusion and Lasting Change,* Pao described this and other aspects of the company's exclusionary boys' club atmosphere, such as all-male dinners, Vegas excursions, and sports events; women were even excluded from work trips when the men thought they would "kill the buzz."[1] Pao sued Kleiner Perkins for gender discrimination and retaliation. (See chapter 5, "Hostility," and chapter 6, "Acquiescence," for further discussion of Pao's case.) During the lawsuit, an investigator asked Pao why men kept women around if the men looked down on them, blocked their opportunities, and excluded them from social events. She replied, "If you had the opportunity to have workers who were overeducated, underpaid, and highly experienced, whom you could dump all the menial tasks you didn't want to do on, whom you could get to clean up all the problems, and whom you could create a second class out of, wouldn't you want them to stay?"[2]

Pao's answer describes an environment built on male privilege, in which men are the leaders, control the resources, set culture standards, and assign women to a second-class status. Male privilege is the bedrock upon which gender bias is built. Between leadership teams and governing boards, many organizations today remain under male control.

In this chapter we describe the components of male-privileged culture, built by men for men. Via *male gatekeeping*, male bosses determine which women have access to leadership positions and the bounds of their authority. Women in this environment may suffer the effects of *tokenism*. In such low numbers, women find it difficult to be heard and to gain support for their perspectives. In addition, when women serve in stereotypically male roles, they may encounter *role incredulity*, in which outsiders assume they are not in charge. Informal conversations and social activities often reflect a *boys' club,* revolving around male interests. In some cases, men may *shun* women, refusing to work with or even to speak to them. People may be *gender blind* and neither question the status quo nor work to change it. *Masculine language* may be used to reinforce notions of who belongs. In some leadership environments, a *two-person career structure* is present, in which there are formal and informal institutional demands placed on both spouses, but only one is employed by the organization. Finally, women may be placed on a *glass cliff,* a perilous leadership position, when the organization is in crisis or a state of decline.

MALE GATEKEEPING

Male gatekeeping occurs when men in charge pick which women are sponsored for leadership and which are not. Throughout history, societal institutions have been constructed by men and for men, enabling them to continually recreate male power structures.[3] Men have also served as the gatekeepers of knowledge, determining what could be learned and who could learn it.[4] Oberlin College was the first to admit women to coeducational baccalaureate programs in 1837, yet many classes remained exclusively male. Oberlin men were required to study Greek and Latin and prepare for the ministry while women were dismissed from Monday classes to do laundry for the male students.[5] As recently as the late 1980s, Leanne was among the first women accepted into a theology program;

previously women had been denied admittance because study of theology was deemed a male prerogative. From the 1960s through the 1980s, White men made up the majority of the "the professions": law, judges, medicine, dentistry, architecture, clergy, hard sciences, and university professors. These were the highest-paid, most respected vocations of the time, giving White men the most autonomy and control.[6] That power enabled them to determine who was admitted into their fields and under what conditions.[7]

Male gatekeeping is a form of bias that replicates itself generation after generation. Former Yahoo! and Autodesk CEO Carol Bartz explained that Fortune 500 companies have made little progress promoting women as heads "because old White men rule . . . the young men are groomed by the older men to run the thing. And they're not predisposed to treat a female as anything more than a female, not a business partner."[8]

Hollywood is an industry with strong male gatekeeping. Even though there are many high-profile female performers, decision makers are mainly men. Actor Meryl Streep explained that sexism in Hollywood perpetuates due to "the distribution of films and how they are financed. It's about who is choosing the films that are put out." Streep further explained that when men are making these decisions, they fall back on "ancient wisdom" that people won't want to see movies on "women's issues."[9]

Male gatekeeping is also prevalent within faith-based organizations, which often use religious doctrine or "God" as their rationale for allowing only the men to lead, a justification known as "sanctified sexism."[10] One mission leader explained, "It is hard to break through when people use the Bible to justify discrimination against women." Another faith-based leader noted that male leaders wanted agreeable women in leadership, not those who "might make a decision." She explained, "Women are valued because they support the existing leadership structure, not because they are good thinkers, managers, etc. Once women begin to exercise their own ideas, all support is dropped and they are scuttled out of their positions." Many faith-based organizations only allow women to serve in leadership as a partner to their husband and only with his approval. (See two-person career structure discussed later in this chapter.) When an organization's president wanted one woman to take a regional director role, he first went to the woman's husband "to find out what he thought."

Religion is not the only industry in which male gatekeeping extends to women's families. One state agency employee who was a trained disaster volunteer asked her supervisor for time off during a wildfire emergency. He responded, "What does your husband think about that?" Similarly, a job interviewer asked another woman what her husband thought of her working full time. She stated, "This was in the past decade, not 1950."

Women in many other industries also experience male gatekeeping. Higher education leaders have difficulties serving under boards of directors, which overwhelmingly tend to be older White men. One community college leader noted the challenge in confronting sexism: "The president serves in her role at the pleasure of the board, and her contract can simply not be renewed if the board members are displeased with her." Another university employee described how six of the ten top earners at her institution are male sports coaches who—despite losing records—"are kept there by a male president and board of trustees made up of, primarily, other men." Men on boards may also ensure staff do not become too diverse. One university vice president explained how board members told her to seek an older man for a vacant position to "complement" her. She noted, "It was just a nightmare for me because what that meant was 'we want what you aren't.'"[11]

Lawyers also experience male gatekeeping. One lawyer worked for a progressive nonprofit with an equity, diversity, and inclusion mission that has never played out in its leadership. Most recently, the organization "made a veteran senior female attorney the interim leader but did not seek to make her the permanent leader, hiring the straight White man instead."

Professional music is another field in which women are kept out of the most prestigious roles. According to one woman who majored in music education, many male band directors refuse to work with female student teachers. (See shunning discussed later in this chapter.) The woman's college roommate landed a student teaching position with a male director but was not invited to conduct; the director explained that "women didn't belong on the podium." While many of her male colleagues have become band directors, this woman and her female music education colleagues "ended up in general music, choir, or very small schools, or quit the profession entirely."

With male gatekeeping, not all women are kept out of leadership; a few "exceptional" women are elevated. Describing certain women as special or extraordinary is a gatekeeping tactic to ensure not too many are let into leadership, especially top roles. A corporate board's sole female member asked the chair if he would find another woman or two to fill three vacant board seats. The chair replied, "There are no good women." She further explained, "I was the exception. He then went on to share that this is because I'm tall and strong, like a man and don't confuse things like a regular woman."

Yet being perceived as "strong" can backfire. A male colleague explained to an advertising agency employee that she lacked promotional opportunities because she was a strong woman, which makes people uncomfortable. He continued, "They don't know how to handle it, it's their problem. But it's intimidating, and when people are intimidated, they do not react well." She was stunned at the mixed messages.

With male gatekeeping women's access to leadership is carefully controlled. Men may admit women they perceive as compliant, non-threatening, or willing to conform. And they block those who might challenge the status quo.

BOYS' CLUB

In a male-privileged culture, a boys' club often exists. Conversations and social activities revolve around stereotypical male interests, such as sports, cars, drinking, and outdoor activities, and may even include lewd images, sexist jokes, and outings to strip clubs. Male entitlement is treated as normal. Women may not feel included in the social events and may feel pressure not to discuss their own interests or speak up about sexist behavior. As college president Dr. Elizabeth Meade noted, "There is still a proverbial boys' club lurking in each of America's cities and towns . . . where a small number of mostly White businessmen golf together, drink together, and do business together, often all at the same time."[12] One woman worked in a male-dominated sales environment in which she "endured [the] only outings being to sporting events, and performance incentives being [National Football League] tickets."

Research among men confirms the existence of the boys' club. In a study that included fifty-two male faculty members at U.S. university medical centers, nearly all discussed networking activities of drinking at bars, thirty mentioned watching or playing sports, five mentioned hunting or fishing, and five referred to strip clubs. One commented, "It bugs the hell out of my female colleagues, because I go fishing with the president and the vice president, and they do not. It gives me special access they do not have." Another noted that even when women come to the bar, men may "hit on them after a few drinks rather than focus on helping their careers."[13] Alcohol-centered events can blur personal and professional lines and make less powerful employees—such as women—feel uncomfortable.[14]

Often originating at the top of organizations, the boys' club occurs even in seemingly progressive industries. One woman noted that although big tech companies may have "free food, scooters in the halls, [and] free commuter buses," they are run by "entitled White males, just like any other big business, and their attitudes and actions are no different when it comes to women." One day, a senior manager at a Boston tech firm had half an hour between meetings to pump breastmilk for her baby, so she darted to the lactation room—the only private space in the office. Opening the door, she discovered her male boss on a phone call. When the manager motioned for her boss to hurry up, he gestured, "hold on" and made her wait. While the company was progressive enough to have a lactation room, the men viewed it as their space.[15]

Sports Metaphors

The boys' club also manifests in sports metaphors, often used with an assumption of universal understanding.

- goal posts
- singles and doubles
- early innings
- hail mary
- game of inches

- layup
- slam dunk
- knocking it out of the park
- low center of gravity
- the ball's in their court
- full-court press
- down for the count
- under the wire / down to the wire
- on the bench / bench strength
- in your wheelhouse
- bush league
- dropped the ball[16]

Not everyone may be familiar with sport metaphor meanings and excessive use may make non-sports fans feel as though they do not belong. One anesthesiologist attended a leadership course in which about 15 percent of attendees were women. In multiple instances, male speakers used metaphors about famous coaches, games, and sporting events to aid their teaching. When men in the room nodded and smiled, she leaned over to a female executive at her table and said, "I have no idea what they are talking about . . . do you?" The executive replied, "Nope." As the anesthesiologist explained, "The most critical examples used to teach us about leadership skills and strategy at a high-level leadership course were ones that not all of the audience could identify with, recall, or use to apply the principle."[17] Relying on sports metaphors may mean that some women, some international participants, and some men walk away baffled.

Sexist Jokes

Sexist humor reinforces solidarity in the boys' club. Sometimes women themselves are the target, such as a trade school student who had to endure being "the brunt of a lot of dirty jokes." Women may tire of enduring such jokes and choose to leave. When a department head attended a meeting with senior management, all but one of whom were men, a discussion ensued about establishing later summer hours. Winking at the department head, the CEO said, "That will give you and your women in sales an extra hour to mop the kitchen floor before you come to work." The department head was understandably irritated: "All the men snickered but looked uncomfortable when they saw me glaring with rage." She quit her job shortly thereafter.

Employee turnover is a costly result when men who make sexist comments are not held accountable. Another woman worked in an office in which a male employee routinely told vulgar, sexist jokes in front of clients and other employees. Though the company president knew of the man's behavior, the woman was told to get over it since the man "just was who he was." When she went to human resources (HR), the man apologized but didn't stop telling such jokes. At that point, the woman quit, perceiving herself as the outcast.

Sexual Images

In 1991, a U.S. federal district court ruled that pictures of naked and scantily-clad women were a form of sexual harassment. In his opinion, Judge Howell Melton wrote that a boys' club atmosphere "that deters women from entering or continuing in a profession or job is no less destructive to and offensive to workplace equality than a sign declaring 'men only.'"[18] Canada had designated sexual images as a form of sexual harassment even earlier, in 1983.[19] (See chapter 5, "Hostility," for more on sexual harassment.)

Yet while technically a form of sexual harassment in the United States and Canada for several decades, sexual images continue to be present in some workplaces. In the mid-1990s when Amy was an information technology (IT) staffer, a male coworker had pin-up calendars of nearly naked women. Being relatively new, she did not feel safe in calling it out. In 1995, when Dr. Elizabeth Rollins Epperly became the first female president of University of Prince Edward Island in Canada, she also encountered this problem. During a tour of campus facilities, Epperly approached the security office, where an officer informed her that she could not enter the locker room. In disbelief, she said, "Is someone taking a shower? I'm not going into the men's washroom." The officer then blocked her as she started through the door. She asked, "What is it that you don't want me to see?" He whispered, "It's some of the posters. You might not . . . like them. . . . We'll take 'em down. We just didn't know you were coming today." Epperly further questioned, "Don't you have one woman officer? What about her? Isn't this her locker room, too?" The officer replied, "She doesn't mind."[20] That women are comfortable with sexist images and behavior is often the presumption in a boys' club environment.

Almost three decades later, sexual images of women still exist in some workplaces, as a woman in tech found: "The CFO of my tech PR firm emailed me a link to porn along with my tax documents." Similarly, an engineer described how her male coworker tested a bot on "pictures of scantily-clad women like Kim Kardashian." When she complained to another male engineer that the bot didn't work properly on pictures of men, he replied that she was "blowing it out of proportion."[21]

Strip Clubs

Holding work events at strip clubs is another manifestation of the boys' club. When web development company CEO Kara Noreika served in a previous role as one of two women programmers at a tech company, "the lead developers and managers within the company felt it was perfectly fine to take lunches at the strip club next door and come back to work with glitter all over their faces."[22] In some cases, women are invited to the clubs. One woman had to go to a meeting in a strip club in 1995, while another commented that the owner at her workplace held the company Christmas party at an exotic dance club.

The boys' club environment puts pressure on women to be "one of the boys" to succeed. One woman reported that two successful female acquaintances in the finance industry climbed the ladder this way: "They will drink, party, talk crap, and happily visit strip clubs as part of a big night out with colleagues." Her female coworkers' perspective is that "it's not a big deal, most of us are just having a drink there—only a few actually pay for anything."

———————————

The boys' club aspect of male culture manifests in a variety of ways, from seemingly innocuous assumptions about space usage and sports to overtly hostile sexist jokes and behaviors. In every case, women are the ones expected to accommodate male preferences, whether by waiting for a man to cede the lactation room, learning to speak the language of sports metaphors, or accepting practices that objectify women as a standard part of business. Men simply assume that women will adjust.

ROLE INCREDULITY

In a male-privileged culture, people may assume women are not in charge. Outsiders may mistake women in a stereotypically male role—leader, engineer, tech support, lawyer, physician—for a stereotypically female role, such as administrative support, court reporter, nurse, or wife. This mistaken assumption is called role incredulity, and even when others learn the woman's actual role, the effects may linger in doubts about her capacity. The story of a digital marketing department head encapsulates this problem. The department head's CEO entrusted her to close strategic deals and build partnerships. However, when she arrived at meetings alone, clients often asked "if we were still waiting for 'him' to arrive." *Him* was an imaginary person, her supposed male superior; the clients assumed that the department head was not the key decision maker. At first the department head downplayed the mistake for fear of offending the customers, but she soon realized that their condescending view limited discussions: "Walking into a negotiation where the other person is basically telling you up front they deem you less than, even before you open your mouth, was and *is* demoralizing."[23] When people assume women are not in charge, their words and actions do not carry weight; the authority of their actual position is diminished.

Role incredulity also wastes women's time when they must assert their role again and again. Consider this phone call between a male pharmacist and a nurse practitioner regarding a prescription:

Pharmacist: "Who is the prescriber?"

Nurse practitioner: "Me."

Pharmacist: "Dr. Me?"

Nurse practitioner: "No, I am."

Pharmacist: "Dr. what? Can you spell that?"

Nurse practitioner: *Spells her name*

Pharmacist: "Listen to me. I have your name. I need the name of the person who is prescribing this medicine."

Nurse practitioner: "*I just did! You are speaking with the prescriber!*"

As the nurse practitioner explained, in the pharmacist's mind, "It's more likely . . . that the young female who politely answers a phone works for a 'Dr. Me' than she is to be the one running the show." She had to state her role *four* times before the pharmacist understood.

Women in many industries face role incredulity. Women lawyers are often assumed to be court reporters, secretaries, receptionists, paralegals, interns, or law students—anything but a lawyer. One lawyer explained how role incredulity caused clients to not take her seriously. After multiple interactions with a client over six months, the client asked if he could speak directly with his attorney. She responded, "I am your lawyer." When another long-time attorney and her male colleague attended trade shows, the attorney was often assumed to be the colleague's assistant or was explicitly asked if she was a lawyer, while no one ever questioned her colleague's occupation. She stated, "It's irritating and insulting."

Women in other male-dominated arenas also experience role incredulity. Golf professional Tina Mickelson was often assumed to be the "shop girl." One day a man entered the store. When Mickelson asked if she could help him, he stated that he had a question for "the pro," motioning towards a teenage male employee who was on the phone. Sensing this man had no desire to talk to her, Mickelson let him wait. When the employee got off the phone, the man asked his question, to which the employee replied, "I'm a cart guy. You need to ask the golf professional. She's right there." The man looked at Mickelson and then—embarrassed—walked out of the shop. To his credit, the man later returned to apologize to Mickelson.[24]

Women of color may frequently experience role incredulity. Several medical doctors expressed dismay at being assumed to be nurses, medical students, or even wives or girlfriends of physicians. One stated, "Because I am a Filipino woman, people . . . assume I am a nurse, and not a doctor and a division chief." Surgeon Dr. Nancy Yen Shipley was assumed to be a physician's wife at an interview event. She commented, "I mean, I'm a wife. Of someone else. Who is not at the fellowship mixer."[25]

And sometimes women in non-male-dominated positions experience mistaken role assumptions. When faculty find out that university staffer Kalani Pickhart is publishing a novel, "You can see their brain short-circuit like, 'Wait, you're not supposed to be capable of anything but making my copies,'" as she explained.[26]

"Where's the Boss?"

In numerous fields, customers outright ask to speak to the boss or to escalate their issue to a man. As an art school and frame shop co-owner described, "After 27 years, I'm still asked, 'Where's the boss?'" Many women experienced role incredulity when on the phone with customers. This happened to a third-tier support engineer at least weekly. Calls are escalated to this engineer for resolution after the customer is routed through two initial support queues without a successful fix. As she explained, customers "would start yelling about having been routed back to 'the secretary' and that they wanted to 'talk to an engineer right (expletive) *now!*'" To counteract the assumption, the engineer asserted her role and informed the customer that she could put them back in the queue "but they were just going to get me again eventually," as she said.

Role incredulity can hamper career paths, making women less likely to be promoted or even hired into male-dominated roles in the first place. It also exacts a toll when women are in these roles, both emotionally and in completing their work. Women must manage their emotions when repeatedly doubted. If women lose their cool or express anger, they may experience backlash for not being warm and agreeable. Additionally, women lose valuable work time in asserting, over and over, that they are the engineer or manager or physician. In situations where evaluations are based on timely responses, such as in tech support or customer service, women's evaluations may be lower because they must spend time defending their expertise before attending to the problem.[27] And the organization loses operational efficiency, with fewer problems solved, fewer patients attended to, and fewer customers served.

SHUNNING

Another aspect of male privilege is shunning, either ignoring directives from female leaders or refusing to work with or even speak to women. Several women described how some men would not follow their orders, such as one music leader who worked with men "who thought it was optional whether or not they would follow my leadership directives because I was a woman. I never saw them treat other men in similar positions like that." Similarly, a male subordinate complained that a department manager was not "nurturing" when she admonished him for arriving to work late and then getting breakfast takeout, which he ate at his desk while talking on the phone to friends. She said, "As a woman manager, I found that my staff expected me to be their Mommy. I was to excuse their faults, give them extra time off, and not be 'so critical.' They did not have these expectations from the male managers who were over me. When the men spoke to them, they were compliant."

Sometimes organizations support men who shun women. Just prior to starting a new position, a faith-based nonprofit leader learned that her work territory was adjusted because of a would-be male subordinate's complaints. He was unwilling to report to a woman due to his religious convictions. Not wanting to lose this male employee, the organization changed the reporting lines instead of insisting that the male employee serve under her.[28]

Attitudes of disrespecting women's authority may be socialized into children from a young age, as an Alabama teacher explained. When contacting parents about behavioral and academic concerns, multiple mothers confided to this teacher that they are "not allowed" to reprimand their child as disciplining is "the husband's place." Furthermore, some fathers instructed children that they do not have to listen to classroom consequences from female teachers and have even come to the school to berate the women, while male administrators did nothing. Not following a woman leader's directions is a way for men to assert their power in the gender hierarchy.

Refusing to Work with Women

Some men decline to work with women, such as one woman who was the only person around when a male maintenance worker needed help getting supplies. Even though the task was simple, the maintenance worker insisted on waiting for a male coworker to return instead of allowing the woman to help.

Other men outright refuse to speak to women. A call center technical support employee noted that at least once per day a female coworker says, "He hung up on me because I'm a woman." Similarly, a big box retail store supervisor experienced shunning: "Sometimes when I get asked to help with manager calls, male customers have told me to get a male manager because they don't think I know what I'm doing."

Sometimes women are treated as if they don't exist. When one woman hosted several out-of-town "bigwigs," she was one of two women present. The visitors greeted each employee, shaking hands and learning their names. When the visitors reached this woman and her female coworker, they "stopped shaking hands and asking names and instead started right in on business questions." Even though this woman was the most senior employee in attendance, the visitors spoke to her male subordinate instead.

It is all too common for women to be overlooked in conversations. A business owner stated that sometimes "the repair man talks to your male employee about the repair while you are standing right there." In another example, a marketing and advertising specialist went to a meeting with her male boss; she was there to discuss marketing, and her boss was there to discuss the contract. During her presentation, the male clients repeatedly interrupted, directing their questions to her male boss, even though he continually motioned to her and even said, "Angela has those answers." Similarly, a communications agency partner who works in Colombia and Mexico finds that men and some women in both countries will not look her in the eye or address her when talking about strategy. As she said, "It gets exhausting to constantly 'try' to be heard, and many times I default to 'not bothering.'"

Glass Partition: "Pence/Graham Rule"

In 2002, Mike Pence (who later became a U.S. vice president) stated in an interview that he doesn't eat alone with a woman who is not his wife. This "Pence rule" originated as the "Billy Graham rule" in the late 1940s when Graham, the famous evangelist, declared that he would not eat or meet alone with a woman other than his wife, Ruth. Not only did evangelical pastors soon adopt the rule, but businessmen did as well.[29] These rules are attempts to avoid the appearance of sexual impropriety as well as the risk of sexual harassment lawsuits.[30] But they result in a "glass partition" between men and women that inhibits cross-gender friendships and more importantly disadvantages women in male-dominated workplaces where networking is crucial for career success.[31]

The Pence/Graham rule creates a challenge for women in entering the "crucial circle of male camaraderie," as retired JPMorgan Chase chief financial officer Dina Dublon noted. Dublon's former male colleagues were reluctant to have dinner or drinks with female subordinates because they worried about being perceived as flirtatious. As she explained, "Once you get to the top of the company, in most cases, you are dealing with a male kingdom. For as long as we are the minority group, it is much more about our capacity to adjust to them than their capacity to open up to us."[32]

The Pence/Graham rule has been used against many women. One woman described how the rule prevents mentoring: "I've tried to work with male mentors, but some have limits due to stigmas they possess. One senior leader would not go to lunch or dinner with female coworkers alone because he did not want to upset his wife." An attorney experienced travel restrictions when "one male partner stated that he wouldn't travel on a case with a woman attorney because they might have sex." Similarly, an account manager lost income due to male colleagues' policies of not traveling with women, promises they made to their wives. The account manager stated, "I was blocked out of all new business development once the time came to pitch new clients in person. And guess what? My male co-worker was given his 15 percent after landing these deals in my place."[33]

In religious contexts, the "stained-glass partition" can be very strong.[34] In research interviews with Leanne, some men noted their preference to maintain their distance from women. One stated, "If I can avoid it [working with a female colleague], I would."[35] He had seen other men work with women and "end up in a sexual relationship with them, or it's been difficult on their marriages." Although the Pence/Graham rule may sound honorable on the surface, lurking underneath is the assumption that women are sexual tempters whom men can't resist. Such caricatures are damaging to men and women, portraying both as enslaved to hormones and incapable of exercising reason, self-control, and common decency.

Shunning thus occurs through multiple means: outright refusal to work under a woman, refusing to work with a woman, or the more noble-sounding Pence/Graham rule to avoid sexual misconduct. Yet the outcome in every case is the same: male privilege is maintained while women's authority is diminished, and their opportunities curtailed.

TOKENISM

The word "tokenism" conjures up an image of an individual who is selected for a position for the appearance of diversity. As one technology worker described, "I was told I was only promoted for my position because my office needed a woman."[36] A faith-based leader had a similar experience: "I may have got the current job partly because I am female as the members of the team selected before me were all male." This type of tokenism is symbolic and suggests that a woman is chosen for a position based on gender rather than qualifications.

Another type of tokenism is numerical, relating strictly to being the only woman or one of a handful of women in a group. Even well-qualified women experience disadvantages when vastly outnumbered by men. In the 1970s, professor Dr. Rosabeth Moss Kanter studied the office culture of a large American manufacturing company and identified numerical tokenism, occurring when women (or any minority group) comprise less than 15 percent of a workgroup. Both symbolic and numerical token women experience performance pressures related to heightened visibility, are isolated even when present, and are expected to act within predefined gender roles.[37] While Dr. Kanter's study was conducted a half-century ago, her conclusions are still relevant in today's workplaces.

Heightened Visibility

Women tokens experience heightened visibility, such as one who took the rest of the room by "surprise" when she spoke up. Similarly, a male colleague told another woman, "I am so impressed how you speak your mind clearly and succinctly . . . in a room full of forty men when you are the only female." Another woman who was the only woman on a tense conference call raised several points that needed a decision. Her boss told her privately that she sounded "really bitchy" and should "tone it down." She described the double standard: "My tone matched that of every other man on the call. . . . What I learned that day was that when tensions are high, as sometimes happens, men are seen as rightly frustrated, women are seen as bitchy. It was extremely disheartening."

Other women experience performance pressures. A technology staffer worked in a department of more than one hundred people, only six of whom were women. Her boss singled her out, making her "look stupid for not knowing how to do things outside of/not required by my job, despite doing my job better than 80 percent of the men there," as she stated. Even worse, another woman worked for a sales manager whose policy was to have one woman on his team at a time. He told the entire team that if she didn't make quota for the month, she would have "to blow the entire team." As she described, "I was so ashamed and embarrassed." (See chapter 4, "Devaluation," for more on sexualizing women.)

Isolation

In contrast to heightened visibility, women in token situations may also be isolated. One university professor was not invited to lunch when she was the only woman in a meeting. The dean told her, "I'm sure you have things you need to get back to in your office."

When token women are present in teams and meetings, they can be isolated in another way—their voices are silenced or ignored. An investment banker explained how she was "loudly shushed by a male colleague" and received looks advising her to "keep mum" in meetings in which she was the only woman present. Similarly, an architect explained how she was frequently the only woman in project meetings yet was often interrupted and her design suggestions "frequently dismissed."

Gender Role Expectations

Token women are often expected to serve traditional female roles and do office housework. As an attorney described, "I have been asked to order lunch or grab coffee, even when I'm not the most junior person in the room." (See chapter 4, "Devaluation" for more on office housework.)

Tokenism intensifies gender role hierarchies. One day in design school, a student was the only woman in a project group. When she spoke up with her ideas, a male classmate tried to shut her down: "You're not leading this project no matter what you think." Describing the experience as "unnerving," the student further explained, "Besides the fact he misread my assertiveness as some sort of threat, he consciously tried to embarrass me in front of others." As the token woman, the student was isolated, silenced, and told to stay in her place as a follower, not a leader.

———————

Tokenism presents opposite messages: "You're only here because we need a woman," and "You're the only woman qualified to be here." Similarly, tokenism can produce both heightened visibility and invisibility at the same time. And tokenism reinforces—above all else—the gender of the token woman, which makes it easier for those around her to fall back on stereotypes in their interactions.

GENDER BLINDNESS

In a male-privileged workplace culture, people may be gender blind, being unaware of the impact of gender. They don't question the gender status quo or work to change it. A faith-based leader described how male leaders in her organization thought they were supportive of women, but "they could not recognize the deeper assumptions and expectations that continued to create hurdles for women and that set the bar higher for their female than for their male colleagues." Another woman described how gender bias can be "nearly impossible to explain to men." In her experience men minimize it: "Some women are just not resilient," or "My wife has not experienced that misogynist phenomenon."

Women themselves can also be unaware of how gender impacts women's experiences. Not all women perceive discrimination or bias in their own experience, adopting an attitude of "because it doesn't happen to me, it must mean it doesn't happen," as one woman explained. A college president told Amy that she didn't believe in the glass ceiling or a gender gap. She believed that people are as successful as they set out to be and that "too often women use the glass ceiling as an excuse." Another professional explained her view that gender-related ceilings are self-imposed, "linked closely to women's own choices to avoid or turn down leadership opportunities in the organization and to favor male leaders over female leaders when positions are voted on by the organization's membership." A result of gender blindness is a lack of resources to support women and overcome gender bias within workplaces, as a faith-based leader described: "We don't have in [our organization] someone who is working on this—women's ministry, empowering women, because there's not a felt need for it."[38]

When top leaders are gender blind, it can be especially damaging to the organization's support of women. Microsoft's male chief executive Satya Nadella commented, "It's not about asking for the raise but knowing and having faith that the system will actually give you the right raises. . . . And that, I think, might be one of the additional superpowers that quite frankly women who don't ask for a raise have. Because that's good karma. It'll come back because somebody's going to know that's the kind of person that I want to trust. That's the kind of person I want to really give more responsibility to."[39] A tough spot for a woman to be in—damned if she asks for a raise, and damned if she doesn't, unless of course "karma" takes care of her. Given that women earn less than men in most every profession (see chapter 4, "Devaluation"), this type of thinking removes responsibility from organizations to fix systemic issues that disadvantage women regardless of their performance.

Merit Principle

Gender-blind individuals may believe that all hiring and promotions are based on "merit" alone. This approach fails to acknowledge that the process itself—qualifications, job advertisements, applications, interview questions—often favors male candidates. A Hewlett-Packard internal report revealed that while men applied for promotions when they met 60 percent of the job criteria, women applied only when they met 100 percent of the criteria.[40] Similarly, a study of LinkedIn data found that while men and women viewed similar numbers of job advertisements, women were 16 percent less likely to apply after viewing the ad, and overall they applied to 20 percent fewer jobs than men on the site.[41]

Job ads are sometimes written in ways that appeal to men, while discouraging women. While it is illegal to advertise jobs specifically to men or women, gender preferences can be hidden in subtle cues. A Canadian study found that women were less likely to see themselves as a fit for jobs that used masculine wording, such as "competitive," "dominant," or "ambitious."[42] One tech startup advertised a "work hard, play hard lifestyle," which included evening Nerf gun battles.[43] Such job descriptions signal that only men should apply.

Some women believe that hiring decisions are made on merit alone. When a male college president suggested it would be great to add another woman to the leadership team, his chief of staff assured him that she wanted a diverse candidate pool and "if the [best qualified person] is a woman, great. . . . But to have women in leadership roles just because they're women is just so wrong."[44] Another woman described this same sentiment: "Irrespective of gender, we should retain the best talent. Also, there is no need to compromise on quality just to get a woman on board." These women fail to recognize the bias that can exist in recruitment and hiring processes.

People may assume that when women are given opportunities, they are less qualified than male counterparts. In the late 1980s, General Electric (GE) CEO Jack Welsh made it a personal goal to advance women. When one GE employee attended management training and became the first woman manager in the engineering department, "some of the engineers were resentful that a less qualified female was promoted in an attempt to correct the inequity," as she stated.

———————————

Male-privileged environments, designed around male standards and life patterns, create systems (i.e., hiring, promotion, behavioral norms) that systematically disadvantage women. Sometimes even women who have survived sexist systems themselves don't perceive the bias. When people don't see the subtle and often unconscious biases built into these systems, they are gender blind.

MASCULINE LANGUAGE

Masculine language is used to reinforce who belongs in male-privileged environments. Consider the use of "guys" to refer to women and mixed-gender groups. In United States slang, the word "guy" means "man" or "fellow" in the singular, but many people use it to mean "persons" in the plural. This creates an inclusivity problem, as women and nonbinary people may feel excluded when referred to as "guys." Even young girls recognize "guys" as leaving them out. As one male teacher found, "I said, 'Hey guys' and one student said, 'I'm a girl' and rolled her eyes so hard I gasped."[45] Guys is not the only masculine term used to refer to women. One woman noted how a male colleague calls all coworkers "dude" regardless of gender.[46] And a physician remarked that masculine language "hurts most when it's an organization/group composed entirely of women."[47]

Research has found that when masculine language is used in the workplace, women can feel ostracized and have a lower sense of belonging.[48] While people who use masculine terms like "guys," "dudes," "lads," "gents," and "men" for mixed-gender and all-women groups may say that they mean everyone, the problem is that not everyone hears it that way.[49] One UK physician described the impact when she was in a group greeted with "Hello Gents": "As the only female neurosurgery [doctor] present, I can't help but feel a little excluded."[50]

Working in the male-dominated field of IT, Amy is often in groups generalized as "guys." Recently she was the only woman on a web conference call that included her male colleagues and an all-male vendor sales team. The male salesperson repeatedly referred to the group as "you guys" even though Amy had her camera on and was the most senior person on the call. It made her feel invisible. Language matters, and how people are referred to in the workplace matters. Masculine language that excludes half of humanity is inadequate in today's workplace.

TWO-PERSON CAREER STRUCTURE

A two-person career structure exists in high-demand and sometimes high-prestige occupations that come with an ingrained expectation that the person who does the job has a fully supportive, available spouse to help. When sociologist Dr. Hanna Papanek named this phenomenon in 1973, she found that it was based on traditional marriages where the husband had the career, but the organization expected the wife to contribute on a voluntary, unpaid basis.[51] Former First Lady Michelle Obama described the two-person career in her memoir *Becoming*. A First Lady has offices in the White House and a paid staff, but "it's not technically a job, nor is it an official government title. It comes with no salary and no spelled-out set of obligations. It's a strange kind of sidecar to the presidency."[52]

High-level government and military positions operate this way. So do clergy and high-ranking business executives. University presidents also encounter this expectation. As one female president explained, "To be a presidential spouse [is] a major sacrifice because your whole life is about this." Spouses are often vetted as part of interview processes. One university president's wife speaks at open houses and other official events when her husband is unavailable.[53]

Times have changed since the two-person career was first identified and the prestigious job holder was typically a man. Women now occupy these high-level roles. In 2020 the United States elected a woman, Kamala Harris, to the office of vice president with her husband, Doug Emhoff, taking the title "Second Gentlemen."[54] For women who hold the formal position, the situation is tricky in three ways. First, if a woman is in a traditional marriage and her husband fills the organizational support role, it may contribute to perceptions that she is overstepping appropriate gender roles by "wearing the pants" in the family. Second, if a woman's husband does not fill the workplace support role, she may wear herself out trying to do the work of two people or find herself not considered for the job. As one university president discovered, "A very large search firm told me I was not likely to be considered because the campus was looking for 'a couple' and my husband works." Third, if the woman is married to a man in a high-level position, she may be expected to do her own job and simultaneously help him in his job. A faith-based nonprofit leader explained, "I struggle with how I can continue to be a team leader while wanting to partner with my husband in his role." Professor Dr. Jill Biden experienced the double demands when she became the first U.S. presidential spouse to keep her full-time job after her husband was elected in 2020. She was described as a "working first lady" even though the First Lady role comes with its own full-time—but unpaid—responsibilities to serve as hostess, coordinate events, travel, make public appearances, and act as an ambassador for the president.[55] In all three scenarios, the woman is the one who must navigate public perceptions and carry the weight of excessive work demands.

For single women or women in relationships other than a traditional marriage, the issues are even more complex. U.S. society has made progress on accepting nontraditional partners and single-parent families. Yet women without a traditional spouse may run into even greater bias when they seek positions that rely on a two-person approach.

GLASS CLIFF

In 2011, Jill Abramson became the first female executive editor of the *New York Times* at a time when the paper was going through a massive transformation to survive in the digital age.[56] Abramson was a hard worker who pushed everyone for excellence; the paper won eight Pulitzer Prizes under her leadership and generated huge revenue from its paywall and advertisements while revenue at other newspapers was suffering.[57] Yet her agentic decision-making style angered some staff, and she was fired based in part on characterizations of being "brusque" and "pushy."[58] Abramson's failure to conform to the male-normed workplace expectations of women as supportive and sympathetic rather than ambitious and decisive led to a tenure of less than three years where the norm was at least eight.[59] The press characterized her firing as a "glass cliff."[60]

A glass cliff occurs when women are hired or promoted into roles with a high risk of failure, such as when an organization is in a downturn or a state of crisis. In this perilous situation, the woman will be blamed and let go if she doesn't perform the miraculous. Abramson's push off the glass cliff was particularly harsh; within minutes of the editorial meeting announcing her firing, her name was removed from the paper's masthead, and she was given no role in a transition.[61] Abramson is not the only high-profile CEO to fall victim to a glass cliff; others include Carol Bartz at Yahoo!, Marissa Mayer at Yahoo!, Ellen Pao at Reddit, Sheri McCoy at Avon, and Carly Fiorina at Hewlett-Packard.[62]

When women are let go, they are often replaced by a man as a return to status quo, as happened to Carol Bartz. Recruited to lead Yahoo! during the Great Recession in 2009, Bartz succeeded a male CEO at a time when online ad revenue was declining, and Google was dominating the search business. When Bartz stood up for her employees, stating, "Let's give this company some friggin' breathing room," the press characterized her as "combative" and "sharp." While Yahoo! profits rose due to the necessary company downsizing Bartz imposed, ad revenues fell.[63] When Bartz's efforts did not work quickly enough to turn the company around, the board abruptly fired her in 2011, two and a half years into a four-year contract, and hired a man to replace her.[64]

Describing how the glass cliff works, Bartz said, "It is absolutely true that women have a better chance to get a directorship or a senior position if there's trouble" because men are often not interested in such risky roles. After men turn down the role, the company will think of a woman who could do it, "and she's so happy that she has a chance to have a senior position as a director or a CEO that she takes it," as Bartz explained.[65]

Bartz's view is backed up by researchers Drs. Christy Glass and Alison Cook who compared the career trajectories of female and male Fortune 500 CEOs through 2010. They found that 42 percent of the fifty-two women studied were appointed when the firm was struggling or in crisis, compared to only 22 percent of the men; 10 percent of the women were appointed at a time of transition, compared to none of the men; and 44 percent of the women were appointed when the firm was doing well, compared to 70 percent of the men. Through interviews with twelve female CEOs, Cook and Glass learned that women may take glass cliff jobs to establish their reputations and prove themselves as transformational leaders or crisis managers.[66]

Women in lower-profile positions may also be set up on a glass cliff. One mission executive was told that she was handed a risky role because she was young, unexperienced, and could be blamed if her project failed.[67] Similarly, a higher education executive was forced to take a vice president role when her predecessor was terminated: "I refused it, and I was basically told, 'you will do it.'" She explained, "Your career is always at risk" at the vice president level. And in fact, it was. Shortly thereafter, her university found itself in a difficult position when its long-time auditors uncovered ten years of accounting errors, which were not on the new vice president's watch. To mitigate damage to themselves, the auditors blamed the new vice president and her division. As she said, "I had walked in the door, hired a new leadership, and we were being held accountable to the point of almost termination."[68]

Even when women produce results, they may still get kicked off the glass cliff. One woman described the experience of her boss, the only woman C-level executive at an online learning company. In less than twelve months, the executive had transformed the department and reported results each quarter that exceeded expectations. Yet, "after eighteen months at the company, she was fired by the CEO because, in his words, she was too strident and 'people didn't like her,'" as her subordinate explained. Like Jill Abramson, she was pushed off the glass cliff for her agentic leadership style, a concern that would be unlikely to damage a man.

––––––––––––––

In this chapter we've broken down the various pressures women encounter that contribute to an environment of male privilege. Male privilege may start with gatekeeping, where men in charge carefully determine which women can enter leadership. The culture of the organization may resemble a boys' club, characterized by stereotypical male interests and approaches to leadership. Due to gatekeeping, there may be very few women admitted to the "club," and those who do enter are treated as tokens, there for appearance but possibly not taken seriously as leaders. A symptom of the skepticism women encounter is role incredulity when people assume a woman is there in a support capacity only. She may also find herself shunned, excluded from meetings and events, in some cases because male colleagues view women as sexual tempters. People may also be gender blind, ignoring or denying that gender has any impact on the privileged nature of the workplace, and thus alleviating themselves of responsibility to change it. Masculine language may be used as an indication that the workplace is primarily for men. Another manifestation of male privilege is the two-person career structure, where jobs are too big for one person to do alone, and the organization expects the unpaid support of a spouse, typically a wife. Finally, women may only gain access to high-level positions when the situation is dire, placing them on a glass cliff.

It's easy to see how these factors benefit men at the expense of women. The overall effect is to keep men firmly in control of the organization and, more importantly, the organization's women. In every case, women are the ones who must conform, and who pay the price associated with men's privilege.

But male privilege isn't the only hindrance women encounter. In fact, male privilege is in some ways the foundation stone upon which the remaining hindrances to women's leadership are built. With a foundation of male privilege firmly in place, the rest of the barriers flow forth to hamper women's leadership and work at every turn.

SHATTERING MALE PRIVILEGE: A DIVERSE ORGANIZATION

Instead of a male-privileged environment, workplaces must adopt diversity as a core value and priority, understanding the long-term benefits of having a workforce that reflects society. Solutions to shatter male privilege and move toward a diverse organization are outlined below. Those serving as leaders must take the lead, while allies—anyone who is supportive—can help advance diversity. Individual women can also take steps to mitigate male privilege if it happens to them.

Male Gatekeeping

LEADERS

- Set organizational diversity goals with reward structures for meeting targets.
- Use inclusive hiring and promotional practices to select employees based on skills rather than "fit." Recognize the value that diversity will bring to your team.

- Use equitable criteria in hiring and promotions, rather than hiring on "potential" for men and demonstrated experience for women.

ALLIES

- Recommend specific women to be hired and promoted.
- Call out biased behavior within hiring searches and promotional discussions. For example, you may say, "We rated John higher than Sarah even though he has less experience. Let's rethink our ratings."

SELF

- Recognize that male gatekeeping is hard to confront directly since you are likely not in the room when the decision is being made.
- If you are looking for a new position, have alternatives on your job search list in case you are denied a position due to male gatekeeping.
- If you are denied a promotion in your existing organization due to male gatekeeping, speak to your boss or HR. If they offer no remedy, consider your options for employment elsewhere and talk to the U.S. federal or your state's equal opportunity employment commission about filing a gender discrimination claim. You may also wish to speak to an employment attorney for advice.

Boys' Club

LEADERS

- Set expectations for zero tolerance for sexual images, sexual jokes, and strip club outings.
- Ask employees to avoid sports metaphors and provide them with inclusive alternatives. For example, "hail mary" can be replaced with "one last attempt."

- Replace male-centric incentives and outings with inclusive options, and don't center events around alcohol. Allow employees to pick from a range of performance incentives or offer cash instead. Survey staff for company outing preferences and provide varied options and times.

ALLIES

- If colleagues display sexual images, tell sexual jokes, or invite you to a strip club, call out their inappropriateness. You can say, "This joke/image/outing is inappropriate and disrespectful to our female colleagues."
- Avoid use of sports metaphors. If you hear them being used, provide a translation.
- Advocate to organizational leaders for inclusive alternatives to male-centric incentives and outings.

SELF

- If you see sexual images, hear sexual jokes, or are aware of outings to strip clubs, bring up your concerns. You may say, "I feel disrespected by these images/jokes/outings." You can also talk to your boss or HR for assistance.
- If you hear a sports metaphor, ask for a translation. You may not be the only person who doesn't understand the meaning.
- Talk to HR or your boss to express your concerns with male-centric incentives or outings. You can say, "I am not a football fan. Could we offer alternative performance incentives?"

Role Incredulity

LEADERS

- Make name and title introductions standard in settings where people don't know each other well.

- Use auto-generated email signatures that include position titles.
- Institute a culture where everyone wears a name tag with position titles prominently displayed.
- Issue nameplates with titles for desks and door labels for physical offices.
- Announce promotions over company-wide email.
- Use diverse staff images—including women in traditionally male positions—on websites, advertisements, and office walls.

ALLIES

- When introducing female colleagues, include their position. "I'd like you to meet Dr. Camila Sanchez, our medical director."
- If a coworker's role is misidentified, speak up on their behalf: "Ana is the lead engineer on this project."
- If you mistake someone's role, apologize: "I'm so sorry, Charlotte; please forgive me." Moving forward, do your research in advance of meetings and events to learn people's roles and titles.

SELF

- Proactively identify your role: "Hi, I'm Dr. Li, your surgeon."
- Put your position title in your email signature.
- Wear a name tag with your position title prominently displayed in situations where you often meet new people.
- If your role is misidentified, correct it: "Actually, I'm your attorney." You can also use a humorous tone: "I've been doing this job for over five years and I'm pretty good at it." [69]

Shunning

LEADERS

- Create a zero-tolerance policy for refusals to work for or with women.

- Include women in hiring committees and value their perspective. Weed out candidates who fail to acknowledge or refuse to communicate with female interviewers, such as by addressing responses only to male interviewers. To help determine if a candidate will have trouble working with women, ask them if they follow the Pence/Graham rule, such as "Do you have any hesitations about working one-on-one with women?"
- Set expectations that women be invited to work lunches and travel.
- If a man refuses to travel with a female colleague, send the woman instead of the man.

ALLIES

- If a man refuses to speak to or work with a woman, speak up on her behalf: "Angela is the manager, and she can help you with your issue."
- If your female colleague is left out of a work lunch or travel opportunity, insist that she be included: "Let's invite Sierra."

SELF

- If someone refuses to work with you, call it out: "I'm the maintenance supervisor who can help you with your project." If this doesn't curtail the shunning, take notes and speak to your supervisor or HR.
- Ask to be included in work lunches and travel opportunities. Discuss the impact on your job with your boss: "I am unable to make deals and relationships with clients when I am excluded from travel."

Tokenism

LEADERS

- Be intentional about equitable representation for women on boards and workplace teams. Ensure there are more than just one or two women.
- Make sure women's voices and perspectives are considered, no matter how many women are in the workgroup or meeting.

ALLIES

- Amplify female colleagues' voices, especially if they are the lone woman. You can say, "Petra's idea is good. Petra, can you elaborate?"
- Advocate for more female representation on workgroups and teams. Suggest specific women to add.
- If you organize committees, ensure women are well represented.

SELF

- Ask your bosses to add more women to teams, suggesting specific women.
- If you are the lone woman on a team and your voice is not being heard, solicit support from a colleague to amplify and give you credit for your ideas.

Gender Blindness

LEADERS

- Train all employees on how to identify and eliminate gender bias.
- Ensure job advertisements are free of subtle male preferences, such as a long list of minimum requirements and masculine

wording (e.g., "competitive," "dominant," "ambitious," "cut-throat," "work hard/play hard").

- Eliminate "merit-based" hiring and promotional criteria that can be exclusionary of women, such as requirements for expensive certifications or significant grant funding.

ALLIES

- When you see gender bias, call it out as a learning opportunity for others: "Did you notice that Alice was cut off every time she tried to speak in the meeting? This is an example of a bias that marginalizes women."

SELF

- If you encounter people who are gender blind, describe some examples: "I've seen many women treated unfairly compared to male colleagues, such as being constantly interrupted in meetings."
- If you encounter a woman who is gender blind, describe your experience while acknowledging hers: "It's great that you haven't dealt with sexism at work. In my experience, I've been treated unfairly compared to male colleagues."

Masculine Language

LEADERS

- Set the example by not using masculine language (e.g., guys, dude, gents) for women or mixed-gender groups.
- Communicate guidelines for use of inclusive language in your organization.

ALLIES

- Become familiar with gender-neutral alternatives for "guys" and other masculine terms. Substitute "you guys" with "you all," "you two," "you both," "you folks," or "you."
- When saying "hey / hi / hello guys," use a "guys" substitute: "all," "everyone," "everybody," "people," "folks," "team," or "colleagues." Or just say "hey," "hi," or "hello" without attaching another word.
- Set a goal to stop using "guys" and other masculine terms to refer to women and mixed-gender groups. Give others permission to call you out if you slip up. Correct yourself if you misspeak: "I meant to say, 'How are you all doing?'"
- If you hear others repeatedly using masculine terms, call it out in private. You may explain, "While many people use 'you guys' to refer to a group, some people don't think of themselves as a 'guy.'"

SELF

- While it can feel tricky to call it out when you are referred to with masculine terms, you can say, "While I don't think it is your intent, I feel excluded when I'm referred to with the term 'guys.'"
- Find an ally who can help by speaking to people about masculine terms on your behalf and vice versa.
- If masculine language is systemic in your organization, solicit support from your boss or HR for gender-inclusive language guidelines and training.[70]

Two-Person Career Structure

LEADERS

- Eliminate expectations for employee spouses to perform unpaid labor. Compensate the spouses or delegate tasks to employees.

- Remove requirements for spouses to be part of employee interviews or vetting processes.
- Remove expectations for employees to bring partners to official work functions.

ALLIES

- Offer to take on tasks (such as hosting or organizing events) handled by employee spouses.
- Advocate to leaders to remove expectations for employee spouses to perform unpaid labor.

SELF

- If you are offered a role that includes expectations for unpaid spousal labor, discuss the types of work your partner will perform and compensation expectations. For example, perhaps they will attend office parties without compensation, but be paid for organizing or planning duties.
- If you are already in a role that includes these expectations, discuss the unpaid work your partner is performing with your board, boss, or HR. Ask that your spouse be compensated or that the duties be delegated to other employees.

Glass Cliff

LEADERS

- When hiring a woman into a risky role, be transparent about the challenges and offer full support and resources to succeed.
- Do not hold women accountable or blame them for organizational problems outside of their control.
- Do not penalize women for their agency or characterizations that would not be said of a man, such as being "aggressive," "pushy," or "brusque."

ALLIES

- If a female colleague is in a risky role, ask, "How can I support you?"
- Highlight to colleagues and bosses the ways in which women are unfairly held responsible for problems that are not in their control. You can say, "The accounting errors are not Dominque's fault. They have existed for years prior to her arrival. Let's help her to resolve them."

SELF

- If you are being hired into a high-risk role, set performance expectations with organizational leaders at the outset. Ask for the support and resources you will need to succeed.
- If your role turns high-risk after your hiring, be forthright with organizational leaders about the challenges and ask for the support you need to succeed. Have your exit options ready in case leaders turn the blame on you.

2

DISPROPORTIONATE
CONSTRAINTS

"I literally have my own words stolen from me and have
to sit by and watch a man take and receive credit for it."

—Florida professional

As First Lady of the United States, Michelle Obama was highly scrutinized. When speaking about serious topics, Obama was criticized
for being "too serious, too severe," while "no one seemed to criticize
Barack for appearing too serious or not smiling enough," as she wrote in
her book *Becoming*.[1] Beyond her demeanor, the media paid excessive attention to her appearance. They reported when she wore flats instead of
heels. Her J. Crew clothing, pearls, belts, cardigans, and white inaugural
gown triggered opinions and immediate feedback. In Summer 2009, the
Obama family took a vacation to the Grand Canyon. After deplaning
from Air Force One in 106-degree heat wearing shorts, Obama was
"lambasted for an apparent lack of dignity." As she recounted, "It seemed
that my clothes mattered more to people than anything I had to say."[2]

Public figures like Obama are not the only women to be disproportionately constrained. It happens to women in all types of careers and workplaces. The purpose is to limit women to positions that are subordinate
to and supportive of men. Women may experience *constrained career choices*
and find their voices *muted*. They may be held to *unequal standards*, which
consists of higher performance expectations than male counterparts. They
may also be expected to undertake emotional labor in ways that men are

not. To ensure that women do not deviate from expectations, their appearance, demeanor, and work are subjected to scrutiny.

CONSTRAINED CAREER CHOICES

Starting when they are young, women's career choices may be constrained through messages that they are better suited for stereotypically female jobs, like teaching, nursing, social work, and administrative assistant rather than stereotypically male domains, such as science, technology, and leadership. Children quickly learn that certain careers are suitable for men, while others are suitable for women. A research study asked eighty-two children ages five to ten to speak in the voices of workers in traditionally masculine and feminine jobs. The study found that both boys and girls lowered their voice pitch for the masculine jobs and raised their voice pitch for the feminine jobs.[3] These findings suggest that children "entertain gender stereotypes even if they are not prepared to say so explicitly."[4]

Adults may unreflectively limit children's options. A pilot asked a five-year-old girl, "Do you know you could be a flight attendant when you grow up?" Fortunately, she retorted, "I could also own the plane."[5] There is nothing demeaning about traditionally female jobs. The problem is when they are presented to girls and young women as their only options, and when traditionally "male" jobs are seemingly off-limits.

When Amy met with an African American college provost, she learned how cultural expectations can constrain career choices for young women of color. Growing up in a rural, predominantly White town, this provost had read about people attending college; in fact, her teachers—all White—encouraged her to go. So, she told her high school guidance counselor that she wanted to go to a four-year college. He responded, "Why do you want to go so far away? . . . Why don't you go to a community college?"[6] She resolved to prove the counselor wrong: "I'm going because you don't think I can go." She taught herself to maneuver through the college financial aid system and apply for scholarships. Then her stepfather became another roadblock, refusing to sign the necessary papers, fearing that he would be financially liable. As a high school teenager, she took a calculated risk: "I signed his name." A self-described "spunky kid," she didn't let the constraints of her counselor or family stop her; she attended college for bachelor's, master's, and doctoral degrees, and worked her way up the academic career ladder to university provost and later to university president.

Even very accomplished women encounter career constraints, such as computer scientist Dr. Barbara Liskov, who received the prestigious Turing award for her programming language work. In the 1960s, Liskov took math and science courses at the University of California, Berkeley—"which girls were not encouraged to do"—and was usually the sole woman in one-hundred-person classes.[7] While male students worked directly with faculty, no professor ever approached Liskov. In fact, she was unaware that such opportunities existed. After finishing her graduate degree at Stanford, again no one presented her with options, while her male counterparts were recruited for academic positions.[8] Sometimes women aren't overtly discouraged, but the supports offered to men aren't provided to women.

Career constraints begin in the educational system. And education for women in the United States has been limited for centuries. When common schools opened in the 1820s to all children, the goal of educating girls was to cultivate skills to make them better wives, homemakers, and mothers.[9] The first post–Civil War women's colleges (Vassar, Wellesley, Smith, and Bryn Mawr) were opened in the late 1800s by religiously-minded individuals to "produce Christian women better prepared to assume their duties in the domestic sphere, as wives and mothers, and only if need be, as schoolteachers."[10] In the 1870s, new "scientific" arguments endangered women's education. Darwinian thought viewed women as intellectually inferior to men, and Dr. Edward Clarke, a retired Harvard Medical School professor, wrote in the widely read book *Sex in Education* that women needed to save their energies to fulfill their societal role as child bearers.[11] The deprioritizing of women's higher education was evident in elite private institutions for men and even some state schools, which remained closed to women until the 1960s and 1970s.[12]

From the beginning of higher education in the United States right up until the 1960s, men vastly outnumbered women in earning bachelor's degrees.[13] Despite the expansion of women's role in society after World War II, as late as the mid-1960s girls and young women were channeled into occupational choices that were limited to four categories: secretarial work, nursing, teaching, or motherhood.[14] It wasn't until 1982 that women finally caught up with men in attaining bachelor's degrees. Now women have surpassed men; in 2020, women earned 57.7 percent of U.S. bachelor's degrees.[15]

Women's choices have broadened, yet the idea persists that certain fields are not desirable for women. Today women are equitably represented in college and in most majors except science, technology, engineering, and mathematics (STEM), where they are severely underrepresented. In 2020 there were 97,047 computer and information science bachelor's degrees awarded; men earned 76,331 (79 percent) of those degrees, while women earned only 20,716 (21 percent).[16] Although women today have more choices than teaching and nursing, lingering occupational stereotypes are limiting their access to the most desirable and high demand fields in the marketplace.

Consider the story of software engineer Tracy Chou. Even though Chou was immersed in tech culture growing up, she had "trouble envisioning a career in software engineering" due to the sexism she encountered in college. As an undergraduate student, Chou enrolled in two introductory computer science classes but soon became convinced that she was too far behind male classmates to catch up. The first-year male students had software engineering internships in high school, skipped prerequisites to take sophomore level courses, and declared themselves unfazed by the challenges that their professors presented. While Chou spent fifteen hours on one assignment in a course meant to "weed out" students from the major, a male classmate bragged about finishing in only three hours. Chou concluded that she was not cut out for computer science. Later, working as a teaching assistant, Chou learned that her performance was on par with the male students.[17] She graduated with a bachelor's degree in electrical engineering and a master's degree in computer science and became an engineer and entrepreneur in Silicon Valley.[18] Chou's example highlights the subtle—and false—cues that women are not suited for technology careers.

Sometimes women are advised not to compete for "male" positions. A physician was told not to pursue medicine because she should "stay home with the kids." Early in her career, U.S. vice president Kamala Harris was dismissed every time she ran for political office: "It's not your time. A Black woman can't do that. It's never been done."[19] Today, women are still discouraged from pursuing stereotypical male careers, especially those with high prestige and earning potential.

MUTED VOICES

Women may find their voices constrained. Their ideas may be appropriated, and they may be ignored, censured, or silenced. Women's communication can't be too authoritative or too tentative, and they must be cautious when self-promoting. They may be interrupted in conversations, or they may have their ideas supported only when restated by a man. The outcome is that women's voices are muted, and they don't get credit for their ideas and work. In our survey research of 1,606 American women, we found that the vast majority reported aspects of being muted (see table 2.1).

Being mindful when expressing authority, downplaying accomplishments, and exercising caution when self-promoting are ways in which women have been conditioned to mute themselves. Interruptions from men actively constrain women's voices. Either way, women's voices are muted, and their contributions limited.

Appropriating

Appropriating women's ideas is all too common. Three words have entered the English lexicon in recent years that relate to this phenomenon: *hepeating*, *bropropriating*, and *mansplaining*. We explain each in turn.

Table 2.1.   Women's Muted Voices Frequencies (N=1,606)

Constraint	Higher Education	Faith-based Nonprofits	Healthcare	Law
Mindful when expressing authority	98%	97%	96%	95%
Downplay accomplishments	87%	92%	89%	83%
Exercise caution when self-promoting	88%	94%	87%	80%
Interrupted by men when speaking	52%	60%	68%	75%

Source: Healthcare data from Amber L. Stephenson et al., "An Exploration of Gender Bias Affecting Women in Medicine," in *The Contributions of Health Care Management to Grand Health Care Challenges (Advances in Health Care Management, Vol. 20),* ed. Jennifer L. Hefner and Ingrid Nembhard (Emerald Publishing Limited, 2021), 81. Higher education, faith-based nonprofit, and law data previously unpublished.
Note: Percentages include women who reported "sometimes," "often," or "always."

Hepeating occurs "when a woman suggests an idea and it's ignored, then a guy says the same thing and everyone loves it."[20] While this behavior may be unconscious, the outcome is that the man gets the credit. As actor Lena Headey described, "Male counterparts can say the same thing [I just did] and everyone's like, 'Oh, that's a great idea,' and I'm like, 'I just said that 19 times, but you chose not to listen or take it on board.'"[21]

Just like Headey, woman after woman has been hepeated. When an engineer's male counterpart repeated her ideas in meetings, questions were addressed to him. This engineer didn't perceive the problem until a vice president pointed it out: "Thank you [coworker], for repeating [engineer's] ideas with a male voice, but she can speak for herself." Hepeating can occur in workplace collaboration tools, too. One woman sometimes sent emails that were ignored, and later when a male colleague sent a reworded version, "everyone thanks him for his wonderful insight."

A transgender engineer noticed a distinct difference in how their ideas were received. Pre-transition—presenting as a man—their ideas were "regarded and considered." But post-transition—presenting as a woman—their opinions and ideas are only taken seriously "when a male colleague affirms the same assertion [and] he will then get credit." This engineer explained, "If anyone wants to proclaim that this type of behavior does not exist, I have my life, lived in two genders, to refute this."

Sometimes women develop strategies to combat hepeating. As a lawyer explained, "When a really important idea needed to be floated, I learned to approach one of these men in advance of the meeting and give them my idea and have them present it." Planting ideas with a "mantermediary" (see chapter 6, "Acquiescence") can be effective in moving them forward, yet it can result in men looking like creative geniuses and women not getting the credit they deserve.

Bropropriating is an intentional attempt to take credit for a woman's ideas or work.[22] Male entitlement underlies this behavior. As one woman described, "[Women's] ideas don't belong to anybody because it's a female body and . . . part of an easy grab-and-play model that helps the men who take them succeed." The male counterpart of a business analyst bropropriated her idea for a solution when they were both asked to produce recommendations. She provided a thorough business case to her manager, who then asked that she give the document to her counterpart to help him along. As the analyst explained, "He literally sent my document in as his own and didn't even bother to change a single word. When I brought this to my manager's attention (a man), I was told not to be petty and focus on my own work."

Sometimes subordinate men bropropriate women's ideas. After a chef instructed her pizza cook to start mixing dough early, the general manager complimented the cook. The male cook responded, "Yeah, I figured if I did it early, I would have time to roll it before I leave." When the general manager left, the cook grinned at the chef and said, "I guess I stole your idea and took your compliment, huh?" The chef felt helpless: "What am I supposed to say to such a blatant display of disrespect?"

Male bosses may be especially likely to bropropriate the work of female subordinates. One woman's new supervisor claimed credit to senior leaders for her research and analysis work completed under the previous supervisor. "He did it right in front of me," she said. "He did not say, 'her work' or 'our work.' He said, 'my work,' [but] he had nothing to do with it." Some bosses shoot down women's ideas and then later reintroduce them. As one woman found, "I have given suggestions to my boss, only to be told that it was a stupid idea. Half an hour later, the same suggestion I made came out of his mouth as his own idea."

Speaking up about misattributed credit can be risky. One woman explained, "When I would point out that it was my idea, I was told that 'it's not about getting credit.'" In another situation, a woman shared an idea in a meeting and was told "it would never work," yet a man then "said almost the exact same thing and was praised." This woman spoke up: "Hey, Dan just repeated what I said." But the meeting participants told her that "he said it better." Later this man received a large monetary award for the idea. When the woman complained, she was told that she "was not acting like a team player." Because gender stereotypes frame women as men's supporters, they may be chastised when they protest bropropriating behaviors.

Mansplaining happens when a man hijacks a woman's own expertise by "explain[ing] something to a woman in a condescending way that assumes she has no knowledge about the topic."[23] Writer Rebecca Solnit identified mansplaining in her essay "Men Explain Things to

Me" in which she described attending a party with a friend. When the party host—an older man—learned that Solnit had published a book on photographer Eadweard Muybridge, he told Solnit that a very important book on that same photographer had just been published. The host was referring to Solnit's book. Solnit's friend had to interrupt several times before the host understood that the book's author was standing right in front of him.[24]

Some men consider themselves experts at women's jobs. A woman's male coworker approached her to explain a new work procedure that she herself had developed. When she told the coworker that she was aware of the procedure, he cut her off, telling her that she should work on her listening skills. As she explained, "I shut my mouth and pretended to listen as he explained to me (in a tone most certainly meant to irritate) something I already knew, as if I were a child."

Mansplaining also occurs on public stages. One company asked employees to participate in a gender equity conference panel held for company leadership. Of the eighteen panelists, only three were women. A question was posed to the panel: "Are women treated differently in this workplace or experiencing any harassment?" Fearing retaliation, the female panelists cautiously explained a few areas that needed improvement, but "they were immediately shut down, talked over, and then told they were perceiving it wrong, and that there were no 'real' problems." Their own experience was mansplained to them.

Even highly successful women encounter mansplaining. Ellevest chief executive officer (CEO) Sallie Krawcheck earned her Wall Street credentials as former chief financial officer (CFO) of Citigroup and head of Bank of America's Merrill Lynch, yet her experience was not enough to stop venture capitalists from mansplaining to her. At one financing meeting, she was the only woman in a room of eighteen men. Even though she was confident, the lead investor insisted that she knew nothing about his questions.[25] She explained, "This man naturally assumed that he knew more about it than I did. It was his ingrained view of women—a view that's costing all of us."[26]

Censuring

When women speak up, they may be censured, which includes being labeled and chastised. Worse, women may experience a communication-style double bind. They may be told to be assertive and speak up and then be censured for doing exactly that. The reason is stereotypes: being too directive breaks female norms while being too tentative breaks leader norms. Prior to a meeting with a male CEO, a male executive told a bank employee, "The CEO doesn't like strong, professional women so try not to act like one." After the meeting, the executive chastised her: "I was hoping you could have been tougher with the CEO and challenged him a bit more."

Women are often censured for communication styles that are acceptable for men. One woman's male colleagues gave very blunt and honest feedback during meetings, yet when this woman did the same, female colleagues chastised her for "not being courteous to the other participants." As she said, "I feel like I'm held to a different standard." And indeed, she was.

LABELING

One way that women are censured is labeling, which consists of words used in a derogatory fashion to describe women. These labels are rarely applied to men. Try putting the word "he's" in front of the labels listed under "Derogatory Labels for Women," such as "he's hysterical" or "he's high maintenance." These sound rather odd. Men are almost never described as "pushy" or "bossy." Yet these words and many more are often applied to silence women.

DEROGATORY LABELS FOR WOMEN

- angry
- aggressive
- argumentative
- bitch
- bossy
- dramatic

- emotional
- feisty
- high maintenance
- high strung
- hormonal
- hysterical
- intimidating
- loud
- outspoken
- overreacting
- pushy
- sensitive
- strident

The purpose of labeling is to discourage women from communicating or behaving in ways that break stereotypical female norms. A frequent label for women is "hysterical," which derives from the Greek word for "uterus." In earlier times, it was used in medicine to describe women who were supposedly unhinged.[27] In June 2017, then U.S. senator Kamala Harris—a former prosecutor—asked pointed questions of then attorney general Jeff Sessions during a Senate investigation. And for that, she was called "hysterical" on cable television news.[28]

Other labels are used for women who supposedly step out of line. In July 2020, U.S. representative Ted Yoho confronted his colleague Representative Alexandria Ocasio-Cortez on the Capitol steps, calling her "disgusting" for suggesting that poverty and unemployment had increased crime in New York City during the coronavirus pandemic. He then said, "You are out of your freaking mind." Ocasio-Cortez pushed back, telling Yoho that he was being "rude." They parted ways, and as he continued down the steps, Yoho said, "F--ing bitch."[29] Yoho's goal was simple: to censure Ocasio-Cortez for expressing an opinion different from his own.

Women who express their views may be labeled as "outspoken," a term rarely applied to men. One woman's husband suggested that a friend appoint her to a company's board because of her experience in the field. The friend said, "Only if she behaves. She is very outspoken."

Apparently, the man only wanted her on the board if she kept her opinions to herself.

Other women are labeled to discourage them from bringing up problems. When one woman's boss disagrees with her, "he tells me that I have 'strong opinions' and dismisses me as stubborn and tells me I only want to be right," as she described. Labeling was used to dismiss another woman's concerns: "My legitimate complaints and outrage over blatant inefficiencies and mistreatment of employees is often taken by my superiors as 'she's emotional' rather than 'there might be a problem with this.'"

CHASTISING

Women may also find themselves chastised—admonished, scolded, or disciplined—when they speak up. A city government employee noted that "speaking up really cost me" when she asserted that the city's constituents deserved to be at the table when decisions were made. Her male boss told her that she was "disrespectful," "pushing back too much," and that she "shouldn't question his decisions." In another situation, an older male constituent verbally berated a congressional aide over the phone. When the aide asked the man to limit his comments to policy concerns, he scolded her: "A girl like you should know better than to speak to a man like that."

Female attorneys—whose job it is to speak up on behalf of others—are frequently chastised. A male judge called a trial lawyer into his chambers to "scold" her because, in his words, "when [she] talked in the courtroom, everyone listened"—which would seem a good quality in a lawyer. Yet when she stopped doing trial work, the judge's clerk told her that "they really miss me because I was a good advocate for my clients," as she explained. Another lawyer was disciplined through dismissal as head of a women's initiative after she discussed gender discrimination and unequal pay with other associates. She was explicitly told "not to talk about it with anyone." While some men may want the appearance of equitable structures, they don't want women to challenge inequity.

Ignoring

Women's voices are also muted when they are outright ignored. Even high-profile women experience this, such as U.S. senator Kirsten Gillibrand: "I don't think I've mentally counted all the times I have been dismissed and not listened to."[30] Many women have similar stories. A nonprofit leader's male colleague was shuffled from one leadership position to another, "despite the objections and evidence presented by five female coworkers" of his lack of qualifications. The women were simply ignored.

Many women have to repeat themselves multiple times—three seems to be the magic number—to be heard. A lab manager restated requests "a minimum of three times" while her male counterpart received immediate compliance. When another woman or her female colleagues suggest ideas or bring up work hindrances, they must repeat it "at least three times before being taken seriously," or "a male colleague will have to say it again before our higher ups take our suggestion seriously." And he gets the credit. Think of how much extra time and effort women must take to make the same points over and over until they are finally heard. And imagine the additional productivity that could result if women were heard and listened to the first time.

INTERRUPTING

Women are actively ignored when they are interrupted and talked over. Women in politics are routinely interrupted. A study of more than twenty-four thousand congressional hearings between 1994 and 2018 found women were more often interrupted than men—10 percent more in Senate committees. The muting was even stronger in hearings on women's issues, where women were more than twice as likely to be cut off than while discussing other issues.[31] In 2020, then U.S. vice presidential candidate Kamala Harris had to assert, "I'm speaking," multiple times during her debate with then vice president Mike Pence to stop his interruptions.[32]

Interruptions of women may be particularly common in male-dominated workplaces. One woman who was the sole woman in her office was "interrupted, corrected, and condescended to on a daily basis," even though her male colleagues all consider themselves to be "feminists." "I don't think they can help themselves," she commented. Male colleagues often cut off and spoke over another woman, without acknowledgement or apology. As she explained, "It seems each time that they are completely unaware that I had been saying something in the first place." Women may make excuses for men's problematic behavior because they've been socialized into a system that prioritizes men's needs and because calling it out could result in backlash.

In the male-dominated field of economics, seminars are events where "researchers disseminate new work, practitioners test out new theories, and young people network and find jobs."[33] They are also venues in which women are interrupted more than men. As an economics professor described, "Women are often interrupted so much they can't finish their presentations. This does not happen to men." Research backs up the professor's observation. A study of 467 seminars found that female presenters were interrupted 12 percent more than male presenters and were more likely to receive hostile questions; the interrupters were "mostly male." The study authors noted that disruptions "throw off the flow of a presentation or interrupt the particular argument that's being made." And while 12 percent may not sound like much, the effect can be damaging over the course of a woman's career, particularly when having to deal with repeated, hostile questioning in seminar after seminar.[34]

Women in female-dominated fields are also interrupted, by "men, young and old, with positions inferior as well as superior to my own," as an education superintendent explained. Two men routinely interrupted and hepeated a nursing school student. She noted the double-standard: "Interruptions and aggression by males are seen as leadership. Those same actions by women are seen as rude, unprofessional, and hysterical. It's infuriating to have to repeatedly say 'excuse me, I wasn't finishing speaking' when I'm being overtly disrespected."

Silencing

Whether figuratively or literally, many women are told to "sit down and shut up." Their voices, ideas, and concerns are silenced. An information technology professional was told not to speak at meetings even if she noticed an oversight because her "quick grasp makes some people feel threatened." A lead aerospace engineer encountered the same mindset when her manager advised her not to bring attention to "any mistakes [other engineers] may have made and let them find out 'on their own.'" She responded, "When should I speak up then, as the plane is being delivered?" Similarly, when a physician clarified a male subordinate's error, the subordinate told her she was being "argumentative and difficult." And she got no support from above: "Male senior staff admonished me to just be quiet and gloss over what was obviously incorrect." Think about the implications of silencing women in these fields. Mistakes in industries like aerospace engineering and medicine can lead to deadly consequences. And for what purpose? To spare men's egos.

Sometimes women are shushed. "I've been face-palmed to man-shush me in a meeting where we were equals but he felt I should take a back seat as a woman," one former government employee recalled. A twenty-one-year-old small business employee was asked to join a meeting to discuss contract changes. The male contractors valued her opinion when she spoke to them on the phone, but when she walked into the meeting, they pretended like she "didn't exist." She explained, "I wasn't allowed to speak. When I did, my boss said I was asking for too much, and [I] was shushed many times."

Other times women are literally told to "shut up." When one woman asked a question during a meeting, a male colleague told her to "shut up a minute." The colleague then completed her thought and her question. When a state appraiser questioned the legality of assigning overinflated rates to homes to raise tax revenue, her supervisor pulled her aside and said, "Shut up! You don't need to say anything about matters that don't concern you." The state was later sued, and thousands of property owners requested reviews over the false property appraisals. Telling a colleague to "shut up" is rude under the best of circumstances; when coupled with a power imbalance of gender and hierarchy, it's doubly damaging.

Some men explicitly state that women should not have the right to speak. When one woman developed laryngitis, an older male colleague told her, "Losing [your] voice makes [you] better because a 'woman without a voice is great.'" While another woman was explaining an accounting process, her boss told her that "she needed to learn how to talk less" and that her husband should "stifle her."

Asking questions can also be problematic. One woman was told not to waste time with questions, "only to have those exact same concerns . . . pop up weeks later," as she explained. In another situation, when a city government employee attended a meeting with her boss, she asked a question. The boss cut her off: "Don't ask questions. It makes you look like you don't know what you're talking about." As she recounted, "Think I felt free to speak up after that?"

Muting in Many Ways

While we have explained one by one the various ways in which women are muted, in practice, women often experience them all. Many women said things like, "Interrupted, ignored, dismissed, credit going to someone else—see it all the time," and "There is not enough room in this comments section for me to list all the times I've been interrupted, mansplained, or had my ideas stolen." One woman was muted in all four ways:

> I was hired as a subject matter expert for an area no one else in the company could support. I was told by my male manager that I'm not allowed to talk in meetings about the very subject I was hired to support. NOT allowed to talk!! (*silenced*). In my current position, I am *constantly* interrupted by both males on my team, with comments such as, "We'll give the conversation back to you, but (Man 1 or Man 2) is going to talk first" (*ignored*). Then they repeat exactly the same thing I was saying as if it's their idea (*appropriated*). It's honestly infuriating. Oh, but if I speak up about it, I'm "too emotional" (*censured*).

———————

Our research has shown that having their communication constrained and voices muted is one of the most prevalent barriers for women. The strength of this barrier may be partly traceable to historical disregard of women's voices, including prohibitions of women speaking in public settings from Greek and Roman philosophers, Jewish rabbis, the Talmud, and Bible.[35] A fifteenth-century clergyman promoted an Old English Proverb: "A mayde [girl] schuld [should] be seen but not herd [heard.]"[36] The new words that have entered our collective vocabulary (hepeat, bropropriate, mansplain) serve to call attention to this persistent, ubiquitous problem. The various facets of muting women show how, even though women may be physically present in the workplace, their ideas may be unwelcome. These behaviors serve to remind women, yet again, of their supposed place in the gender hierarchy of serving and empowering men, but not being men's equals.

UNEQUAL STANDARDS

Women are often held to different standards than their male colleagues, leading them to overprepare and work twice as hard to earn respect and succeed. They may be expected to undertake emotional labor, by being caring and nurturing, maintaining a positive demeanor, and buffering men's emotions. To ensure that women do not deviate from performance expectations, their dress, appearance, demeanor, and even the sound of their voice are scrutinized in ways that men's are not.

Many women find they must work harder than men to succeed. One woman's male manager admitted his preference for hiring women, who "work harder because they always feel they have to prove something." Similarly, a banker noted that the few women who made it to senior levels in commercial banking had to "work harder and smarter and accept the fact that that alone would not (necessarily) get them the recognition and promotions they sought."

Many women experience differing standards for opportunities. An overseas project team leader worked for months, making contacts, setting up details, and recruiting and training team members. Yet a few weeks before the team departed, the leadership role was given to a young man because "he needs the experience," as she was told. This woman was "crushed" and had to fix problems caused by the man's poor decisions. In another case, an Australian police detective investigated a death in custody for a man who had been arrested for rape, run from police, and then jumped to his death from a high-rise building. She spent hours managing the chaos and hundreds of traumatized witnesses. When she began the internal investigation of the arresting police officers, her male boss told her that a junior male officer would take over. She explained, "When I said that was a breach of policy, I was simply told I couldn't do it as I was a woman."

Unequal standards also affect women entrepreneurs in their ability to raise venture capital funds. While U.S. employment law prevents questions about relationship and family status in job interviews, the same rules do not apply to venture pitches. When entrepreneurs Yada Piyajomkwan and Anderson Sumarli pitched their online investment startup to over fifty venture firms and angel investors from Silicon Valley to Singapore, they received very different questions. Business-related questions were more often directed to Sumarli, while Piyajomkwan received lots of personal questions. Did she have a boyfriend? When did she plan on marrying? Was she dating Sumarli? The personal questioning was worse in Asia, yet even in the United States, a venture firm partner commented, "I'm worried about investing in them because Yada may get married and drop out of the company."[37] Men's ideas matter, but what apparently matters for women is their relationship status.

Unequal performance expectations affect women in many industries. Entertainer Jennifer Lopez experienced differing standards in Hollywood. While it was acceptable for a man to be late or belligerent, Lopez was "berated" when she was fifteen minutes late and labeled as "difficult" when she expressed certain opinions or was passionate about a topic.[38] In education, male coaches in one district were "given a pass to skip meetings," while female coaches were formally reprimanded if not present, as a teacher explained. In another case, a male supervisor gave a manager performance feedback that she was "the most manipulative person he'd ever met." When she asked for an example, he said that she observes people to determine what motivates them and then uses that to get them to do what she wants. She asked her supervisor to consider how he would characterize the behavior if she were a man, suggesting that he would "call that leadership." At least the supervisor recognized the flaw in his thinking, as she explained: "He did have the grace to admit that I was correct, and he never realized that he viewed female and male employees differently." But such acknowledgements are rare.

Emotional Labor

While people are hired for physical and mental labor, women are also often expected to perform emotional labor, a term coined by sociologist Dr. Arlie Hochschild to describe producing and managing feelings, such as being constantly cheerful. Teaching, nursing, childcare, and flight attendant are professions typically thought of as "female," and in which emotional labor is expected.[39] But even women in male-dominated professions are expected to perform emotional labor. A lawyer had to "maintain a bright, cheerful, almost cheerleader-like attitude;" several male bosses became "threatened, indignant, and despondent" when she opted for neutral professionalism. At one point, she was written up on a performance evaluation and given thirty days to improve or lose her job because a male partner thought she didn't want to work with him anymore. When challenged, the partner confirmed that her work performance was still satisfactory. This lawyer explained, "I 'got my job back' in thirty days after spending one to two hours a day in [the male partner's] office asking questions about cases, complimenting him, and talking about him."

Expectations to carry out emotional labor are made explicit every time women are commanded to "smile," which is "like telling a dog to 'sit, stay, or heel,'" as one woman pointed out. Other women noted that only men asked them to smile and that they could not recall a man being told to smile. In another case, a woman's male manager told her that "though it's unfair, women are held to a different standard and so [you] should smile more." He continued, "Fake it until [you] make it." Several women were given the feedback to "smile more" during performance evaluations. One said, "I was ranked as a top performer last year. My only constructive feedback was that I should smile more. Really? I'm sure no man has ever been given that feedback!"

Buffering men's emotions is another type of emotional labor. Amy performed this task in a previous role during almost daily conversations with her boss about his personal life and feelings. In another example, a male C-level officer became offended with a colleague when he stopped by her office and she was busy. He refused to speak to her and avoided eye contact even in meetings where they needed to communicate. However, she was responsible for rectifying the situation: "I had to buy him a latte and apologize for him to 'forgive' me."

Scrutiny

To ensure that women do not deviate from behavior and performance expectations, they are often subject to scrutiny of their work, appearance, demeanor, and even the tone and sound of their voice. Probably no woman in U.S. politics has been scrutinized more than Hillary Clinton. As secretary of state, Clinton used a private email server to send emails on unclassified topics. The Department of State spent three years on an investigation, finally concluding in October 2019 that "there was no systemic or deliberate mishandling of classified information."[40] After all the debunked scandals and investigations over the years—Vince Foster's death, emails, Benghazi—Clinton has said, "I'm the most investigated innocent person in America."[41] Not only were Clinton's work practices heavily scrutinized, her hair, dress, and demeanor have been monitored throughout her career.[42]

U.S. representative Alexandria Ocasio-Cortez has also had her share of scrutiny, especially related to her appearance. Shortly after her election, a journalist tweeted a photo of her with the comment "that jacket and coat don't look like a girl who struggles."[43] A newspaper also criticized Ocasio-Cortez for spending "nearly $300" on hair services— an estimate of $80 for a haircut, $180 for lowlights, plus a 20 percent tip—even though these prices are not unusual for Washington, DC.[44] The time and money women spend to maintain societal expectations for their appearance—makeup, hair, jewelry, clothing, shoes, accessories— add up fast. According to psychology professor Dr. Renee Englen, the goal of scrutiny and criticism of female politicians' appearance is to keep the focus off their ideas, with the result that "powerful women are silenced . . . and other women are dissuaded from entering the political arena."[45]

Extreme scrutiny of appearance is common for actors. Jennifer Aniston and Jennifer Lawrence were both told to lose weight at the start of their careers. While Aniston was "hardly fat" before she landed her *Friends* role, she was told that she was too heavy to get acting jobs and that she should "lose 30 lbs."[46] While working on a film, producers told Lawrence "to lose 15 pounds in two weeks," while another young female actor on the same project "had already been fired for not losing weight fast enough," as Lawrence recounted. As actor Lena Headey stated, "[Male] actors can be 'interesting,' but there's real pressure on women to be beautiful and skinny."[47]

Some women in Hollywood have been advised to get plastic surgery. The first agent who actor Elizabeth Banks met told her "to get a boob job." She was thankful that she didn't have the money to follow through. Similarly, when actor Debra Messing was doing a love scene in her first film, a director screamed, "Cut! How quickly can we get a plastic surgeon in here? Her nose is ruining my movie."[48]

Women in all types of roles experience scrutiny. A college provost noted that while it is important for women to be in visible leadership roles, it is also scary because "everybody's watching your every move." Professor Dr. Kristina Mitchell was scrutinized on student evaluations that ranged from "She's a bit prickly in her demeanor" to "I like it when she wears skinny jeans and heels." As she explained, it is "commentary my male counterparts say they never receive."[49]

Women lawyers also face disproportionate scrutiny. Law professor and former trial attorney Lara Bazelon noted that as long as male lawyers "stuck to a basic uniform: a dark suit, a crisp button-down shirt, an inoffensive tie, and a close shave or neatly trimmed beard, [then] their physicality was unremarkable—essentially invisible." Yet women's clothing was scrutinized by everyone from judges to other lawyers to jurors to witnesses to clients. Bazelon found that she had to be attractive but not provocative, yet not frumpy or cheap. Observing the appearance of her female colleagues, medium-length or long hair was appropriate, "but not too long." At trial, heels that were "not too high" and skirts that were "not too short" were preferred, and pantyhose were a requirement as women's bare legs were considered taboo.[50]

Correctional facilities also have rules that place an undue burden on women. When public defender Emily Galvin-Almanza drove five hours to visit a client, a male officer turned her away because her underwire bra set off the metal detector. She went to her car and tore up the stitching on the bra to remove the wire so that she could enter the facility to do her job.[51]

Because women are socialized into the same gendered system, sometimes they also internalize stereotypes and enforce sexist norms by scrutinizing other women's appearance. A college provost told Amy about a search committee's discussion of a female candidate. A woman on the committee said, "I could never take her seriously. . . . Didn't you notice? She didn't have on pantyhose?" The provost explained, "I wasn't looking at the woman's legs. I was listening to what she had to say, which were really good ideas for the position."

Women's tone of voice is also scrutinized. When Oprah Winfrey worked for the television show *60 Minutes*, she had to do *seven* takes to say her name because producers thought her voice had "too much emotion" and needed to be "flattened."[52] Conversely news anchor Norah O'Donnell was criticized for not speaking with enough emotion. A male television critic wrote, "She's an OK news reader, but nothing special. She lacks energy and often reads the news robotically. She changes her tone so infrequently that you occasionally don't get the sense she has empathy even when stories demand it."[53] Actor Jennifer Lawrence described her own dismay at tone policing: "I'm over trying to find the 'adorable' way to state my opinion and still be likable! F*ck that. I don't think I've ever worked for a man in charge who spent time contemplating what angle he should use to have his voice heard. It's just heard."[54]

Women are criticized no matter their tone. As nonprofit executive Dr. Mariko Silver, explained, "Women leaders are expected to be both personable and authoritative, both analytic and affable, both warm (including being open to any question, no matter how off-putting) and clearly commanding."[55] Even in life-or-death situations, women's tones may be policed. A resident physician was told she was too "bossy" during a code blue, which is a time when decisiveness is required to resuscitate a patient.[56]

Women are similarly criticized over the sound of their voices. One woman was told that the inflection of her voice came across as "bitchy" and if she were younger, she would sound like she was "whining." Female lawyers "routinely report that male judges critique their voices as too loud or too shrill," as law professor Lara Bazelon explained.[57] One marketing professional was excited to lead her first committee meeting, which included executive leadership. About ten minutes into her presentation, the CFO asked, "Does your voice always sound like Scarlett Johansson's?" She commented, "I was crestfallen." And while physician Dr. Lara Devgan often receives good feedback for the content of her medical talks, she explained, "I have been given the 'constructive criticism' that my voice is 'girly' or 'immature.'"[58]

The voices of prominent women are also highly scrutinized. Media critics have called Hillary Clinton's voice too "nagging," while former U.S. vice presidential candidate Sarah Palin's voice "causes ears to bleed," and pundit Ann Coulter's "whiny voice is so distracting."[59] Due to their roles, audiences typically hear voices of prominent women through broadcast technology, which distorts the sound. In 1927, when the U.S. Congress regulated bandwidth assigned to radio stations, broadcasters and equipment manufacturers limited their signals to ranges optimal for men's lower voices. Today, data-compression algorithms and Bluetooth speakers impact higher frequencies and consonants; hence, women's voices lose definition and sound "thin and tinny." Instead of improving the technology, women have been told to lower their voices and not to show too much emotion. But when they do, they get the criticism—like Norah O'Donnell's experience—of sounding "forced" and "unnatural."[60]

―――――――――――――

The breadth and variety of unequal standards applied to women is staggering. They range from the requirement that women work harder and achieve more, to expectations that women perform emotional labor to manage the feelings of those around them, to scrutiny of literally everything about a woman. The combined load can feel exhausting and overwhelming. Not surprisingly, many women have simply decided not to play along. Yet not playing is risky, as some of the stories have shown. Too often, the standards are not only unequal, but nonnegotiable.

―――――――――――――

Women at work are disproportionately constrained in many ways. Early on they may be pressured into careers that have been deemed "suitable" for women and discouraged from pursuing high-paid, high-reward careers considered to be men's domain. Once in the workplace, they find their voices are muted, and they are subjected to unequal standards for their work and behavior. The source of these pressures as well as the intended purpose is clear: they flow directly from the male privilege to limit women's presence and authority in the workplace. And they are enacted in ways designed to increase male power and male comfort. If women work harder at their jobs and achieve more, then organizations do indeed get "a bargain" when they hire a woman, as one woman explained to Leanne.[61] At this same time, women are pressured to self-monitor and to please the men around them. Every minute that women spend worrying about what to wear, how to speak, or how to manage their male colleagues' emotions is time taken away from productive work they could be investing for the organization. Yet all too often, those in power fail to recognize the real loss that results from these constraints.

SHATTERING DISPROPORTIONATE CONSTRAINTS: AN EQUITABLE ORGANIZATION

Instead of constraining women, workplaces must adopt equity as a value and priority, rooted in the concept of *equalism*, that all people are of equal value and deserve equal access, treatment, rights, and opportunity.[62] Acknowledging that people are starting from different places, equitable organizations allocate resources and supports such that equal outcomes are attainable. Solutions to shatter disproportionate constraints and move toward an equitable organization are outlined below. Those serving as leaders must take the lead, while allies—anyone who is supportive—can help advance equity. Individual women can also take steps to mitigate constraints.

Constrained Career Choices

LEADERS

- Establish programs, sponsor scholarships, and fund training to encourage girls and young women into traditionally male career paths. Partner with existing organizations that aim to increase women in these fields.
- Connect new female hires—especially those in traditionally male fields—with mentors. Ensure these women are fully supported.

- Use diverse staff images—including women in stereotypically male positions—on websites, advertisements, and office walls.

ALLIES

- Be a role model. Offer to speak to girls and young women at schools, clubs, and colleges about your career field.
- Volunteer in organizations that aim to increase women in stereotypically male fields.
- Mentor women who are new to your field.

SELF

- If you are considering career paths, research your options. Talk to teachers, guidance counselors, and college and trade school faculty about possibilities. Reach out to people currently working in the field to learn about their experience. Ask to shadow them.
- Don't let discouragement from others dissuade you from a career path that interests you.
- Don't compare yourself to men in the field. Recognize that men's confidence, knowledge, and accomplishments may be exaggerated.

Muted Voices

LEADERS

- Require training for staff on identifying and avoiding muting behaviors. Train meeting facilitators how to ensure all voices are heard.
- Set norms that allow everyone to have a voice. Do not penalize people for speaking up or asking questions.
- Establish a "no interruptions" rule for meetings. Facilitators should call out interruptions and allow the interrupted person to finish.

ALLIES

- Amplify women's voices. When a woman says a key idea, repeat it and give her credit, which will force others to recognize the contribution and stop it from being bropropriated or hepeated.[63]
- Call out muting behaviors and revert attention back to the woman. If a woman is interrupted, you can say, "Let Agnes finish her thought." If a woman is hepeated, you can say, "Meng just mentioned that idea. Let's hear her thoughts." If she is being mansplained, interrupt the speaker with, "Sofia is an expert on this topic. Let's hear what she thinks."
- Push back against censuring. Highlight how men are not treated the same way. If a woman is labeled, you can explain, "We would never say that men are hysterical. It's not appropriate to label women that way." If a woman is chastised for asking questions, you may say, "Jess brings up good questions. Men aren't admonished for speaking up and neither should women be."

SELF

- Recognize that calling out interruptions when they happen to you can be tricky. You may interrupt the interrupter: "Excuse me, Mike, may I finish my thought?" or "Excuse me, Mike, let me finish my thought." You may also choose to wait for the interrupter to finish, especially if they are your superior in the hierarchy: "As I was saying before Mike jumped in . . ." If the interruption has caused the conversation to go in another direction, you can continue your point at any time: "Let me circle back to what I was saying earlier."
- If certain colleagues repeatedly mute you, speak to them privately. You can explain, "I find that you often speak over me in meetings. When I am not able to make my points, I can't do my job. Let's discuss ways that ensure we are both able to get our thoughts on the table."

- Solicit support from colleagues to watch for muting behaviors and call them out on your behalf. Establish a buddy system with another person to help reinforce each other's ideas.
- If these behaviors are systemic, ask for support from your boss or human resources (HR).

Unequal Standards

LEADERS

- Ensure performance standards are equitable for everyone.
- Train managers how to avoid gender bias in performance evaluations, such as not penalizing women for decisive behavior and not judging them for emotional labor, such as not smiling or being nurturing enough.
- Train managers to spot bias in customer evaluations and to not hold biased comments against women. Give managers guidelines to disregard comments about women's appearance and demeanor.

ALLIES

- Do not make comments about women's appearance, demeanor, or sound of their voice.
- If you hear others unfairly scrutinizing women, call it out: "We wouldn't mention a man's attire. It is not appropriate to scrutinize women's attire."
- Do not tell women to "smile" or expect women to listen to your personal problems.

SELF

- If you receive biased criticism on a performance evaluation, discuss the unfairness with your supervisor: "This criticism describes a leadership behavior that I use to accomplish my job. Would I be given this feedback if I were a man?"

- If someone tells you to smile, you can say, "Thanks, but smiling isn't necessary for me to do my job." Or, "I don't feel like smiling right now." You can also explain the problem, "Women are often asked to smile while men are not. It's emotional labor on which women are unfairly judged."
- If a colleague continually expects you to listen to their personal problems, redirect them to other sources of support: "I'm sorry to hear you are having a hard time. Perhaps someone in HR can point you toward some helpful resources."

3

INSUFFICIENT SUPPORT

"I witnessed incompetent men get hired and promoted and invited to male-only outings, while exceptionally talented women were ignored."

—Lawyer

The COVID-19 pandemic has perhaps done more to draw attention to the inequities faced by women than any other event in recent history. Professor Chiara Saraceno pointed out that governments worked on reopening plans for businesses without considering that schools remained closed: "They didn't even think of it."[1] For women, this presented a nightmare-like conundrum. How could they go to work and take care of their children? Around the globe, the pandemic showed how women in all types of work suffer from insufficient support. From garment factory workers without contracts to high-level professionals in developed nations saddled with "the double-double shift," women were the ones most severely impacted by the pandemic.[2]

Under-resourced at home and work, women saw their unpaid labor skyrocket and their work productivity plummet.[3] One in five U.S. working-aged adults was unemployed as of August 2020 because the pandemic upended their childcare. Women were three times more likely than men to be the parent who dropped out of the paid workforce.[4] In academia, a study of 1,893 medical journal articles from January through June 2020 found that the proportion of women first authors was 19 percent lower than for papers published in the same journals from January through June 2019. This reduction was particularly noticeable during the first two months of the pandemic (March and April 2020) when female first-author publications were 23 percent lower than the prior year.[5]

For women with children who kept their paid job by working from home during pandemic shut down orders, their work was more likely to be erratic compared to male partners, who tended to have priority in uninterrupted time and private physical space for their jobs.[6] Author Virginia Woolfe pointed out this problem a century ago; for women to write they needed a room of their own.[7] While professor Dr. Vanessa LoBue and her husband were both working at home at the beginning of the pandemic, her productivity took a hit with her two- and five-year old children at home. "There is more of an expectation that [my husband] can be working all the time than there is for me," as she stated.[8]

The reality for women working in a male-run world is that support is all too often missing. Even in the best of times in the West, women lack access to social structures and networks that would help them advance. There are few *communal resources*, like subsidized childcare or paid family leave, that would help women maintain a job and a family. Women often *lack mentors* to aid their professional growth and *sponsors* to recommend them for advancement. They face *exclusion* from informal networks, social events, and even formal leadership events. In addition, *unsupportive leaders* may fail to help women dealing with discrimination or harassment in favor of protecting men in the organization.

LACK OF COMMUNAL RESOURCES

Societal and organizational supports are critical for women to be available for the workforce, yet the United States offers very few resources. While other countries have policies and programs to support work and families, such as paid family leave, affordable childcare, universal pre-school, and longer school days, the United States does not.[9] Parents have a huge burden in caregiving, but according to economist Dr. Kathryn Edwards, "the [U.S.] federal response to that has been, women, try to do more. And we have never made an investment in working women in this country."[10] As sociologist Dr. Jessica Calarco pointed out, "Other countries have social safety nets. The U.S. has women."[11]

Women are disproportionately responsible for both housework and childcare. As of 2020, women spent an average of 2.4 hours per day on household activities; men 1.6 hours. Similarly, women spent 1.7 hours per day caring for children; men 45 minutes. While the amount of time men spent on childcare was about the same as 2019, women's time rose by 13 minutes, likely a result of pandemic stay-at-home orders. This disparity means that men have about an hour more per day to spend on leisure and sports (6.0 hours for men; 5.1 for women).[12]

An expectation that male partners step up would help, as would federal programs and mandates for organizations. While some states and organizations have implemented family supports, workers face disparities across the country. Someone fortunate enough to work for a company that offers paid parental leave, paid sick leave, and onsite subsidized childcare is likely a professional worker in a competitive and well-funded industry. Unfortunately, most corporations view parenting challenges as individual and not communal problems.[13] Too often organizations offer few resources, assuming employees have stay-at-home partners to watch children, take them to doctor visits, and oversee schooling and homework. Amy previously worked in a state without mandated paid maternity or family leave. Her organization offered neither paid parental leave nor short-term disability insurance, often used to substitute for paid maternity leave. New mothers used accrued sick or vacation leave to cover the absence or went without pay. Partners were able to use just one week of their paid sick leave to help with a new child. If the mother or child had extended illnesses, there was no sick leave left. There was also no leave left for vacation.

The resources provided to Leanne were even less. When she was pregnant in the mid-1990s, not only did her health insurance not cover maternity costs, but her employer had a reputation for firing pregnant women. Hence, Leanne hid the pregnancy; she was successful for more than six months. To keep healthcare costs down, Leanne went for prenatal care every other month, instead of monthly as recommended. Fortunately, Leanne delivered a healthy baby, but the stress impacted her productivity and health.

Due to the closure of daycares and schools during the COVID-19 pandemic, many women were forced to leave the workforce to care for children. Proposal coordinator Teresa Derdianian left her job to care for her two small children and is considering not returning in part due to the high cost of childcare—thousands of dollars per month.[14] Similarly, prosecutor Youli Lee hit a breaking point at the start of the pandemic in spring 2020. With her physician husband working seven days per week, Lee was left at home to manage her work plus online learning for three children. She took a leave of absence from her job when she realized that it was too much.[15]

For single mothers, the lack of societal resources for parenting creates an even more dire situation. Single parent Rocio Flores had started a new daycare job when the pandemic hit, closing the daycare center. While the daycare soon reopened, her children's school did not. In need of a paycheck, she had no other choice but to her leave her two children—ages seven and twelve—home alone.[16]

While there was pressure to get businesses open during early stages of the pandemic, there was no federal priority in the United States to get children in school safely, forcing many women to choose between their job and taking care of their children.[17] At the start of the pandemic, employment for married women with school-aged children fell by 15 percent. When schools reopened in 2021, their employment regained only 21 percent of the losses (3.2 percentage points).[18] These statistics are evidence of the competition between career and caregiving that women face every day because the burden for caregiving falls to individual women.

LACK OF MENTORING AND SPONSORING

Mentors are experienced employees who provide career guidance and support to less-experienced individuals. Mentoring relationships can be established informally where two people connect directly or formally where the organization matches the mentor and protégé.[19] Sponsors are high-ranking individuals who advocate for and provide advancement opportunities to less-experienced employees. As professor Dr. Herminia Ibarra explained, "While a mentor is someone who has knowledge and will share it with you, a sponsor is a person who has power and will use it for you."[20]

Along with opportunities, sponsors provide preparation for new roles, skill development for advancement, increased visibility, and a means of overcoming obstacles.[21] Even with good mentors, women can still lag behind men; a sponsor, however, can increase women's chances of promotion.[22] Clearly, the lack of these crucial relationships can limit a woman's career. Yet all too often, women are left to navigate on their own with neither a mentor nor a sponsor.

In our research of 1,606 women leaders, less than half (47.6 percent) received significant mentoring while about two-thirds (64.7 percent) had to learn to lead on their own. The results were slightly better in terms of sponsorship with 63.7 percent having been sponsored for promotion. Still, of these highly successful women, more than one-third did not have the benefit of a sponsor. In a McKinsey & Company survey of women employees at all levels, only 30 percent said they have the sponsorship needed to advance their careers; that number dropped to 24 percent for the Black women surveyed.[23]

Lack of Mentoring

Amy met with two university presidents who both lacked mentors in their careers. While one attended women's leadership seminars, she never had anyone reach out and say, "Let me help you." The other president had to teach herself how to lead. She described herself as "highly competent" yet "organizationally incompetent," which led to a risk of being fired. She expressed, "I very much feel the absence of a mentor."[24]

Leaders often fail to be proactive about women's professional development and mentoring. One lawyer lamented, "[I was] left to learn to lead on my own and from my clients." She pinpointed a reason why she lacked mentors as "not being put on teams where I would have made stronger connections with my colleagues. [I was] more often assigned cases and clients I would handle by myself or with teams of those below me in [the] organization."

Women in male-dominated professions may have extra difficulty in finding willing mentors. Photojournalist Katie Orlinsky explained how the "bro network" makes mentoring difficult for women photographers: "People like to see a young version of themselves. A man might not see that in a young woman."[25] Similarly, when butcher Jessica Wragg worked at a meat counter as a teenager, she quickly learned that none of the men wanted to help her learn. She spent hours researching the cuts online and then asked to be shown the process. The male butchers' response was always the same: "I haven't got the time." As she said, "I was expected to pick it up, but that's the thing with butchery: Picking it up just isn't that easy."[26]

In the faith-based industry, it can be common for women to wait until their children are grown to work directly for the organization; hence, they enter leadership positions at much later ages than men. But by then, women may be thought of as "too old" for mentoring. One woman explained, "Once I was over sixty, no one thinks I am worth investing in with training or mentoring." And investing in women's professional development may not be prioritized. Another leader noted, "I would have loved to have another woman mentor me, but the organization didn't have funds to cover this."

Even when formal mentoring relationships are established, they may not work out. One physician was bullied by an assigned mentor, her female colleague, "as if I work at her discretion," as the physician stated.[27] She continued, "No mentoring ever occurred. It was more of condescension." (See chapter 5, "Hostility," for more on mean girl behavior.)

Lack of Sponsoring

While many women lack sponsors, some are explicitly denied the opportunity. One boss informed a woman with ten years of experience and a PhD that she would "*never* get a promotion," despite being qualified for both her job and the one above hers. According to the boss, she was "too ambitious," "too big for her britches," and "overstepping [her] role." (see chapter 2, "Disproportionate Constraints" for more on labeling.)

A retired emergency medicine physician was also denied a sponsor. While Dr. Elizabeth Edwardsen began her residency in internal medicine, she found emergency medicine to be a better fit. After completing four of the required five years of clinical emergency medicine practice, she asked a male administrator for a letter of recommendation for board certification. Although this administrator was helping a male classmate through the same process, he refused Edwardsen's request. An internal medicine administrator also failed to write a letter when asked. As a result, Edwardsen was unable to sit for the emergency medicine board. As she described it, "My inability to demonstrate 'appropriate' credentialing greatly affected my career mobility to other institutions and communities, my credibility for my chosen practice setting, and future leadership in my career of choice."[28]

Women of color may be especially challenged in finding mentors and sponsors. A Black fifth-year associate attorney described having neither a mentor nor a sponsor: "To ultimately continue advancing [in a law firm], you need to have a partner and/or senior associates that take a liking to you. And in terms of taking a liking, that's a very personal choice. . . . People tend to gravitate to people who are similar to them, and I know I'm different than a lot of the people at the firm."[29] Without mentors and sponsors, women find career progress to be a struggle or halted altogether.

EXCLUSION

Women are often excluded from informal networks, social events, and sometimes formal work events, places where work relationships are built and decisions made. As a lawyer described, "I witnessed incompetent men get hired and promoted and invited to male-only outings, while exceptionally talented women were ignored." While exclusion may seem more benign than overt discrimination or harassment, it is more likely to cause job dissatisfaction and turnover. A study of 1,300 full-time workers found that exclusion was more common than harassment (70 percent had experienced exclusion in the previous six months, while 48 percent experienced harassment). The researchers then looked at an employment survey that included isolation and harassment questions and compared the data to turnover rates three years later. Those who felt excluded were more likely to have suffered health problems and to have left their jobs. While not diminishing the harms of harassment, the researchers argued that exclusion was "more likely to douse individuals' sense of belonging and their organizational commitment and engagement."[30] Both turnover and disengagement have a high organizational cost, yet exclusion may be tolerated as part of a boys' club atmosphere (see chapter 1, "Male Privilege").

Social Events

Lunches and dinners are social activities from which women are often excluded, as a town planning director described: "The town manager routinely [went] to lunch with the public works director, his assistant, and the finance director—all male. Through the grapevine I heard they were discussing my budget and department scope of responsibilities." When the planning director brought this up, she was viewed as a "complainer." A lumber company accountant experienced similar exclusion. After she completed the audit each year, the audit partner (a man) took everyone to dinner except for her, even though she ran the project. Her two male superiors were friends with the audit partner, yet they never stood up for her to say, "She's got to come, she did the whole thing."[31]

Sometimes promotions and other opportunities result from socializing outside of work. A software architect learned from a male mentor that recruiting for "prize" projects happens socially. The mentor explained to her, "I don't really do networking; it is more friendship based. [A male leader] offered me to lead this project because we play golf together, and we started talking about it, and he asked [about] my interest." The architect noted that it is an "impossible game to win" as not having high-visibility projects on a résumé turns into "proof why a woman is less suited for big times." Another woman observed the same pattern in both industry and academia; top jobs go to those with social connections to male leaders, and women can be "locked out of opportunities to be part of their circle because the male leaders may not feel comfortable socializing with [them]." In addition, wives of male leaders "are more likely to view you with suspicion and exclude you from social events that they organize," as she noted.

Exclusion from social events may especially impact women of color. An African American higher education leader found that colleagues "engaged in external affairs outside of the office and oftentimes made business decisions during these external events." She explained, "I was expected to comply with the decisions made at these external events when I had no prior knowledge."

The problem is not that men socialize on their off-time—it is that they do business at these nonwork events. When deals and decisions are made and "friends" promoted through personal socializing, women are too often left out. Many women (and others) have neither time nor interest in attending after-hours and weekend social events such as going to the bar or golfing. Doing business when socializing instead of doing business at work creates an exclusionary boys' club atmosphere and leaves key stakeholders out of discussions and decisions.

Work Events

Not only are women excluded from unofficial social activities, they also may be excluded from official work events and meetings. One chief information officer was left out of meetings; when she was invited, it was often as an afterthought with her male boss saying, "Oh, we forgot about you." A male coworker once told another woman, "Feel free to leave the room. [Another male colleague] and I are going to talk about metrics. We don't want to bore you." This woman pushed back: "If it's alright with you, I'd like to stay. My team's work contributes directly to your metrics."

Exclusion from work events may be especially prevalent for women in faith-based organizations, as they are subject to a "stained-glass partition." [32] One-on-one lunch meetings are often "same sex in order to avoid the appearance of impropriety," according to one leader. As another woman explained, single women are often grouped with wives instead of male counterparts during work retreats, even though "a lot of business takes place in those social settings among the men." In one organization, men may travel with other men for work-related activities, but women are prevented from traveling alone with male colleagues. As a leader in the organization noted, "Qualified, competent women are overlooked for positions of leadership because of the convenience of sending a man to travel to conduct leadership trainings or broker leadership interventions." (See chapter 1, "Male Privilege," for more on shunning.)

Included Yet Excluded

Sometimes even when women are present at meetings or events, they may still be excluded or even ostracized, something that both Amy and Leanne have experienced. On multiple occasions when Amy posed a question in meetings that included her boss and a male subordinate, the boss turned and responded to Amy's subordinate instead of Amy. At an academic conference, Leanne was talking with a presenter when a male audience member approached. Physically inserting himself between Leanne and the presenter, he asked a question about the talk. The presenter turned away from Leanne and engaged the man; neither man acknowledged her presence or apologized for the interruption.

Women may be excluded even in settings in which they have an official role, such as one co-counsel who was not acknowledged during a capital punishment case. Throughout the trial, the judge identified the male attorneys included in bench conferences: "Will the attorneys Mr. X, Mr. Y, and Mr. Z please approach the bench," while excluding this female lawyer. On the last day of the trial, the lawyer's name was finally included. As it turns out, her opinion was "needed to determine whether the bailiff could be allowed to go out and purchase feminine hygiene products for one of the jurors."

Women may also be subtly ostracized in informal settings. When professor Dr. Alice Silverberg sat down next to her department chair at seminar dinners, "he would get up and make his wife change places with him, so that I sat next to her instead of him. He didn't do that with anyone else." This made it much harder for Silverberg to participate in conversations with her colleagues.[33] The problem with such "trivial" events is that they mount up over the months and years, and the results of repeated exclusions, even if small, are detrimental to women's careers.

UNSUPPORTIVE LEADERSHIP

Unsupportive leaders may fail to help women who face discrimination or harassment, prioritize men's needs, and overlook men's bad behavior. There are several forms of unsupportive leadership: disbelieving and victim blaming women, trivializing and ignoring their concerns, overriding women's decisions, and not having policies that would protect women. When not supported, women draw the very real conclusion that the organization values men—even problematic men—more than women.

Amy first discovered this barrier when she interviewed higher education leaders about their experiences with adversity. Unsupportive leadership was especially difficult for the women to understand, in part because it was hard to not take it personally. As one college president noted, "You're prone to say maybe it's about me." And dealing with an unsupportive leader does not stop at work. A vice president explained, "I certainly came home with less energy and frustrated many a night, so it took its toll . . . on my family." Several women executives who experienced active resistance from their supervisors had no recourse but to find other employment. One vice president who was forced out remarked, "I couldn't find a job for 15 months, so I supported my husband and [myself] for 15 months by borrowing against my credit cards."

Disbelief

Sometimes when women report discrimination or harassment, they are not believed, which is a form of credibility deficit. (See chapter 4, "Devaluation.") When one male boss sexually harassed, verbally abused, criticized, and demeaned a psychotherapist at a treatment center, she informed the center's executive director. The director stated that while she was aware of the behavior, the center's male owner "refused to believe or act on any of it." Not receiving any support, the psychotherapist resigned, detailing the abuse in a letter. She stated, "When it was finally all in writing, they fired him a month after I quit."

It's all too easy and acceptable to disbelieve women when they are mistreated in private settings. When women in another workplace reported men's sexist comments, they were told to "confront the person directly and have witnesses" but were given no guidance if confrontation didn't change the men's behavior. As one of the women noted, "There is no victory for women in the workplaces when it comes to this type of behavior."

Victim Blaming

Sometimes when women report sexism, harassment, or other discriminatory behavior, they are blamed, as if they—the victim—are at fault. One woman was sexually harassed, but when she reported it, her boss told her she was "difficult to work with." Similarly, when a coworker lashed out at another woman, a supervisor asked the woman what she said to cause the temper tantrum. When a third woman shared complaints about obvious inefficiencies and mistreatment of her co-workers, her supervisors blamed her for being "emotional" rather than taking action to correct the problems.

Victim blaming happens to many women. After an older male supervisor groped a nineteen-year-old woman, she reported the harass-ment to another male supervisor who said, "You must have a problem with authority." In a different case, when an older male partner continu-ally called a female attorney from another firm "sweetie" or "honey" (pet names) during depositions, she "told him off." The male attorney reported her "disrespectful" behavior to the managing partner at *her* firm. As she described, "*My* managing partner told me I was being dis-respectful and how dare I speak to another attorney like that. And we wonder why women don't speak up."

Trivializing

When news anchor Roma Torre and four female colleagues real-ized they were losing airtime and opportunities and being treated differ-ently because they were "older women," they each filed age discrimina-tion complaints with human resources (HR) and various news station managers. But their complaints were trivialized. In response to one complaint, Torre's supervisor said, "That's just the way it is. Too bad. Boo hoo."[34] (See chapter 5, "Hostility," for more on the discrimination cases filed by Torre and her colleagues.)

Many women find their concerns trivialized. Some women are advised to ignore men's bad behavior because it's "not a big deal." A project manager was told she was "overreacting" when some men in the information technology department skipped her product development meetings. Similarly, an HR representative told another woman that she should "grow a pair" to deal with her male boss and that she wouldn't be successful in her job "without a thicker skin." Later when this woman stood up to the boss while he was having a tantrum, he made it clear that she "was to bend." Instead, she quit her job.

Women are sometimes told to keep working with male customers who mistreat them. When a drunk customer sexually harassed a bartender, she asked for him to be banned from the establishment. But the manager said, "He's good business and usually well-behaved. So, can you try to think of it as a compliment or something?" In another situation, an editor received an email from a male author with a dinner invitation and other things that violated the author-editor relationship. When the editor told her male boss about it, the boss said, "He's being nice. You're overreacting."

Harassment and abusive behavior from male bosses and coworkers are also trivialized, especially when those men are seen as top performers. One woman worked for a man who "bragged when [he] made female employees cry because of his abusive rants." When this woman complained about the man, she was told that "he had a file of complaints but brought in the dollars, so they kinda looked the other way."

Even sexual harassment is trivialized. One woman was told to ignore being hit on by her boss and not to wear V-neck shirts (thus also victim blaming her). Similarly, a company executive "grabbed the breast and buttocks" of former Vice Media employee Helen Donahue at a party; when she reported the incident, the HR director said it was "not sexual harassment but rather someone making a move on her." Donahue quit Vice shortly thereafter.[35]

Sometimes concern for men's ability to earn a living overrides women's safety in the workplace. When a male coworker sexually harassed Ford assembly plant worker Suzette Wright, she asked her union representative for help. The representative encouraged her not to file a claim because the coworker "would lose his job, his benefits, his pension." The union official then told her, "Suzette, you're a pretty woman—take it as a compliment."[36] An exposé found sexual harassment of other blue-collar women at Ford was similarly trivialized, which took a toll on them: "Some women quit. Others were emotionally spent."[37]

Laughing at women's reports of men's bad behavior also trivializes women's concerns. One woman was told to collaborate with a male colleague, but he refused to comply, saying he was holding back from treating her worse "because you are a woman," as she recounted. When she reported the colleague's behavior to her male supervisor, the supervisor laughed in her face.

Even health concerns are trivialized, as happened to a retail worker dealing with menstrual problems. Although the retail staff were primarily women, the supervisors and corporate staff were primarily men. When she had a conversation with HR about her issues, the representative "acted as if it wouldn't go through for FMLA [U.S. Family and Medical Leave Act] and didn't even want me to put that my cramps were the reason on the form."

Ignoring

In some cases, women and their concerns are outright ignored. This happens when supervisors fail to give women performance feedback. Male leaders neither mentioned areas for improvement for one nonprofit professional nor gave her "acknowledgement and affirmation to know that I was doing well," as she stated. Leaders may also ignore differential treatment. When clients disregarded a lawyer's advice and made inappropriate comments, she received no support. "My superiors have either not addressed or questioned why [the clients] refuse to listen to me but take the same advice from them," as she explained.

By ignoring women's reports, leaders communicate that they will continue to tolerate men's sexist behavior. When a tenure-track assistant professor made complaints about her male supervisor's belittling to "everyone superior to him," she was "completely ignored." She quit her job. In another situation, a male coworker made clucking sounds to two female coworkers, stating they "sounded like a couple of old hens." He later made a mooing sound at one of the women when she entered a meeting full of men to deliver a message from the boss. Although this woman spoke to the man privately both times, asking him to not speak to her in a disrespectful tone, the man ignored her and developed a negative attitude toward her. As she recounted, "I spoke to our human resources representatives and told them all of this and to the best of my knowledge nothing ever happened, and this man was never spoken to. Nobody ever followed up with me."

Overriding

Sometimes male leaders override women's decisions. One woman worked out a timeline for a customer project and got approval from her male boss. During the meeting with the all-male client group, one of them made a face as she was discussing the timeline. Before the client could explain, her boss grabbed her hand and patted it, saying, "She doesn't understand. She's trying to be too nice to the team. We can cut that time in half."

Leaders may also blame women as an excuse to override their decisions. An event space manager fired a repair person because he refused to complete agreed-upon tasks, invoiced for non-approved expenses, worked on building circuitry without an electrical license, and had a physical confrontation with a female event organizer. After being dismissed, the repair person sent the manager "manic emails and physical letters multiple times a day for *months*." Due to the threatening nature of the communications, the manager banned him from further contact with the organization. However, the manager's male boss overrode the ban and blamed her handling of the firing for the repair person's behavior. As the manager explained, "I quit."

Lack of Policies

Sometimes organizational leaders use policies—or lack thereof—to undermine women. After a tech startup employee had a stressful and only partly paid maternity leave, she asked her boss why company policy only allowed for six weeks of leave at reduced pay. Her boss responded that since women tend to quit after having children, a terrible maternity leave policy would dissuade them from joining so that "the company is not out of luck when they leave." As she said, "I was just so shocked and horrified that somebody would think that way, not to mention that they would say that out loud."[38]

Some workers and companies lack policy protections altogether. One woman, who experienced pay discrimination and verbal abuse from past bosses, explained, "Women that are subjected to this kind of treatment at small firms feel trapped because they have no one to go to and have no protection other than to leave, which is what I did." Similarly, when freelancers experience bias and discrimination, including sexual harassment, there is no HR department to support them. As journalist David Walker pointed out, in the photo industry this lack of supportive structures explains why "so many women give up their dreams of shooting to become photo editors instead (or quit the photo industry entirely). At least desk jobs provide some protection, in the form of a corporate HR department, that freelance photographers lack."[39]

When the chief executive officer or board members treat women badly, there is often no formal process or policy for dealing with it. A chief financial officer explained, "I have nowhere to go when the president behaves poorly, discriminates, or is outright inappropriate. No one requires him to have training for leadership over women." Similarly, a college executive noticed the lack of protection for female college presidents who serve under governing boards elected among community members. This executive has seen "overt gender bias" against the college's female president among the board members, such as labeling her strong leadership skills as "pushy, arrogant, abrasive, etc." As the executive explained, "It is very difficult to confront the sexism directly, as the president serves in her role at the pleasure of the board, and her contract can simply not be renewed if the board members are displeased with her."

The problem of insufficient support is pervasive, as the COVID-19 pandemic made abundantly clear. Women are expected to "go it alone" at work without help and support that men may receive or may not need. And when women are mistreated, unsupportive leaders may victim blame or punish women instead of helping them.

The expectation that women accept sexual harassment as a "compliment" is particularly troubling. Demanding that women recast men's overt misuse of power—because harassment is about power, not about sex—as a positive response toward women's physical attractiveness conflates not sex and desire, but power and submission. When men define sexual harassment as a compliment, they are suggesting that women should be receptive to the behavior rather than viewing it as an aggressive move to be resisted. It's a way of communicating that male domination is good, positive, benevolent, and normal and that women should submit. And it's a type of gaslighting because it tells a woman that what she thinks, feels, or believes is false; that her sense of violation is wrong; that what she *should* feel is positive. Finally, it serves as a reminder that a woman is first a woman, and only secondarily an employed professional. In this view women's role is to support men including serving their sexual needs and desires. In all cases, the underlying assumption is that women are tolerated in the workplace, but only to the extent they don't place any needs or expectations on those around them.

SHATTERING INSUFFICIENT SUPPORT: A SUPPORTIVE ORGANIZATION

Workplaces must support all employees, not just the men. Solutions to shatter insufficient support and move toward a supportive organization are outlined below. Those serving as leaders must take the lead, while allies—anyone who is supportive—can help support women. Individual women can also take steps to mitigate insufficient support.

Lack of Communal Resources

LEADERS

- Provide paid family leave, paid sick leave, and childcare to all employees.
- Advocate to governmental officials for paid family and sick leave mandates and family-friendly programs such as affordable child-care, universal preschool, and longer school days.

ALLIES

- Contribute to equitable distribution of caretaking and house-work in your own household.
- Advocate for paid family and sick leave and childcare in your organization. Describe the benefits, such as, "Offering paid fam-ily leave will help us to hire and retain women."

SELF

- If housework and childcare are inequitably distributed in your household, speak to your partner about redistributing tasks or outsourcing. You may say, "I am handling most of the childcare and housework, which leaves little time for taking care of myself. Let's talk about how we can accomplish these tasks more equitably." If this conflict with your partner seems unresolvable, consider seeking external relationship support. Many companies have employee assistance programs (EAPs) and healthcare coverage for counseling to assist with personal problems.
- Advocate for paid family and sick leave and childcare in your organization. Describe the impact, "Without paid leave, I may have to quit my job." Or, "Subsidized childcare would enable me to be more productive and help us recruit more women."

Lack of Mentoring and Sponsoring

LEADERS

- Create mentoring programs for new and established employees at all levels. Ensure that every woman has a mentor. Provide alternative mentors when connections don't work out. Compensate mentors with time, financial incentives, and recognition.
- Use a "train-the-trainer" approach to help the mentee become the future mentor.
- Create sponsorship programs in which employees with interest in advancing are matched with leaders. Actively recruit female employees to take part. Train sponsors to help protégés develop skills and overcome obstacles, publicly recognize protégé's achievements, and provide promotional opportunities.
- Incentivize promotions of women including rewards and acknowledgement for sponsors.[40]

ALLIES

- Mentor women. Share your experience with them. Connect them with other professionals. Listen to their concerns and provide advice.
- Sponsor women. Help them learn skills to advance and strategies to overcome obstacles. Publicly recognize their achievements. Advocate for their advancement and provide them with opportunities.

SELF

- Look for mentors—of any gender—inside and outside your organization. Participate in your organization's formal mentoring program. Invite potential informal mentors to chat in person or via web conferencing. Aim to have multiple mentors with various backgrounds.
- Use peer mentoring in which you and a colleague support each other.
- Make connections with leaders at various levels in your organization. Tell them about your desire to advance. Ask them to help you with professional development and opportunities for new assignments and roles.

Exclusion

LEADERS

- Require that work be done during working hours—and not at after-hours social events—with decisions made when all stakeholders are present. While people may socialize with colleagues outside of work, set the expectation that work discussions are not appropriate at such events.
- Offer networking events during the workday in both in-person and virtual formats. Vary activities and make sure they are inclusive.

- Ensure that employees are considered for promotions using equitable criteria. Don't advantage "friends" of leaders.

ALLIES

- Advocate for inclusive work-sponsored networking events.
- Make sure women are included in work events you organize. If you are in a meeting and your colleague should be there to discuss a topic, you can say, "Let's ask Raven to join us."
- If you hear work being discussed at nonwork events, redirect the conversation: "Let's talk about this issue tomorrow at work and include Raven and Uma."
- Invite women to group lunches and other social events. If they don't wish or are unable to attend such events, help them overcome disadvantages of not being there. For example, recommend them for promotions and new assignments. You may say, "I think we should consider Erica for the director of sales position. She has outstanding relationship skills and has hit her sales target every month since coming on board."

SELF

- Share your suggestions for inclusive work-sponsored networking events with your boss or HR.
- If you are excluded from nonwork social events and you would like to attend, ask to be included: "I'm learning to play golf. Invite me the next time you are going."
- Don't push yourself to attend nonwork social events in which you have no time or interest to attend. Watch for signs that work is being done or decisions made at these events. Ask your boss or HR to set expectations that business discussions only be held with all stakeholders present. You can say, "I learned that my department's budget was discussed when I was not present. It impedes my work and hurts this organization when decisions are made without my input."

- If you are excluded from a work event or discussion, you can say, "I'd like to join. My team's work contributes directly to your metrics."

Unsupportive Leadership

LEADERS

- Set expectations in your organization that women are to be believed and their concerns addressed. Do not victim blame women or trivialize their concerns.
- Do not override women's decisions. If a decision needs to be rethought, discuss options privately with the woman to mutually develop a path forward.
- Create anti-discrimination and anti-harassment policies. Develop complaint procedures that include steps to protect victims. Ensure that every complaint is addressed and that the harasser is disciplined, not the victim.

ALLIES

- Be a trusted confidant for women who express concerns about unsupportive leaders. Believe them and don't trivialize their issues. Help them brainstorm solutions.
- If you notice a woman who is not being supported, offer to help her. If she doesn't feel comfortable sharing her situation with you, suggest other colleagues with whom she could speak.

SELF

- Seek out trusted colleagues and mentors with whom you can discuss your situation and brainstorm options.
- Keep in mind that HR works for the organization, and therefore they may be required to support organizational leaders, even for abuse and harassment complaints.

- If you decide to reach out to your boss's superiors, be thoughtful about your approach. Superiors may see your boss's positive persona but be in the dark about how your boss treats subordinates. When talking to superiors, describe how your work is affected: "I have discussed being harassed with my boss and HR. Neither have addressed my concerns. While I endeavor to do my best every day, the quality of my work is suffering. I ask for your assistance in resolving this issue."
- Recognize that unsupportive leadership is challenging to overcome. Consider your options for employment elsewhere and talk to the U.S. federal or your state's equal opportunity employment commission about filing a gender discrimination claim. You may also wish to speak to an employment attorney for advice.

4

DEVALUATION

"They're only girls. . . . What do they need more money for?"

—Oprah Winfrey's former male boss

When Oprah Winfrey was co-hosting a local television show in the late 1970s, she discovered that her co-host Richard Sher was making more money than she was. She said to her boss, "I don't think that's fair because we are doing the same job. We sit on the same show." Her boss questioned why Oprah should earn as much: "He has children. Do you have children? . . . He has to pay for college educations. He owns his own home. Do you own your home?" Being asked to justify her salary based on expenses instead of workplace contributions led Oprah to realize that the television station leadership would not take her seriously. So, she left. Years later as host of *The Oprah Winfrey Show*, she ran into a similar attitude. Oprah was making more money, but her female producers were not. She went to her boss and said, "Everybody needs a raise." The boss replied, "They're only girls. . . . What do they need more money for?" Fortunately, given the popularity of her national show, Oprah was successful at obtaining raises for her staffers but only by threatening to quit the show herself.[1]

Oprah and her producers experienced devaluation, which makes women seem less important and detracts from their authority. Women's contributions in the workplace are often devalued or even ignored. People assume they will handle administrative work, called *office housework*, and they may experience backlash if they refuse. Devaluation manifests when women are compensated less than men for similar work. They may be told that *salary inequality* stems from their marital status, parental status, or family situation, particularly in comparison to male colleagues. They may experience *diminishment* in the form of put-downs, pet names, belittling, and condescending remarks. Some devaluing behaviors fall into the category of *benevolent sexism*, which includes seemingly positive compliments based on stereotypes and assumptions that women lack capacity to do the job. If all this isn't enough, women may find themselves subjected to a *credibility deficit*, in which their statements are questioned or flat-out disbelieved.

Oprah's illustration of being devalued occurred several decades ago, yet little has changed. In the twenty-first century, women still experience this form of sexism, which can be subtle or overt. Either way, women find themselves and their workplace contributions considered to be less than.

OFFICE HOUSEWORK

One day a Hollywood publishing executive and her male colleagues showed up for a meeting with other Hollywood executives—all men. Not recognizing her, one of the men turned to her and said, "Honey, will you please get me a cup of coffee." Although the publishing executive was "steaming mad," she complied so as not to jeopardize the meeting. Not only did the man assume she was in a support role, her colleagues did nothing to correct the misperception.

If you've been asked to get coffee, order lunch, organize a party, or take notes in a meeting, you are doing office housework. There's nothing wrong with these jobs, which keep the workplace running smoothly. The problem is the assumption that women will perform these tasks or that women are "best suited" for them. Lots of women are expected to do office housework while men are not. Office housework tasks include the following:

- Taking notes in meetings
- Cleaning up anything
- Diversity, equity, inclusion, and justice work

- Getting coffee, lunch, or snacks
- Helping colleagues
- Organizing events
- Serving on committees
- Scheduling meetings
- Initiating conference calls
- Purchasing flowers or gifts for colleagues
- Printing documents or making copies

A lawyer experienced expectations to do office housework when she found books in her mailbox. Her boss explained that returning the books to the library was part of her job. Even though the men had to walk "twice as far" to her mailbox, returning books was her responsibility. Similarly, another woman's office had a mat to use on slippery floors. However, the men never put it out; instead, they waited until a female coworker arrived and then asked her to put out the mat. Returning books and putting out a mat are simple tasks, yet these men refused to do them.

Sometimes women are asked to do office housework because of role incredulity, described in chapter 1, when newcomers assume women are in a support role. But it also happens when the woman's role is known. During a critical project meeting, one woman gave her status update and then her colleagues (all men) gave theirs. At that point, the vice president running the meeting turned to the woman and said, "How about you get us some coffee?"

Many women have been marginalized in meetings by being asked to take notes, hampering their active participation. Other times it's assumed women will take notes, such as a human resources (HR) specialist who attended a meeting on behalf of her male supervisor. The next day he asked for meeting minutes. She commented, "If I had known I was supposed to take minutes, I would have paid more attention." Sometimes women develop resistance strategies for this type of work. A science teacher explained that she stopped taking notebooks and pens to meetings because her male peers so often asked her to write things down.

Occasionally companies attempt solutions for office housework. A law firm partner described how the men always wanted her to take notes and do other uncompensated work. She said, "It got better when the firm established a relative contribution index, and everyone who did un-compensated service to the firm got some 'credits' that were put on our year-end balance sheet. . . . At least comparatively, I moved up in the performance matrix against the guys who never did any uncompensated service." Yet even with the more equitable "contribution index," there was still no expectation that the men share the non-billable workload. Another woman worked in an office that had a kitchen cleaning rota-tion. However, only women were assigned to clean. Being young at the time, this woman didn't feel she could ask why. Having a rotation for office housework is a great solution—if everyone is included.

Women of color are especially impacted by expectations to perform unrewarded work, which benefits colleagues throughout the organiza-tion. A study in engineering found that 66 percent of women of color but only 26 percent of White men reported doing more undervalued work than peers, while 61 percent of White men, but less than half of women of color, reported being more likely to do high-profile work. A Black engineering product manager who was also her company's diver-sity and inclusion program manager explained to the researchers that the company "lacked the budget" to compensate her. Ironically the women in the study were penalized for diversity work because their performance assessments were based solely on technical work, and they lacked time to accomplish both.[2]

Backlash

Like the young woman afraid to speak up about kitchen duties and the Hollywood executive fearful of jeopardizing her meeting, many women recognize that they risk backlash if they question office house-work. Due to gender stereotypes, women are penalized for not acting altruistically.[3] So women are under social pressure to volunteer for office housework. And if they decline, they may be labeled as egotistical or "not a team player."[4] Women of color are especially at risk. As a tech-nology manager explained, "If I don't accept the office housework, I'm considered an 'Angry Black' woman."[5]

Yet men rarely experience backlash for refusing office housework; they can get away with declining or doing the job poorly.[6] As business executive Sheryl Sandberg and professor Dr. Adam Grant wrote, "A man who doesn't help is 'busy'; a woman is 'selfish.'"[7] When a male childcare facility manager encouraged the women to teach their male coworkers to change diapers, the men simply "refused to learn" with no negative consequences, according to a female employee. Similarly, when a factory worker complained that the men rarely cleaned up their workstations, she was told, "They're not homemakers." She commented, "At least a third of our employees are female, so we aren't homemakers either."

While women receive backlash for refusing office housework, men are excused from these tasks altogether. Women also experience the negative consequences of office housework. They have less time for duties in their job description, while men's time is freed up to focus on high-profile, career-enhancing work.

DIMINISHMENT

Diminishment comprises the myriad ways women are made to seem less important in the workplace. Some diminishing behaviors seem innocuous, such as referring to women by pet names or by first name instead of their professional title. Other forms go unseen like failing to acknowledge women's contributions. Diminishment can also be aggressive, such as infantilizing, belittling, and sexualizing women. Whatever the form, diminishment functions to devalue women and their workplace contributions.

Pet Names and Diminutives

Have you ever been called "missy" or "kiddo" or referred to as a "girl" in a professional setting? If so, you are not alone. These terms are pet names and diminutives—shortened forms of address, typically used in close relationships. While such terms may be used affectionately in family or romantic relationships, they are not appropriate professionally.[8] People rarely refer to their male accountant as "little boy" or "sweetheart." Such terms of endearment addressed to a man in the workplace sound ridiculous yet are a common experience for women. A nurse described how some older male patients call nurses "babe" or "honey." When she told a patient, "My name is Sara, call me Sara," the patient's wife defended him: "He calls everyone that." This nurse noted, "I'm pretty sure he didn't call the surgeon (who's a man) 'babe.'" Here is a list of common pet names and diminutives:

- babe
- baby
- dear
- girl
- hon
- honey
- kiddo
- little girl
- little lady
- miss
- missy
- sweetheart
- sweetie
- sugar
- young lady

The underlying message of pet names is that women don't belong in the workplace. Male bosses referred to a mathematician as "sweetie" and "honey." She commented, "It's like they are intimidated by my abilities and so to 'put me in my place' they need to use demoralizing pet names to make me seem not as competent."[9]

Referring to women with pet names and diminutives is an example of what researchers Drs. Marta Calás and Linda Smircich call moving the home realm into the workplace.[10] Rather than treating women as professionals, they are treated as family members or caretakers. Male executives called one nonprofit leader "sweetie," "dear," and "hon." She explained, "They are meaning it in a nice way, like they see me like a granddaughter, but it comes off condescending and somewhat demeaning because I'm not a child and this is a professional setting." Even some male subordinates called an engineer "sweetie," "dear," and "baby."[11]

Sometimes customers are referred to by diminishing pet names. Bank employees greeted a customer with "Good morning, sweetie." Upon learning the customer's name, they asked, "What can I do for you, Miss Debbie?"—even though she never used that diminutive form of her name. The customer commented, "If Mr. John Smith came to the same window, would you ask him, 'What can I do for you, Mr. Johnny?' *Never*!" She took her business elsewhere.

An especially common diminutive is the word "girl" to refer to an adult woman. Everyday professional women such as firm partners, engineers, and architects reported being diminished as "girls." A flight attendant explained, "I'm sick of the cabin crew being called 'girls' by the male cockpit crew. It's really condescending." Similarly, an oil rig engineer was labeled "girl." On rigs, personnel are routinely paged over an intercom using their first names, such as "Melinda, page 232. Melinda, 232" or their title: "Electrician, call 232 please. Electrician, 232." However, this engineer was routinely paged as "Girl, page 232. Girl, 232." She felt helpless: "They also knew I was not in a position to not answer, being a [contractor] and due to the sensitive nature of actively drilling."

It's not just men who use these terms; sometimes women use them as a subtle way to assert dominance over other women. One thirty-seven-year-old woman noted this tendency: "I also HATE when grown men (and women) call me honey or sweetie or girl to try to diminish my position in a negotiation or the value of my opinion."

Diminutives reduce women's perceived professional capacity, suggesting they are of lower status than workplace peers. The point is to communicate that they are out of place and to stop them from speaking up. As U.S. representative Alexandria Ocasio-Cortez noted, "I usually know my questions of power are getting somewhere when the powerful stop referring to me as 'Congresswoman' and start referring to me as 'young lady' instead."[12]

Untitling and Uncredentialing

Omitting women's titles or credentials in professional settings is another form of diminishment. Untitling occurs when women are called by their first names instead of their appropriate title and is a common occurrence for women physicians, professors, clergy, coaches, government officials, and military personnel (especially when out of uniform). Uncredentialing occurs when credentials (e.g., MD, PhD, EdD) are used after men's names but not women's. For example, a hospital newsletter omitted "MD" after a female physician's name, while including credentials for three male physicians.[13]

Many women are untitled while male colleagues are referred to as "Dr. So-and-So." Hospital staff routinely asked for a physician by first name when calling her home for instructions, yet those same staff addressed her male counterparts as "Dr." Other women with doctorates were referred to as "Mrs." A male patient greeted oncologist Dr. Jennifer Lycette: "I'm so glad you're back—that I get to see *Mrs.* Lycette today!" She noted, "Most male physicians in our society are referred to as 'Doctor' in all aspects of their lives. Why shouldn't female physicians be as well?"[14] A case in point is Dr. Anu Kathiresan, a surgeon who married a surgeon and kept her birth name. She is often called "Mrs. Johnson" (her husband's last name) outside of work, such as at her children's pediatrician's office and school. Formal party invitations are often addressed to "Dr. and Mrs. Johnson" or "Drs. Johnson."[15] Both her title and her name are rendered invisible.

Untitling is even more diminishing when women's titles are replaced with pet names. One physician explained, "I can't tell you how often male clients call me 'sweetie' or 'miss' instead of doctor." When the pastor of a large congregation called a funeral home to discuss an upcoming service that she was officiating, she introduced herself as "Pastor Williams." Yet the male employee addressed her as "Miss" throughout the phone call. Even if it was meant to be polite, using "Miss" instead of a professional title communicates disrespect for the woman's authority.

Invisible Contributions

Failing to acknowledge women's work is diminishment that renders their contributions invisible. Consider what happened to assistant professor Dr. Sarah Milov, author of *The Cigarette: A Political History*. After the publisher sent her book to two male historians, National Public Radio (NPR) invited them to discuss tobacco regulation. During the segment, "every cited fact was taken from [her book]," yet neither the historians nor the male host credited Milov. Whereas the historians were tenured faculty, Milov was untenured, a career stage in which it is essential to have media-cited work. Though the segment relied heavily on her book, Milov was not invited on the show. She explained, "My book is about tobacco, and I live in Virginia. I would have been a reasonable person to talk about the topic. But they wanted the history guys."[16]

Unfortunately, Dr. Milov is not the only case of NPR excluding women's contributions. Dr. Silke-Maria Weineck coauthored a book with sports economist Dr. Stefan Szymanski on the histories of sports and words. Both authors were invited to record a segment for NPR's *All Things Considered*. On the day the segment was slated to air, a producer emailed them: "Because of the way the story came together, I was only able to use clips from Stefan—sorry, Silke!!!!!" And not only were there no quotes from Weineck, but her coauthored book was exclusively attributed to Szymanski.[17] What happened to Milov and Weineck in public forums happens to professional women every day. While their work is used, their names and contributions go unrecognized.

Invisible contributions mean "no praise or recognition for women who are doing the work," as a higher education executive noted. Administrative professionals deal with this sort of treatment often. A secretary was accustomed to being considered "furniture," while an administrative assistant was not thanked or acknowledged when helping her male coworker with his sales work.

Being overlooked is demoralizing for women. One nonprofit leader commented that there is an "assumption that women don't want to have any job titles, nor do they need affirmation like men do. This is a widespread presumption and is highly demotivating to women." Similarly, a lawyer noted, "I feel very unfulfilled at work and, even if I can get a great result for my client, my work is never actually appreciated by them." Yet men's work may be publicly credited. As one woman found, "I've also gotten few accolades for doing certain hard work, and male colleagues doing the same hard work have been openly praised."

Infantilizing

Infantilizing, or considering women as immature, also diminishes them. Many women are treated like children and talked down to. A technology professional was hugged when she did something right, which made her feel "like a child." Similarly, in product design meetings, engineers told a software developer that she was "precious" and said "the cutest things." They also laughed in her face, even though she was the most senior team member. As she said, "In my 18 years working on the product, I have never seen a man treated this way."

Women are sometimes admonished as if they were children. When band students damaged a doorway, a male custodian cornered an English teacher. He was "very rude and condescending, lecturing me like I was 12," the teacher explained. When the custodian finally let the teacher speak, she suggested that he go see the band director. The teacher watched as the custodian asked the male band director for a "favor" of having a talk with the kids. She commented, "He was extremely polite, respectful, and professional when talking to the band director."

Sometimes infantilizing intersects with other factors like race. An African American nonprofit executive explained, "I am all but invisible, even when I'm the one who has called the meeting and set the agenda. Men—White men—will still take over and usually talk to me like I'm about 5 years old. . . . They all but pat me on the head." Women's body size is also used to diminish them. A "petite" higher education vice president was often talked down to; one male colleague went so far as to lift her up, commenting, "I can just pick you up!"[18] Quite a few women were discounted because of their young age. After one woman presented a $3 million project, the client said, "What are you, about 14 years old?" She commented, "I felt belittled, humiliated, and singled out." Youthful appearance can lead to assumptions of lack of experience or commitment, thus further diminishing women's contributions.

Belittling

Another category of diminishment consists of belittling, disparaging, and dismissive remarks that are often used to communicate that women don't belong in "male" roles or in the workplace at all. Male passersby often stopped to watch an outdoor laborer, commenting to her, "Why don't they find a man to do that?" During his job interview, a mid-career engineer answered a technical question incorrectly and then told the hiring manager that his response wasn't wrong and that she was "a newbie who didn't know any better."[19] In a single interaction, the engineer exhibited three forms of bias: credibility deficit, benevolent sexism, and belittling ("newbie"), all of which presumed the hiring manager was incompetent.

Belittling comments are also used to reduce competition. As one woman noted, "It's about fear—fear that women will take it all away from [men], and they won't have their big chunk of the pie." A mathematician on medical leave was told that a "real" mathematician (a man) would be taking over her classes, implying that she had usurped a male job.

Sometimes disparaging comments relate to women's menstrual cycles. When one publishing manager presented a calendar, she was told that her copy "was organized in 28-day intervals." A grocery store deli employee worked with a male manager, one male employee, and eleven female employees. When one of the women had a bad day, the manager said things like, "Throw some chocolate at [her]; she must be on her period." Calling attention to a woman's reproductive functions serves to foreground a woman's gender rather than her abilities and supports the narrative that women are emotional rather than rational due to their monthly cycles.

Sexualizing

Reducing women to sex objects is yet another way to diminish them, suggesting they not be taken seriously. Many women are labeled with sexualized terms, catcalled, propositioned, or seen as sexual partners instead of coworkers. One woman was in a meeting in which an older man greeted the room with "Good afternoon, gentleman and chicka-boobs." She remarked, "Guess how the women's thoughts and opinions were received after that opening." Similarly, when a client thanked a college professional in a meeting, the college's dean compared her to a prostitute: "She would stand on a street corner to get a contract." In another case, a male executive asked a technology manager's female team members to work with a customer who was "crotchety and old but has been a lady's man his whole life." The officer hoped that the women's "feminine charms" would be helpful. Fear of backlash over her own position kept the manager from speaking up about it.[20]

Men in male-dominated workplaces may be particularly prone to viewing women as sexual objects. The boss of a newly hired oil pump meter reader told her to stop because she "distracted the truck drivers." Eventually the meter reader quit to go to graduate school, at which point she was told she had been hired because she "had nice legs" and that they would "never hire someone smart again." This woman's story illustrates a double bind in being attractive: she was hired for her beauty and then penalized for it, while being told that her intelligence was not a valuable quality.

The technology industry can be particularly egregious in sexualizing women. Male coworkers of a technology professional referred to her breasts as "maracas." The male coworker of another woman told her, "If I weren't married, I would be on you like white on rice."[21] Male colleagues made it clear to Silicon Valley engineer Tracy Chou that they used work as a place to find dating relationships.[22] They were flirty towards Chou, tried "awkward pick-up lines," and complimented her appearance, rather than her work. One offered to give her a massage while another invited her to watch a movie in a dark locked room and later gave her a t-shirt with his name across the front.[23] Another technology employee was valued for her flirtatious behavior, which gained her direct access to men in upper management. At first, this employee was considered "just the fun girl," but later she was invited to after-work parties. Pretty soon, every time the CEO was in town, he scheduled meetings with her, ending with drinks afterward. As the employee's manager explained, "I'm a confident, MBA professional with twenty years of experience in my field, but I've never been more undermined, disrespected, and made to feel useless and like a piece of ass in my entire career."[24]

Perhaps not surprisingly, Hollywood is also rife with examples of women being treated like sexual objects, starting when they are young. The media sexualized actor Emma Watson "as early as age 14," as she stated.[25] Other female actors were coached to act and dress sexually for auditions and be flirty with male directors and producers, giving "blowjob eyes," as actor Zoe Kazan noted. Women auditioning for roles have been explicitly told to "wear something body-conscious," allowing casting directors to check out their bodies. Kazan commented, "It's the sense that your sexuality is somehow baked into the situation." The effect is detrimental to the women, as they leave the situation feeling uneasy about what happened and unable to explain why. As Kazan further explained, "It makes you feel guilty, and bad, as if it's somehow your fault—that you're somehow giving that person the signal that it's OK to treat you that way. And none of that is stuff that [male actors have] to deal with."[26]

Via sexualizing, male colleagues and high-powered men communicate that they value women as sexual objects or potential sexual partners more than for their work. Just as with the other forms of diminishment, the goal is to communicate that women don't belong in the workplace.

BENEVOLENT SEXISM

Benevolent sexism consists of seemingly chivalrous comments and behavior based on stereotypical assumptions about women. These assumptions and behaviors have a diminishing effect on women. Benevolent sexism can take the form of compliments about women's appearance and caring behavior. Such accolades may seem harmless; however, they reinforce ideas that women should conform to feminine standards and be helpful to men, their protectors and superiors in the gender hierarchy. The result is an undermining of women's capacity and even their careers. Although it may look like positive behavior, the underlying belief is that women are inferior.

The insidious nature of benevolent sexism is hard to overestimate. If men are confronted, they may say that their intention was to be kind and considerate. What's unrecognized, however, is that such behavior undermines women's opportunities and professional authority.

"Look Pretty"

Benevolent sexist remarks on appearance offer women seemingly positive compliments and encouragement to be physically attractive. Such remarks call attention to stereotypical requirements that women should please the male gaze. One physician was proud of her scientific conference presentation, yet afterward a male colleague told her that she "looked like a Barbie doll up there."[27]

Sometimes women are told they should serve no other purpose than to "look pretty." A male supervisor moved a medical assistant's desk to a central location, making it more difficult for her to concentrate on her work. When she complained, he told her to "sit and look pretty." Another woman started a new job and asked one of six men standing around her what exactly the job consisted of. The man replied that it was to "sit there and look pretty" while the others laughed. As she said, "Imagine them replying like that to another man, no way." A well-respected theologian evaluated Bible teacher Beth Moore on her physical attractiveness. As she described, "The instant I met him, he looked me up and down, smiled approvingly and said, 'You are better looking than _____.' He didn't leave it blank. He filled it in with the name of another woman Bible teacher."[28] In all these cases, the women are told that their priority is to please men visually.

At Hollywood red carpet award shows reporters routinely ask men about their achievements. But they ask women about their appearance: "Who are you wearing?" meaning who designed their attire.[29] Actor Sandra Bullock commented, "I'm going to be asked about my dress and my hair, while the man standing next to me will be asked about his performance and political issues."[30]

Such actions are not limited to Hollywood; they also show up in the corporate world. As a salesperson discovered, "The first time I met my boss, he kissed my hand and said, 'Enchanté, mademoiselle,' and proceeded to let me know I was but the second most beautiful woman, after his own daughter." In one swoop, her boss used a social behavior rather than a workplace one and infantilized her with the comparison to his daughter. Coworkers informed her that this was standard behavior, and she should not make a big deal of it. But it didn't stop there. This boss told her "what to wear to events" and had a "creepy way" of remembering what she had worn on past occasions. She eventually realized he was using her appearance "as a selling point" to clients, thereby undermining her professional capacity.

"Protecting" Women

Benevolent sexism is also at play when men offer to "protect" women. One male supervisor referred to female subordinates as "his girls" (diminutive term) and told them he was protecting them from "all the mean people," as one woman described. Men who think like this see it as their role to protect women from supposed dangers in public life.

Some men assume women don't want to travel for work and therefore offer to "protect" women's home and family time. But by withholding professional opportunities, these men imply that women belong in the home. A higher education administrator worked with a male leader who expressed concerns about young women traveling, questioning whether they would want to be in leadership due to time away from home. When women are denied opportunities for job-related travel, their careers may stall. Women may also not be considered for out-of-state or international assignments on the assumption that they don't want to uproot their families. Or they may not be encouraged to expand their education, as happened to an information technology (IT) professional who was a single mother. An executive discouraged her from pursuing company-funded education because he "knew" she would soon "hit the husband jackpot and be outta here." Acknowledging that the executive likely intended it as a compliment, the IT professional added, "It definitely made me feel less valued."

Men may outright communicate to women that they are better off in the home. When a male consulting firm partner asked a colleague about her plans for marriage and children, she replied that she did not want to be married or have children, so that she could focus on her career. The partner launched into a story about another career-oriented woman who said the same thing but now stays home to take care of four children and "is so happy." In another situation, a woman and her male coworker were at a work standstill after their boss had left. The coworker said, "It's much worse for me. After all, you're a woman and you can just get married."

Sometimes "protection" involves discouraging women from making their own choices. A school professional's boss asked her, "As a wife and mother, what do you foresee as your future with this school district?" His question implied that the professional's family roles should be primary, superseding her career. The same assumption happened to an attorney who had a near-miss on a project deadline. When she apologized to a senior manager, he responded, "I know you have other priorities. You are a wife and a mother first. I get that." This lawyer was rendered speechless because, as she said, "First of all, what does that have to do with it? Second, I had to completely rearrange priorities with work, family, etc. to meet that particular deadline. It really stung to have my efforts diminished and marginalized like that."

Women are sometimes not offered overtime or challenging assignments to keep them from working "too much." But women's visibility and skills are reduced when they are prevented from working "too late at night, too much travel, too 'dirty' a job," as one lawyer described. When another attorney was busy, she suggested giving an assignment to an associate who happened to be pregnant. The firm partner said, "She might have a doctor's appointment or something." The attorney was taken aback: "He thought he was doing her a favor but holding back billable work for any reason is the worst thing you can do for an associate," she reflected. By making such assumptions, men communicate that they know best and deny women agency.

Assumptions of Incompetence

A software engineer's boss told her that since she was a "girl," she "ought to be good at the less complicated tasks." That's how benevolent sexism is used to communicate that women are not competent. Some women were told they were good at their jobs "for a woman" or asked, "Did you come up with that yourself?" An information technology executive labeled such assumptions as a "she's the girl" mentality meaning, "She can't do the job."

Some benevolent sexist comments communicate that women professionals are seen as a woman first, a professional second. One lawyer's supervisor told her that she could be "the best female litigator in the city." Not the best litigator, the best female litigator.

Sometimes men tell women, "Don't worry your pretty little head about it," referring to details deemed too complex. Another lawyer commented, "Pretty much every time I've been told that, it's because he was pulling a fast one, and I absolutely needed to worry about it."

Men—even those with no experience—may try to mansplain women's jobs to women in stereotypical male fields. Male customers told butcher Jessica Wragg that she didn't know how to do her job. One customer said, "Look, you're too young and pretty to be doing this work. If you're going to have a go at least let me show you how."[31] An organic farmer's story is similar. This farmer was highly athletic, working twelve to seventeen hours per day digging hard in the dirt and processing animals and vegetables. Yet a stranger commented, "Look! It's a girl with a mattock [a hand tool], about to chop her hands off!" When the farmer was around less-experienced men, they took the more challenging jobs, which she could have handled better and faster. At one point she started her own rabbitry and invited a male friend to join her first harvest. The male friend took over and dressed the whole rabbit even though he had never done it before. As she said, "It was frustrating. I appreciated that we all need our chance to learn . . . but their motives were what bothered me."

The perception that women are physically weaker creates barriers for them in some professions. Photographer Gina Santucci was told that male photographers wouldn't hire female assistants because the men would have to carry their own equipment.[32] Another male photographer told his assistant Brook Pifer that "girls aren't strong, they can't lift things, they don't know how to do things properly."[33]

Sometimes women are discouraged from taking risks. An environmental engineering lecturer was told "maybe you shouldn't do this because it might not work out," referring to opportunities such as promotions, challenging roles, and grant funding. In a similar vein, economics and international relations professor Dr. Lisa Cook was advised not to protest when her ideas were rejected. She said, "There was a certain sense about who has big, original ideas that might make an impact. Typically, those ideas weren't delivered by people who look like me—a 6-foot-1.5-inch African American woman. A young woman."[34]

Some people blame biology for the gender gap in male-dominated fields. In 2017, a male Google employee wrote an anti-diversity memo, which argued that women are underrepresented in tech only because of inherent personality differences between men and women.[35] YouTube CEO Susan Wojcicki explained, "My experience in the tech industry has shown me just how pervasive that question is." Wojcicki described a thought experiment: "What if the memo said that biological differences amongst Black, Hispanic, or LGBTQ employees explained their underrepresentation in tech and leadership roles? . . . I don't ask this to compare one group to another, but rather to point out that the language of discrimination can take many different forms."[36]And yet for some reason it is acceptable to suggest that women as a group are inherently incompetent in traditionally male jobs.

Men may think complimenting women's appearance, "protecting" them from opportunities, or mansplaining women's jobs to them is "benevolent." But it is not. It's another way of asserting that women belong in the home, not the workplace.

SALARY INEQUALITY

As a young professor at Rutgers Law School in the 1960s, Ruth Bader Ginsburg discovered that she was making significantly less than male colleagues. So she asked the dean how much a comparable male colleague was making. The dean responded, "Ruth, he has a wife and two children to support. You have a husband with a good paying job in New York."[37]

Although Ginsburg filed and won an equal pay lawsuit against Rutgers, the problem of salary inequality has not gone away. In 2018, broadcast journalist Hoda Kotb was named co-anchor of NBC's *The Today Show* after co-host Matt Lauer was fired for alleged inappropriate sexual behavior. Neither Kotb nor co-anchor Savannah Guthrie made a salary equal to the reported $20 million that the network had paid Lauer. And Kotb even kept her co-host duties for the third hour of *The Today Show*. Yet as Kotb said, "I'm not making Matt Lauer money. Not even close."[38] The network valued neither woman as much as the male co-host.

The entertainment business is rife with examples of female actors who are not compensated equally to male actors, and the gap can be very wide. In the mid-1990s, Demi Moore became the highest paid female actor in Hollywood when she earned $12 million for the movie *Striptease*. At the same time, her then-husband Bruce Willis was paid $20 million to star in *Die Hard with a Vengeance*. Instead of celebrating Moore's achievement, the press gave her a demeaning nickname: "Gimme Moore." As Moore said, "Nobody gave [Willis] a grabby, greedy nickname. He was just a guy doing what guys are supposed to do: earn as much as possible to take care of his family. Women, for some reason, are supposed to earn less . . . and never push back."[39]

Little has changed three decades later. In 2020, the highest paid male actor, Dwayne Johnson, earned $87.5 million, while the highest paid female actor, Sofia Vergara earned $43 million.[40] Between June 1, 2019, and June 1, 2020, the top ten male actors cumulatively earned $545.5 million, while the top ten female actors earned $254 million—a gender wage gap of 46.6 percent.[41] Even comparing co-stars of the same film reveals disparities. When Sony Pictures was hacked in 2014, it was revealed that producers paid the male stars of the film *American Hustle* 9 percent of back-end royalties, but paid only 7 percent to the female stars, Jennifer Lawrence and Amy Adams.[42]

Gender Pay Gap

While many famous women earn less than men, not surprisingly, the pay gap affects women no matter their race, ethnicity, age, or position. According to 2020 U.S. Census data, on average women earn 83 percent of what men earn. Broken down by race, the data is somewhat varied but still less than White men's earnings. White women are paid 79 percent compared to White men's salaries. Black women's comparative pay rate is 64 percent, Hispanic women's is 57 percent, and American Asian and Pacific Islander's is 85 percent with a wide range between subpopulations—Burmese women make just 52 percent of White men's earnings.[43] According to the 2020 U.S. Census data, there are no ages in which women earn the same median income as men. Median earnings of women ages fifteen to twenty-four are 89.6 percent of men's earnings. From there the gap only widens to 59.3 percent of men's earnings for ages sixty-five and older.[44]

And women earn less than men in comparable positions. As of 2022, female financial managers earned 73 percent of male financial managers' pay. Female healthcare providers earned 80 percent of what their male colleagues earned. Female retail supervisors earned 78 percent of their male colleagues' earnings. But perhaps most surprisingly, even when professions are female-dominated, men still earn more. Take teaching, for example. The average female elementary or middle school teacher earns 87 percent of the average male teacher's wage. Similarly, the average female registered nurse earns 89 percent of her male counterpart's pay.[45]

Furthermore, unpaid housework is not included in the U.S. Gross Domestic Product (GDP)—leading to conflation of women's work in the home with the workplace. When two male economists developed GDP in the mid-twentieth century to measure value of goods and services, they ignored research assistant Phyllis Dean who argued to include unpaid household labor.[46] Without counting unpaid work, the GDP fails to fully assess the health of an economy. It's socially acceptable to not only pay women less for the same work as men but also to treat their labor in the home as not benefiting the economy.

Underpaying women communicates that their work is unimportant and their income discretionary. Yet poverty rates for women, both nationally and globally, are substantially higher than for men. In the United States, poverty rates for women in 2021 outpaced men by three percentage points overall, and while the percentage differs by state, there was no state in which the rates for women were lower than those for men.[47]

In times of economic depression, women's poverty rates go up more than men's. The global pandemic has disproportionately impacted women both in loss of paid employment and in pressures to perform more unpaid labor in the home, especially care and schooling of children when daycare and schools shut down.[48] Women's jobs accounted for 63.3 percent of the total lost during the pandemic. As of February 2022, men had recouped all their job losses since February 2020, while women still lacked over 1.8 million jobs compared to February 2020.[49]

The United Nations and the World Bank have called attention to the increasing health, income, and education risks to women and girls due to the pandemic.[50] Prior to the pandemic, single mothers in both developed and developing countries had higher poverty rates than single fathers, and substantially higher poverty rates than two-parent households.[51] The pandemic increased these disparities. Between 2019 and 2020 in the United States, poverty rates increased for single mothers (22.2 percent to 23.4 percent) and married couples (4.0 percent to 4.7 percent) but remained steady for single fathers (11.4 percent).[52] The majority of the world's poor are women because they are paid less than men (24 percent less on average globally) and do most of the unpaid care work (estimated at $10.8 trillion globally, per year!).[53] Since women are far more likely than men to live below the poverty line, this argument that women's earnings are "luxury" or "discretionary" is not accurate.

The Family Excuse

Just like Ruth Bader Ginsburg and Oprah Winfrey, numerous women have been given family-related excuses for lower pay. One lawyer was told that her younger male colleague was making more because he was getting divorced and needed the money. As she commented, "This was said to my single mom face, putting a daughter through college and having just lost my house to Superstorm Sandy." In other cases, men received a direct fatherhood premium—raises with the birth of children—while pregnant women did not get the same benefit. One woman stated, "Four times in one year, men in my department were promoted . . . given a raise, shortly after the birth of their child."

Other women are denied promotions and raises and told that men need to be promoted to support their families. One woman was asked why she wanted a promotion so badly: "Is it because of the money? Are you struggling financially?" She commented in her social media post, "Nope, don't need the money, who needs extra money? Money is for suckers. C'moooooon. :)." When a boss told another woman that her male colleague made more because he was the head of his household, she replied, "I am the head of MY household." But her boss refused the request for a raise, saying, "That's just the way it is." There is still a pervasive view that women's work is optional. When one woman questioned why she was denied an annual raise, her manager responded, "It doesn't matter. Your money is just for fun, anyway."

Due to fear of backlash, women may not push back. One woman worked a job where the men started at higher salaries than the women. When the women questioned it, they were told that they could be fired for discussing pay. As this woman said, "I believe this was illegal, but who wants to take a lawyer to court over an extra dollar an hour?" Similarly, another woman discovered that a male counterpart with lesser credentials and experience was making twice as much as she was, but her supervisors were unresponsive to her request to equalize the pay. She felt her choices were to quit or sue. She chose to quit rather than acquire the stigma of a troublemaker. As she said, companies "lose great talent because women have no possibilities for advancement and the company sees men as more valuable. Women move on or start their own companies—suing is a no-win scenario."

Other Excuses

Beyond the family excuse, employers come up with other reasons to pay women less. One London transport worker asked why a lower-achieving male colleague was getting a pay raise when she wasn't. As she learned, "I was considered more capable, so everyone expected far more from me. . . . Because I knocked myself out to negotiate good deals, that's what was expected of me, but a male doing basic admin work and [who] didn't stretch himself deserved to be on far more money!"

Considering women to be cheap labor is another excuse. One woman's boss stated, "I like to hire women because I can pay them less because they don't have to support their family." And one large company hired an advertising and film consultant because she was a woman and "was cheaper than the guys." It seems that any excuse at all is reason enough to not pay women equitably.

Retirement Effect

For women, decades of earning less than men leads to less money in retirement. In the United States, retirement income comes from three sources: Social Security, retirement plans, and individual savings. Today's older women may not have pensions or savings, and lower earnings leave them with less money to invest. In the United States, 61 percent of unpaid caregivers are women, for which Social Security does not provide benefits.[54] Women also need more money in retirement because they can expect to live about three years longer than men.[55] In 2020, women retirees received an average Social Security monthly benefit of $1,378—just 80.4 percent of their male counterpart's average benefit ($1,714).[56]

Women are shortchanged throughout their working years and in the retirement system. One woman who has worked since 1971 noted that "Social Security will pay my husband a lot more than I will [get] when I'm 62. It's not fair." Another woman wrote her boss's meeting talking points in the 1970s but was never allowed to attend meetings or present them as her own. Although she "did all the work," she received only a small raise once per year, while her boss received bonus after bonus. Though her position and pay improved in the 1980s and 1990s, she commented, "Now I am retired, and my Social Security reflects the discrimination in the workplace. It follows you from birth to death."

CREDIBILITY DEFICIT

During the January 6, 2021, attack on the U.S. Capitol, *New York Times* reporter Erin Schaff was caught in the mayhem; rioters threw her to the ground, stole her press pass and one camera, and broke the other. To conceal her identity as a reporter, Schaff filmed from her phone. When police deployed tear gas, she hid in a hallway, but they found her. As she recounted, "I told [the police] that I was a photojournalist and that my pass had been stolen, but they didn't believe me." The officers drew their guns, ordering Schaff to get down on hands and knees. Fortunately, two other photojournalists shouted, "She's a journalist," at which point the officers helped all of them find a room in which to barricade.[57] In a life-or-death moment, Schaff suffered from credibility deficit in which she was disbelieved.

If you have ever been asked, "Are you sure that's right?" or had others turn to a man to ask, "Is that correct?" after you made a statement, then you've experienced credibility deficit. Credibility deficit occurs when women's words and accounts of events are discredited or flat-out disbelieved. This problem has existed throughout recorded history from the time of the Greeks and the Romans and the Jews. The Talmud, the Jewish law text that dates to the second century AD, stated that women were not to be considered reliable witnesses.[58] In the 1600s, England's chief justice Matthew Hale warned that those alleging rape (i.e., women) were not to be trusted as it "is an accusation easily to be made and hard to be proved, and harder to be defended by the party accused." In the United States, this "Hale warning"—that the law requires testimony of rape victims to be examined "with caution"—was read to juries until at least the 1980s.[59] Distrust of women's testimony lingers still today.

Professor Dr. Miranda Fricker calls this problem of women not being believed because they are women "testimonial injustice."[60] Women who've been sexually assaulted or harassed are routinely doubted. Law professor Anita Hill is a case in point. In 1991, a report leaked that Hill told FBI investigators that U.S. Supreme Court nominee Clarence

Thomas had made unwanted sexual advances toward her. Although Hill never intended to go public, she was called to testify before an all-male Senate committee. She calmly described her experiences and answered the senators' questions. Yet afterward, Hill was called "a little bit nutty and a little bit slutty" and accused of fantasizing about Thomas and making it all up.[61] (See chapter 5, "Hostility," and chapter 6, "Acquiescence," for more about Hill's experience.)

Almost three decades later in 2018, professor Dr. Christine Blasey Ford suffered the same fate when she testified that Supreme Court nominee Brett Kavanaugh had sexually assaulted her at a high school party. Her testimony was discredited, and she was told she had "misremembered" what had happened.[62] At the time, then-president Donald Trump tweeted, "If the attack on Dr. Ford was as bad as she says, charges would have been immediately filed with local Law Enforcement Authorities by either her or her loving parents."[63] But regarding Kavanaugh, he tweeted, "Judge Kavanaugh showed America exactly why I nominated him. His testimony was powerful, honest, and riveting."[64]

This type of blatant disbelief of women's accounts is enormously demoralizing—especially when accompanied by statements of a man's "honesty." It presents men as dispassionate, factual, and reliable witnesses and women as unreliable and inconsistent. The responses to Dr. Ford's testimony were horrendous; she received death threats, had to move multiple times, and was unable to resume her career.[65]

Anita Hill and Dr. Christine Blasey Ford may seem like extreme examples, but credibility deficit is a common experience for many women. Lots of women have answered a question only to have a male counterpart be asked to confirm. Other women's ideas are not deemed valid until "seconded" by a man. Even men in lower positions are able to endorse women's ideas with "Actually, that's a pretty good idea," and then it becomes okay for others to take the idea seriously.

Men must second women's words in many fields. Gaming company cofounder Mary Min noticed a pattern when meeting with investors to raise money. When she finished presentations, the investors often turned to her cofounder, Kevin Li, to ask, "What do you think?" Yet investors never asked for Min's opinion after Li spoke.[66] In another case, a department head could not convince her male bosses to let her restructure her area to handle significant growth, even though she had already grown the business 300 percent in less than two years. Instead, they brought in a man to take over the department, who told the male bosses to "do it" and to get out of the woman's way. This woman went on to grow the business from less than $1 million to over $15 million, but it took a man to convince the male bosses that her idea was a good one.

The public may not trust women experts either. Male tourists often questioned a space museum tour guide: "Sweetie, are you sure that's right?" It became tempting for the guide to respond, "Yes, you idiot, I studied for months in order to make up lies about people who gave their lives for our nation." Her frustration is understandable. When women's knowledge is disbelieved, they're being told that they are of less value than the men, even when men have no expertise in the subject at hand.

Like office housework, diminishment, salary inequality, and benevolent sexism, the overall impact of credibility deficit is to undermine the woman's value in the workplace. Even while working on this chapter, we personally experienced the things we were writing about. One day a man asked Leanne a question in her area of expertise and she answered, then he turned to her husband and repeated the question. That's how pervasive, endless, and routine such treatment of women is.

Devaluation tells women in subtle and overt ways that they are not valued. Toward the subtle end of the continuum are familial conversational styles and put-downs (*diminishment*) and compliments on women's appearance (*benevolent sexism*). More overt ways of communicating the same message are disbelieving women's statements (*credibility deficit*), assigning them unrecognized work (*office housework*), and paying them less than men for the same job (*salary inequality*). In reviewing the components of devaluation, the purpose becomes clear:

- Communicate to women that they do not belong in the workplace.
- Communicate to women that they do belong in the home.

One day a male anesthetist walked into a surgeons' lounge with several women present. He said, "Look at this! It's like a goddamned Tupperware party in here." As surgeon Dr. Arghavan Salles explained, "He reduced these highly trained specialists to women who, in his view, belong in the home. Never mind the fact that to become a surgeon, these women would have completed four years of college, four years of medical school, and four to nine additional years of surgical training. In his mind, they were only good for selling Tupperware."[67]

Devaluation carries a heavy weight. When repeated consistently over the course of a woman's career, being devalued becomes demoralizing. It damages their careers, reduces their earnings and their retirement, and prioritizes men over women every step of the way.

SHATTERING DEVALUATION: A VALUING ORGANIZATION

We've described the myriad of ways in which women are devalued in the workplace. The antidote is a workplace that values all employees, demonstrated through pay, credit, and expectations. Solutions to shatter devaluation and move toward a valuing organization are outlined below. Those serving as leaders must take the lead, while allies—anyone who is supportive—can help reinforce the valuing organization. Individual women can also take steps to mitigate devaluation if it happens to them.

Office Housework

LEADERS

- Ensure that everyone—no matter their gender or level in the organization—shares office housework, including note taking, cleaning duties, getting food, party planning, and committee assignments.
- Implement a tangible reward structure for office housework responsibilities.
- Include office housework and diversity work in performance assessments.

- Don't penalize women or dismiss their concerns if they speak up about unfair distribution of office housework.

ALLIES

- Offer to help with office housework responsibilities.
- If you notice women being assigned an unfair distribution of office housework, express your concerns to organizational leadership on their behalf.

SELF

- If someone asks you to do office housework, you can say, "I took meeting notes last time; could you take them this time?" Or "I'll clean out the refrigerator this week, but let's create a cleaning rotation for the future."
- Explain to your boss that when you take on disproportionate office housework, it impacts your ability to complete the job you were hired to do.
- Discuss with your colleagues ways to share office housework duties.
- If self-appraisals are a part of performance reviews, highlight your office housework duties and include a description of their value in keeping your organization running smoothly.

Diminishment

LEADERS

- Set the example by not diminishing women.
- Communicate guidelines for respectful treatment of women (e.g., not using pet names, using proper titles).
- Ensure women's contributions are acknowledged in private and public settings.

- Establish disciplinary consequences for individuals who infantilize, sexualize, belittle, or disparage women.

ALLIES

- If you hear or see diminishing behaviors, call them out: "That statement diminished our colleague. Let's treat her respectfully." Or, "It's disrespectful to call women by first names when we refer to men with their title and last name."
- If you catch yourself diminishing someone, such as using a pet name or untitling women, apologize and correct the mistake.
- Give women credit for their work in public events, meetings, and private settings with colleagues and bosses. You can say, "Did you hear about the excellent work that Wendy did on this contract? Her negotiations saved our company thousands of dollars."

SELF

- If you are diminished, call it out. If you are untitled, you can say, "My name is Dr. Brown." You could add, "It is disrespectful to call me by my first name when we refer to male doctors with their title and last name."
- If you are disparaged, belittled, or sexualized, consider saying, "I don't appreciate that comment. I am going to focus on my job. If these comments continue, I will have to report them."
- Speak privately to the individual who is diminishing you to explain the effect on you and express your expectation for respectful treatment.
- Self-promote. Share your accomplishments with your boss and colleagues and in meetings, social media, and other public settings. It may feel uncomfortable but don't let that stop you. You can say, "In the past month, I've closed three sales deals and attained five new leads." When credit belongs to a group that

includes you, be sure to acknowledge your own role: "My colleagues and I identified $40,000 in budget savings."

- Set up a buddy system with colleagues to share each other's accomplishments in public settings and meetings. If you are in an environment that uses professional titles, you and your colleagues can also reinforce their proper use, by using them when naming the other.
- For repeated diminishing treatment, keep notes of the behaviors and ask your boss or HR for assistance. Explain the impact to your morale and others' perceptions of your work.[68]

Benevolent Sexism

LEADERS

- Communicate expectations that women be treated as equal colleagues and judged based on their skills and work, rather than appearance or stereotypical feminine behaviors (e.g., caring, nurturing, kindness).
- Assume that women can do the job. Ensure women are offered opportunities for challenging assignments, overtime, and work travel to the same extent men are.

ALLIES

- Compliment women on their skills and accomplishments. But be careful when complimenting women on appearance or feminine behavior. Consider if you would compliment a man in the same way.
- Don't assume that women need men's protection or that they can't do the job.
- If you see benevolent sexist behavior, call it out, explaining why it is demeaning to women.

SELF

- In the moment, stand up to benevolent sexist behavior. If someone compliments your appearance, you can say, "I appreciate the compliment, but let's focus on my work." If you are told to "sit and look pretty," you can say, "I am going to help with this task." You can also push back more strongly, "While I appreciate compliments about my work, comments about my appearance aren't relevant here."
- Speak privately to the individual who has made patronizing or other benevolent sexist comments to explain their impact on you.
- If speaking the person directly doesn't help or benevolent sexist behavior is systemic in your organization, ask for assistance from HR or your boss.
- Find a colleague who can watch for and call out benevolent sexist behavior on your behalf.

Salary Inequality

LEADERS

- Establish standardized pay structures that reflect the value of each job in the external market and the internal value to the organization.
- Review new hire offers and promotional pay to ensure equity.
- Do not consider salary history or employee family situations in determining salaries or raises.
- Examine salaries across the organization and rectify any gender pay disparities. Establish an annual salary audit to ensure disparities do not creep in.
- Provide pay transparency throughout the organization and allow employees to freely discuss pay.

ALLIES

- Share your salary information with others if not prohibited by company policy.
- If you are aware that women are being paid less for similar work, speak up on their behalf to HR or organizational leadership.

SELF

- Do research on what others are earning in your organization and field. Ask your colleagues for their salary information if not prohibited by company policy.
- If you find you are being paid less than others for comparable work, speak to your boss or HR. Present the salary data you have gathered and explain the impact of not paying you an equitable wage. You can say, "I know that this organization values my work, but it impacts my morale knowing that my labor is not paid at the same rate as men."
- If your organization is unwilling to rectify your pay discrepancy, then consider other employment options as well as action through the U.S. federal or your state's equal opportunity employment commission. You may also wish to consult with an employment attorney for advice.

Credibility Deficit

LEADERS

- Recognize that credibility deficit is often very subtle. Train your staff on how to identify it and to avoid asking women, "Are you sure that's right?" or asking men to back up women's statements. Set expectations that women are to be trusted.
- Trust the expertise and skills that women bring to their role.
- If you observe individuals disbelieving women's statements, use it as a teachable moment for that individual or the entire team.

ALLIES

- Assume that women's statements are credible to the same extent that men's statements are assumed to be credible.
- Don't ask men to confirm women's statements.
- Unless you can back it up with a rationale, don't ask women, "Are you sure that's right?"
- If you observe individuals disbelieving women's statements, back up the women: "Jane is the expert. Let's trust her."

SELF

- If you are asked, "Are you sure that's right?" you can simply say, "Yes." You may add, "Your question implies that my words are not credible. I would not have made the statement if I thought it was inaccurate." If your male colleague is asked to back up your statement, you may interject, "Thank you for asking Jamel to back me up but I've done the research and am confident about this point."
- Speak privately to individuals who repeatedly express disbelief in your statements.
- If engaging the disbelieving person directly doesn't help or if credibility deficit is systemic in your organization, ask HR or your boss for assistance.
- Form a buddy system to watch for unfair disbelief and back up each other: "Janetha is the expert. Let's trust her knowledge."

5

HOSTILITY

"Because I spoke out against my male boss for his bullying
conduct, he hated me and sought to retaliate."

—Lawyer[1]

In November 2015, Susan Fowler joined the ride-sharing company
Uber as a software engineer. On her first day, she received chat messages from her manager stating that he was looking for sexual partners.
Fowler took screen shots and reported the manager to human resources
(HR). Although propositioning was sexual harassment, it was the manager's first offense and as a top performer, upper management didn't feel
comfortable punishing him for an "innocent" mistake. Fowler could
find another team or stay, knowing the manager would probably give
her a bad performance review. HR claimed that it would not count as
retaliation since they had given her an option. Fowler left the team, but
over the subsequent months, she met women engineers who had similar
stories; some had even reported the same manager. Eventually Fowler
requested a transfer to a third engineering team. While other managers wanted her and she had perfect performance scores, her transfer was
blocked. She waited until the next review cycle and made another transfer request. This time her performance score was lowered, which stopped
the transfer. As it turns out, having a woman on the team made Fowler's
manager look good. Fowler left the company in December 2016.[2]

In February 2017, Fowler published a blog post that described her
experiences at Uber.[3] Her post went viral and was part of a water-shed
moment against workplace sexual misconduct. But soon things changed
for Fowler. Family, friends, and acquaintances were contacted by people
who wanted information on her personal life and past. Private investigators

contacted Fowler directly, including a firm that had been previously hired to discredit victims of sexual misconduct. Fowler was attacked in other ways, too; her social media accounts were hacked, and she was followed.[4] During this time, Fowler was sick to her stomach, had trouble sleeping, and experienced intense periods of crying. While Fowler's blog post led to investigations of Uber's culture and the departure of chief executive officer Travis Kalanick, it came a great personal cost to Fowler herself.[5]

Susan Fowler experienced hostility consisting of discrimination and sexual harassment while employed at Uber and retaliation after leaving. Hostility is an active resistance to women's presence in the workplace. The goal is to keep women in their supposed place underneath men in the gender hierarchy.

In this chapter, we break down hostility into four components: discrimination, workplace harassment, female hostility, and retaliation. *Discrimination* occurs when women are denied opportunities or equal pay based on gender. *Workplace harassment* consists of verbal abuse, bullying, sabotage, and sexual harassment. Not all harassment comes from men. *Female hostility* stems from women's learned mistrust of, dislike for, or prejudice against other women. And if enduring hostility isn't enough, women experience *retaliation* when their employers punish them for reporting discrimination or harassment. Unfortunately, workplace hostility against women is still all too common.

DISCRIMINATION

In 1989, when journalist Meredith Viera was hired part-time for the television news show *60 Minutes*, she made an agreement with then executive producer Don Hewitt to move to full-time after two years. When Viera became pregnant in 1991, she asked to remain part-time. Hewitt turned down her request and released Viera from her contract, stating that it was unfair to the other journalists—all men—to bear the extra work burden. Defending his action, Hewitt said, "You don't come looking for a job you can't do, and convince [your employers] you can do it, and then one day say, 'No, I gotta tell you, I can't.'"[6] While *60 Minutes* had the opportunity to set an example by providing work flexibility and support to mothers, it chose to discriminate. More than three decades since Viera's experience, women continue to face discrimination in hiring, pay, promotions, and firing. Discrimination against women also often involves motherhood, age, race, and other identity characteristics.

Gender discrimination occurs when an employee or job applicant is treated less favorably because of their sex or gender. While sex is biological and gender is socially constructed, these terms are often used interchangeably in discrimination laws. The U.S. Equal Pay Act of 1963 made it illegal to pay women less than men for the same job under the same conditions.[7] In 1964, Title VII of the Civil Rights Act made discrimination based on sex, race, color, religion, or national origin illegal for employers of fifteen or more people. It is not lawful to pay less, fire, not hire, or provide discriminatory working conditions based on these categories. Title VII also made it illegal to retaliate against employees who report discrimination or pursue legal action.[8] In 2009, the Lilly Ledbetter Fair Pay Act amended Title VII to extend the time in which workers can file suit to 180 days after the last pay violation.[9]

Even though U.S. law renders discrimination illegal, it continues to happen, and challenging it in federal court is difficult. When women bring discrimination suits based on the Equal Pay Act, companies can easily find reasons—such as employee performance, seniority, experience, or education—to justify differences in pay. Alternatively, women may file a pay gap suit based on Title VII. Underpaying women based on sex is generally easier to prove than discrimination under the Equal Pay Act, since the plaintiff doesn't have to prove she was doing the same job as a man who was paid more. However, she must prove that she was paid less due to gender, which is not a requirement of the Equal Pay Act. In addition, judges dismiss job discrimination and equal pay claims at a higher rate than other civil lawsuits. Only about 4 percent of discrimination lawsuits succeed.[10]

Furthermore, the U.S. legal system favors those with power and money. When investor Ellen Pao (discussed in chapter 1, "Male Privilege,") sued her employer, venture capital firm Kleiner Perkins, for gender discrimination and retaliation, she could not compete with the firm's vast wealth ($7 billion in 2012, the year Pao filed her suit).[11] And the company's clout in Silicon Valley made it challenging for Pao to find anyone willing to testify on her behalf.[12] Pao's legal expenses totaled $2.7 million. After the jury ruled in favor of Kleiner Perkins, a judge ordered Pao to pay $276,000 to Kleiner Perkins toward *their* legal costs.[13] Pao chose not to appeal because she could not "afford the risk of even more costs to fight against a firm with tremendous financial resources and massive legal and PR armies."[14]

The U.S. legal system also favors corporations over women. In 2019, the Northern District of California court ruled that a group of Walmart store employees who alleged systemic sex discrimination due to lack of promotions and pay inequity must file eighteen separate lawsuits. The court's rationale was that since "each woman worked for a different supervisor at a different Walmart at different times," the bias didn't arise out of the same occurrence.[15] Without the ability to band together, women who experience comparable discrimination within the same company have near-impossible battles to fight on their own.

Even when women win discrimination lawsuits, there is a personal cost. Sandra Robertson endured six years of pay discrimination and harassment from male colleagues when she worked as a shipping supervisor. She filed a lawsuit after being fired in 2012 for "job performance" and "management style"; a federal jury found her the victim of discrimination, hostile work environment, and retaliation. Yet during the suit, "she lost weight, became depressed, and could not find a new job because she had to reveal to prospective employers that she had been fired."[16]

Hiring

Some women experience blatant discrimination during hiring interviews. After a lengthy interview, a male manager told one woman, "I only hire young men in this position." He also said that the last time he hired a woman, "she dressed provocatively and would always cat fight with the women in the office." An interviewer told another woman that if it were up to him, he "wouldn't hire a woman of childbearing age." Even so, the woman was offered the job. She turned it down. Interviewers sometimes ask women about future family plans. As one woman said, "It's been asked casually, but it's very jarring."

Pay

Pay discrimination is common but due to legal barriers, relatively few women file lawsuits. Those who do face long, uphill battles. In 2017, Walt Disney Company employee LaRonda Rasmussen asked the HR department for a pay audit, which found that men were paid more. Even though Disney claimed that the differences were "not due to gender," it raised Rasmussen's salary by $25,000 due to "an evaluation of market forces." But her pay was still less than men in similar positions. Disney employee Karen Moore was discouraged from applying for a manager position. A man was hired and paid significantly more than Moore, even though they "perform[ed] the same or substantially similar work." Rasmussen and Moore filed a joint pay discrimination lawsuit against Disney in 2019.[17] In 2021, the suit was expanded to include pay secrecy, a violation of California law, and eight more women have since joined. Just like Walmart, Disney is fighting in court to require the women to file their suits individually.[18]

Sometimes retention raises lead to gender pay disparities. Psychology professor Dr. Jennifer Freyd of the University of Oregon was paid substantially less than several male colleagues even though she was more senior. A departmental self-study found that the average difference between male and female full professors was $25,000 per year due to raises given to faculty who pursued outside offers. The university claimed that there was no need to equalize pay because Freyd had not pursued retention raises like the men. Freyd filed a sex discrimination case against the university in U.S. District Court, arguing that retention raises have a disparate impact on women.[19] With the case about to go to a jury trial, the university settled, agreeing to pay $450,000 to Freyd and her attorneys for damages and fees spanning the four-year lawsuit.[20]

Promotion

Many women experience discrimination in promotional opportunities. One woman was told that she would not get a promotion because "elderly male clients wouldn't take advice from a young woman." Yet the person who received the promotion was a man barely older than she was. In another case, a senior nonprofit professional was passed over for an interim position "in favor of the zero-experience board member/

friend of the founder." She was told, "He doesn't know anything about this kind of work. Think how much he'll need you!"

Sometimes qualified women in interim roles are passed over for permanent positions. One woman served as acting department manager for nineteen months, yet a man was promoted to the job, and she was asked to train him. She noted, "I declined." In another case, a marketing manager served as acting sales manager. One day the general manager asked her opinion of three choices for the permanent role—all men, only one with sales experience. Seeing the look on her face, the general manager explained that the all-male sales staff would have trouble working under her, even though they had done so for six months. She asked, "Why? Because I'm a woman?" The general manager replied, "Yes." Within a week, her job responsibilities were changed. She was given three months to do a research project. After three weeks, she was told that she had not made enough progress and was let go.

Firing

Women may be fired from their jobs for discriminatory reasons. The manager of the second-highest-grossing retail location in a liquor store chain experienced a sales decline of 12 percent compared to the previous year, a drop similar to other retailers. Her biggest competitor was another location overseen by her district manager. During her annual review, the district manager noted the decline. When the store manager tried to discuss it, the district manager stopped her: "I don't care if you have to stand on a corner in a bikini holding a sign if that's what it takes to increase sales." Four days later she was fired. When she asked the district manager why, he said, "It isn't open for discussion."

Independent contractors may be especially at risk of being let go for discriminatory reasons. When a former contract reporter for the *Washington Post* found she was underpaid compared to male colleagues, she asked her boss's boss, editor Doug Jehl, for a pay increase. But Jehl became angry, telling her that "she'd have to leave the paper if she brought up the issue again." The next morning Jehl told the reporter that her recent job application to a staff position was not being considered and that her contract would not be renewed. A few months later, the reporter wrote a letter to *Post* executive editor Martin Baron, explaining that she had not made a demand but had expressed her "perceived value to the company and as a reporter." Yet Baron dug in, stating that the decision was "part of a rethink of the entire bureau." The reporter discussed a discrimination suit with an attorney but was told nothing could be done since she was a contractor.[21]

Motherhood

Women also experience discrimination based on being mothers. When one woman told her boss she was pregnant, she was denied benefits she had been promised when hired a few months earlier. When this woman returned from maternity leave, her hours were cut because someone else had been hired to cover her leave. As she said, "I was slowly edged out by being deemed incapable of doing my job properly, despite communicating the issues and the best way to move forward." Not considering the fight to be worth it, she and her boss mutually agreed to let her contract run out two months early.

Brands that sponsor professional athletes often view pregnancy and motherhood "as inconveniences or as aberrations" and therefore penalize women who try to combine career and family.[22] When long-distance runner Kara Goucher and her husband Adam wanted to start a family, her Nike-sponsored coach told them, "As long as she stays relevant, everything will be fine." While pregnant, Goucher wrote a book, did every appearance requested by Nike plus a dozen more, and worked out with her coach. Yet six months into the pregnancy, her contract was suspended without pay until she could compete. A Nike representative told Goucher that she "had not done her job in a year, and that she was not paid to share her journey, she was paid to race." This pressure meant Goucher was back in training two weeks after delivery and running 100 miles per week within two months. Goucher also dealt with physical and emotional stress when her son was hospitalized, yet she continued to train, competing in a half marathon three months postpartum to stop the "clock ticking" on her return. All the while Nike was using her likeness in ads without compensating her. As her husband explained, "I was watching someone abuse their power over her again and again, breaking her will and her body. . . . We were even told by her coach that it would be a bad idea to pursue any type of serious legal action [as] there would be no way Nike would keep us around, and it would be the end of our careers."[23] Goucher's experience with Nike may seem egregious, but far too frequently women encounter the power of a corporation leveraged against their personal motherhood and realize they cannot win.

Mothers of older children also face assumptions that they can't do their job. When one mother of teenagers was up for a promotion, she was asked if her "family responsibilities" would interfere with her job duties. It was an unnecessary and discriminatory question, as she had already been doing the job on an interim basis for months.

Even childless women are subject to discrimination due to an assumed motherhood potential. When one woman applied for a job at an art museum, the general counsel asked if she was dating anyone and if she planned to have children soon. A lawyer described how she avoided this discrimination when male partners asked if she wanted to have kids: "I lied to them by saying that I wasn't sure and I'm just focusing on my career now."

Because of awareness of discrimination law, employers may not outright fire current or aspiring mothers but instead make the work undesirable so that women leave on their own accord. A newspaper publisher asked a female employee if she planned to have children. When she replied, "Someday," he said, "then that will be your career." The publisher subsequently moved her around the newsroom to position after position, never let her advance, and assigned her unappealing night hours. She eventually quit.

Age

Age discrimination is also common for women. Sometimes women are outright told they are too young for promotions or leadership positions. Early in her career, at age twenty-four, an HR professional was appointed interim director of her department, but "the good old guy down the hall" got the permanent job. Her boss explained, "You've done a great job for the last three months, and you're going to be the support system that keeps this office going. But we just really felt that you were . . . too young and a female."[24] While recognizing her boss's behavior as illegal discrimination, this woman chose not to fight it. Instead, she left for a new employer.

Other women are considered too old. After working in television news for more than three decades and receiving dozens of awards, news anchor Roma Torre found her airtime shrinking after her news station NY1 was acquired by Charter Communications. Four female colleagues with eleven to twenty-five years of experience had the same problem. While these women filed complaints with NY1 management, the responses were dismissive. In 2019, Torre and her colleagues filed an age and gender discrimination lawsuit against Charter. As Torre said, "For decades, experienced female news anchors have been pushed out of highly visible roles and denied promotional opportunities due to age and appearance. This rarely happens to men."[25] Charter settled the lawsuit in 2020 with the condition that all five women leave NY1.[26] It is no gain for women's equality when those who file lawsuits are pushed out of their roles.

Age discrimination against women is sometimes disguised by suggestions that they are overqualified. When mathematics professor Dr. Alice Silverberg inquired about a job at Hewlett Packard Labs, she was told mathematics is a "young man's game" and that she was "much better than the people they hire." Hence the answer was no.[27]

Intersectionality

Beyond motherhood and age, women may have additional identities upon which they experience discrimination, such as race, ethnicity, religion, sexual orientation, physical ability, and health, just to name a few. Intersectionality refers to overlapping systems of discrimination based on marginalized identity characteristics. Professor Kimberlé Crenshaw observed intersectionality in the legal field when courts declined to treat Black women as a protected class, ignoring the specific challenges they face as a group.[28] Women with simultaneous marginalized identities often suffer from compounding effects of discrimination and hostility, resulting in "multiple jeopardy."[29] As one woman explained, "Being a Black out lesbian can present challenges that are less in my face than they are expressions of lack of confidence in my abilities. This constant strain of microaggressions is wearying to say the least."

Women are subject to discrimination in myriad ways throughout their careers. When they're hired, or fired, or have children, or are assumed to want children, when they're young, or when they're old, when they seek promotion or want equal pay, or have any marginalized identity characteristic, they routinely encounter discrimination. In essence, employers are saying to the women "we want what you aren't." And laws that are supposed to protect them too often fail.

WORKPLACE HARASSMENT

One Tuesday morning, a manager repeatedly questioned a woman about a department that was not hers. Exasperated, the woman reminded the manager which department she did oversee and answered, "I don't know." The manager then berated her in a mocking, whiny voice: "All I ever hear is 'I don't know.'" When the woman broke down in tears, the manager responded, "Geez, I didn't mean to make you cry," to which the woman replied, "Don't flatter yourself. I am having a horrible morning. I don't know where my husband is, and I may have lost two cousins." It was September 11, 2001.

Workplace harassment consists of behaviors that provoke, frighten, intimidate, or bring discomfort to victims and includes verbal abuse, bullying, sabotage, and sexual harassment. According to U.S. law, harassment is illegal when enduring it is a condition of employment or when it is so severe that a reasonable person would find the work environment to be intimidating, hostile, or abusive.[30] Unfortunately, harassment is a common occurrence for women at work. In our survey research of 1,606 women leaders, 54 percent reported that the behavior of their male coworkers had sometimes made them uncomfortable, 41 percent had experienced verbal abuse at work, and 29 percent had been sexually harassed at work.

However, reporting harassment is not common. In 2016, the U.S. Equal Employment Opportunity Commission (EEOC) found that the least common response to harassment is taking formal action; an estimated 75 percent of individuals who experience harassment never report it. Fearing disbelief or retaliation, victims instead may avoid the harasser or attempt to downplay, ignore, forget, or even endure the harassment.[31] These fears may be realistic; a 2003 study found that 66 percent of employees who reported harassment experienced subtle or

overt retaliation.[32] Harassment is particularly prevalent in male-dominated fields, service-based industries that rely on tips and customer approval, and low-wage jobs like hotel cleaners and farm workers in which
women have no bargaining power to push back.[33] The organizational
harms of workplace harassment go beyond direct legal costs (an average
of $125,000 per claim for small and mid-sized businesses) to include
decreased productivity, increased turnover, and reputational damage. As
the EEOC concluded, "All of this is a drag on performance—and the
bottom-line."[34]

Harassment is about control; the goal of harassing women is to
communicate that they are not welcome in the workplace and must stay
in their assigned place supporting but not competing with men. Harassers use organizational, economic, physical, and social power, leaving
victims with little recourse for self-defense. The primary motivation
for harassment is to protect one's social status. The more an individual
believes in a gender hierarchy, the more they are likely to define their
own and other's status according to the hierarchy and want to defend
their own status.[35]

General Harassment

General workplace harassment includes verbal attacks, bullying, undermining, and sabotage. It happens not only face-to-face but in virtual
environments too. Unfortunately, women are affected by all three types
and are sometimes even blamed.

VERBAL ATTACKS

Many women are screamed at, sworn at, berated, and even threatened at
work. One woman worked for a man who verbally abused women and
then bragged when he made them cry. When this woman reported the
behavior, she was told that he had many complaints but since his work
brought in revenue, the company would do nothing. Another woman
recounted how a male coworker lashed out at her during a meeting: "A
supervisor asked what I may have said to cause his temper tantrum as
though I must have done something to deserve it."

BULLYING

Bullying is another common form of harassment. A program manager worked for a director who intimidated the women to get him coffee, bring him food, and even cook for his family events lest they lose their jobs. While this manager didn't allow the director to bully her into serving him food, she spoke up about the behavior. But he retaliated. "I became a good target. I was eventually run out of the department [by] him and upper management for speaking for the women," as she said.

Bullying can accomplish the harasser's goal of pushing women out of the workforce. The male boss of an information technology (IT) director bullied her daily for seven years. When she finally filed a complaint, the boss retaliated and "got rid of me in the most inhumane way possible," as she described. She was so emotionally scarred that she stopped working altogether.

UNDERMINING

Undermining is a pernicious form of harassment in which a woman's abilities or integrity are questioned. After a Fortune 500 executive was promoted over three men, they started a rumor that she slept with the boss to get the job. "This was five years ago, and the allegations still resurface every now and then," as she explained. Men may spread rumors and lies about women colleagues because the risks are low. As another executive explained, "There is rarely a negative consequence for the 'players'—and it often pays off. So why not give it a shot?"

The goal of undermining is to encourage women to quit, as happened to a young Hispanic marketing department head. The woman's coworker explained, "They continually ignored her input, patronized her, questioned her knowledge. It seemed that they resented the fact that she knew more than they did, that they wanted to break her down. . . . They made her quit!"

SABOTAGE

While undermining can be subtle and may take place over a long time, sabotage is an outright attack. An executive helped a man get a C-suite position, but later he attacked her, saying, "She's not doing this right," in front of other executives. Soon after, male colleagues outmaneuvered this executive during a corporate reorganization, causing her exit from the company. As she explained, "Women are prey. [The men] can smell it in the water, that women are not going to play the same game. Those men think, 'If I kick her, she's not going to kick back, but the men will. So, I'll go after her.' It's keeping women in their place."[36]

Women at all levels can be targets of sabotage. While men who started as temps in a machine shop were hired permanently after five hundred hours of work, a female temp never was. She lost her job when some men "made up bad work orders under my name . . . because [they] didn't like a woman there," as she explained.

Men may use stereotypes about women to sabotage them. Attorney David O. Doyle, Jr. filed a motion before trial started to "preclude emotional displays" from opposing lawyer Elizabeth Faiella. The judge denied Doyle's request, indicating both attorneys should "behave themselves." Yet the damage was done, as the idea that Faiella would become emotional to get her way had been planted. As Faiella noted, "Because I am a woman, I have to act like it doesn't bother me, but I tell you that it does. The arrow lands every time."[37]

VIRTUAL HARASSMENT

Harassment can also happen virtually. The shift to remote work during the COVID-19 pandemic made it easier for some employees to exert power over others. The channels through which remote work occurs—text, phone, video—are often unmonitored, unrecorded, or occur outside employer-sponsored platforms. It can be easy to harass due to the privacy in those interactions. There are no colleagues nearby while a harasser is yelling at somebody, so nobody to see or overhear the harassment or help stop it. Research of three thousand tech workers across forty-eight countries—97 percent working remotely—from May

2020 to February 2021 found 36 percent of women reported an increase in gender-based harassment since the start of the pandemic.[38] Harassment included "public bullying attacks on group video calls to berating 1:1 over email to racist and sexist link-sharing in chat."[39] Virtual harassment is all too possible, and some harassers are undeterred even in group virtual conferencing settings.

Sexual Harassment

While people may think that sexual harassment is about sexual desire, it is meant to demean and humiliate and to protect one's own sex-based status.[40] While "sexual harassment" was named in the 1970s, the term wasn't used widely until 1991, when Anita Hill (discussed in chapter 4, "Devaluation,") testified before an all-male U.S. Senate panel during the Supreme Court confirmation process for Clarence Thomas, her former boss.[41] According to Hill's testimony, Thomas pressured Hill to go out with him and she refused. Thomas continued to pressure her, discussing "his sexual prowess and his porn-watching habits." While Hill was "horrified," and told Thomas that she was uncomfortable, her approach was to try to change the subject. Under Senate questioning, Hill described the motive: "He wanted me at a disadvantage." Hill understood that the point wasn't to have sex with her; it was to make her vulnerable. In fact, the harassment took a toll on Hill's health; she was hospitalized for stress-induced stomach pain.[42]

Prior to Hill's testimony, many people had no idea what "sexual harassment" meant. In the five years following, sexual harassment complaints filed to the EEOC more than doubled.[43] In recent years, complaints rose from 6,696 in 2017 to 7,609 in 2018 and 7,514 in 2019,[44] likely spurred by the #MeToo movement, started by activist Tarana Burke and popularized by actor Alyssa Milano to demonstrate the scale of sexual harassment and assault.[45] This section will cover six types of sexually harassing behavior: sexual remarks, physical touching, sexual advances, sexual relationships, sexual assault, and institutional assault.

SEXUAL REMARKS

Many women suffer through sexual remarks and innuendoes. A male creative director praised a female journalist: "I could kiss you on the mouth for that headline!" The journalist noted that the director "thought it was a compliment." In another case, the male coworkers of a then fifteen-year-old fast food cashier routinely asked her sexually explicit questions, such as "Did you give your boyfriend a blowjob this weekend, or did you punish him?" As she explained, "I was an object before I even got hired and never told anyone about the harassment. I didn't realize what was happening at the time."

Even religious men make sexual remarks toward women. When a reporter covered an event at St. Peter's Basilica in Rome, she dressed conservatively with her press credentials attached to her suit lapel. A priest smirked and pointed at her chest, saying, "Whenever I see a woman with a tag on that says, 'Hi, my name is _____ ,' I want to ask her, 'What's the name of the other one.'" The reporter informed the priest he was "disgusting" at which point a bishop told her not to be "so sensitive," since the priest was "just kidding." While the reporter would have liked to report the priest for sexual harassment, she explained, "It would have been my word against his, and he was in a very powerful position."

Workers in service industries frequently encounter sexual remarks. To not jeopardize tips and because "the customer is always right," servers may ignore comments about their bodies and deflect sexual advances. When server Jaime Brittain was offered $30 to answer a question about pubic hair, she debated, but then provided a "snappy answer," which earned her the tip. As Brittain stated, "Every time it happens, I will have this inner monologue with myself: 'Is this worth saying something or is it not?'"[46]

Women in non-tipped service roles also face inappropriate remarks from customers. One jewelry store employee assisted a man shopping for a diamond for his wife. The man told the employee that he "wanted to f#@k me 'in the worst way,'" as she described. After he left, the woman went to the back of the store to cry: "I have no idea why he felt he could say that to me." Another woman described the power imbalance between customers and service workers as "too much for some men to resist. They know they won't be challenged."

PHYSICAL TOUCHING

Many women experience harassment via unwanted physical touching, which can leave them feeling deeply uncomfortable and unsure what to do. A software engineer's boss tried "to put his hands on my shoulders for a back rub at a company party," as the engineer explained. One summer day an older male subordinate grabbed Amy's bare arm in a car during a work trip. On previous occasions he touched her shoulders from behind. Situations like that can be confusing; the victim may not want to cause a scene or may not recognize such behavior as harassment. Yet saying nothing may lead the perpetrator to think that the behavior is acceptable, which may result in further escalation. In Amy's case, she felt embarrassed and said nothing, choosing instead to avoid situations in which she was alone with the subordinate.

SEXUAL ADVANCES

One day a male director asked entertainer Jennifer Lopez to see her breasts while off set. Lopez said "no" but recalls "being so panicked in the moment."[47] Fortunately, Lopez had the power to reject the advance and not face backlash. The same cannot be said for others. Some male directors forced female stars to sit on their laps, as happened to actors Sharon Stone and Geena Davis.[48] When Stone refused, the director declined to shoot her scenes until she complied.[49] Davis felt powerless: "You can't say anything, because it will kill your career."[50]

Noncelebrities also experience sexual advances. Male coworkers treated one woman as if she "owed them sexual favors for simply existing as a female," even though she attempted to avoid them. As she stated, "Earphones, a hoodie over my head, and reading a book apparently is code for 'come hither.'" A boss made an advance on another woman by tricking her into thinking she was meeting with a group. When she entered the room and was alone with him, "he took the opportunity to kiss me," she explained. Nor are public officials immune. A major donor made advances on Mayor Breea Clark of Norman, Oklahoma. She commented, "People still see me as a woman and an object, which is really unfortunate."[51]

Backlash is often a consequence for refusing advances. When one woman called the head of IT for a technical issue, she was subjected to "inappropriate verbal sexual advances and harassment." When the woman said she wasn't interested, the IT head refused to answer future calls. Other women in the office were treated the same way. "The minute you refused an advance, you were . . . punished professionally," as the woman explained.

SEXUAL RELATIONSHIPS

When powerful men initiate sexual relationships, women are put in a difficult situation. Whether the women accept or decline, they are likely to suffer negative consequences personally and professionally. A famous example is the relationship between former President Bill Clinton and White House intern Monica Lewinsky. While their affair was consensual, when it was exposed, Lewinsky—not Clinton—was publicly shamed, humiliated, and stigmatized, even though there were numerous other sexual harassment and assault allegations against Clinton.[52] Impeached for lying under oath about the relationship, Clinton was nevertheless acquitted and finished out his presidency, remaining a respected elder stateman. Meanwhile, Lewinsky was unable to find an employer willing to hire her. As she said, "I was made a scapegoat in order to protect his powerful position."[53]

Men in powerful positions may use flattery to pressure women—especially those of lower workplace status—into sexual relationships. An example occurred with former TV news personality Matt Lauer and twenty-four-year-old production assistant Addie Collins at the *Today Show*. The then-married Lauer sent Collins flirtatious instant messages, such as, "OK . . . NOW YOU'RE KILLING ME. . . . YOU LOOK GREAT TODAY! A BIT TOUGH TO CONCENTRATE." When Collins met Lauer for lunch hoping for some professional mentoring, Lauer hit on her. As she said, "It was flattering, confusing, overwhelming. I was nervous. I didn't know what to do with it." Their month-long sexual relationship ended when she left for a local anchor position in another state. When the *National Enquirer* tabloid picked up the story, Lauer ghosted her, and Collins quit her anchor job due to the stress.

Collins wrote, "This man who I'd held on a pedestal had made me feel like my looks and my body were my true assets. He made it clear that he wasn't interested in my skills or my talent. It just shattered everything."[54]

These powerful men often have inappropriate relationships with more than one colleague. Lauer was fired from *Today* in 2017 but only after another staffer complained about similar conduct. An investigation found that "Lauer had a history of inviting colleagues into his office for sexual activity."[55] While Lauer was finally held accountable, the power imbalance leaves women with few good options. If they decline the relationship, their career is likely harmed. If they accept the relationship and it goes sour or is found out—like Addie Collins—their career and self-worth are left in tatters.

SEXUAL ASSAULT

Some women are sexually assaulted. One form is groping, which is fondling or touching someone in an unwanted sexual way. Even celebrities have been groped. In one incident, actor Ben Affleck "tweaked" the breast of fellow actor Hilarie Burton—then just nineteen years old—on the MTV show *Total Request Live*. She laughed it off on camera, and an MTV executive called to tell her that she handled it well. At the time, Burton didn't realize that she was being groomed, "trained to be a good girl and *a good sport*, someone who would put up with much worse behavior," as she recounted.[56]

Sometimes customers grope women. One surgeon had to deal with "grabbing, groping, and verbal abuse" from intoxicated patients in the emergency room. Wait staff can also suffer. A male customer grabbed server Dana Angelo's crotch under her skirt. Stifling the urge to scream and fighting back tears, she pointed out the assailant to her manager. Instead of taking action, the manager shook the man's hand.[57]

Some managers use their positional power to touch women's private body parts. As one woman recounted, "I was cornered and groped by my managers on a near-daily basis for 8 years."[58] And perpetrators may laugh off the harassment. The male colleague of one woman apologized for grabbing her behind at a party but a week later grabbed her breast. He said it was a "joke."[59] Calling it a joke is an attempt to gaslight the victim into believing it's not harassment.

Worse, sexual assault sometimes goes beyond groping to include sexual abuse and even rape. A case in point is Hollywood producer Harvey Weinstein. In the late 1990s, Weinstein invited actor Ashley Judd to a hotel for a business breakfast meeting. When Judd arrived, he requested she come to his room, where he was dressed in a bathrobe. Weinstein asked Judd to give him a massage or watch him shower. Judd recalls thinking, "How do I get out of the room as fast as possible without alienating Harvey Weinstein?" On October 5, 2017, the *New York Times* published a story detailing years of sexual harassment allegations against Weinstein.[60] Five days later, the *New Yorker* published allegations from thirteen additional women including three accusations of rape.[61] Weinstein forced many victims to massage him and watch him naked, while promising to advance their careers.[62] In May 2018, Weinstein was officially charged in New York with rape and sexual abuse of two women; two years later a jury found him guilty of a criminal sexual act and rape.[63] In total at least one hundred women publicly accused Weinstein of encounters that ranged from unwelcome, harassing behaviors to rape.[64] Weinstein bought the silence of at least eight women with a settlement that prevented them from sharing their stories.[65]

Weinstein is not the only high-powered man to be accused of sexual assault in workplace contexts. Dozens of women have described sexual harassment and quid pro quos (job benefits tied to submission to unwelcome sexual advances) against Roger Ailes, former chairman of Fox News. In 1990, Ailes told twenty-nine-year-old Republican operative Kellie Boyle, "If you want to play with the big boys, you have to lay with the big boys." She refused and was "professionally blackballed." In 2016, Gretchen Carlson sued Ailes for sexual harassment. Ailes subsequently left Fox News, with a $40 million "golden parachute," and then died in 2017.[66] Meanwhile, Carlson received a settlement and a public apology from 21st Century Fox in exchange for her silence about her experiences at Fox News. While Carlson felt no choice but to sign the settlement, she recognized that nondisclosure agreements and forced arbitration "foster a culture that gives predators cover to commit the same crimes again."[67] Carlson has since successfully advocated for a U.S.

federal law—Ending Forced Arbitration of Sexual Assault and Sexual Harassment Act—which allows survivors to file lawsuits in court.[68]

INSTITUTIONAL ASSAULT

Sometimes powerful organizations assault women by condoning sexual harassment and abuse, silencing victims, and vilifying those who report it. A case of such institutional assault is the Southern Baptist Convention (SBC). In 2022 an independent investigation concluded that the SBC had a twenty-plus year pattern of sexual abuse (over seven hundred instances including abuse by executive committee members) and had mishandled reports, intimidated victims and their advocates, and resisted reforms.[69] In one case, a seminary professor sexually abused his student, Jennifer Lyell. Years later, Lyell agreed to go public with the abuse at the request of her employer, Lifeway Christian Resources, and the SBC. But the SBC's news service "drastically changed her history and mischaracterized the abuse as a 'morally inappropriate relationship.'" Lyell was harassed in person and online, and she lost her career, friends, and health.[70]

When a powerful organization is run by powerful men who do everything possible to protect their privilege and status, victim blaming and silencing are the outcomes. SBC general counsel D. August Boto characterized victim reports as "a satanic scheme to completely distract us from evangelism," thus equating victims to the devil.[71] Disclosure comes at a cost, as one survivor said: "Imagine telling [your story] for decades to a non-receptive audience, to an audience who abuses you with their shame and their hateful words against you."[72] Indeed, it took decades of telling and an independent investigation to begin shedding light on the SBC's institutional hostility.

Similar reports have come from the Roman Catholic Church. In 2019, the Vatican's women's magazine published an article detailing rape and abuse of nuns by priests, including forced abortions and children fathered but not recognized by priests.[73] Yet the priests went unpunished, allowing them to rape repeatedly. Victims had to see their abusers every day. As nun Doris Wagner described, "He was preaching at the chapel. He was giving me holy communion. He was sitting at breakfast, at lunch, at dinner . . . at the same table. I was ironing his shirts."[74] A particularly egregious instance that included sexual slavery led Pope Francis to recognize that the Church has an ongoing problem of "seeing women as second-class."[75] As Wagner further explained, "Anybody who wants to become a nun wants to serve and wants to give herself to God. And that's why it's so easy to abuse nuns, because they are so ready to listen to others who tell them how they are supposed to be."[76]

Like the SBC, the Vatican women's group named abuse of power and an intent to preserve the Church's reputation as motivations for the secrecy of institutional assault.[77] Conservative religious culture socializes women as men's supporters and to consider male authority as beneficent.[78] When men abuse their power, the culture requires silent assent, thus making women vulnerable to institutional abuse. Such socialization isn't limited to religious organizations, but male organizational control and lack of external oversight may make these organizations especially ripe for abuse to occur and to fester.

Harassment, whether general or sexual, is an attempt to stop women from competing for "male" jobs, with the goal to push them to supporting roles or out of the workforce altogether. Harassment serves to remind women that they are only tolerated in roles that support men, including pleasing the male gaze or serving men's sexual desires. Harassment is a blatant attempt to communicate to women that some men will use all their power to maintain their position above women in the gender hierarchy.

FEMALE HOSTILITY

Not all harassment or mistreatment comes from men. To protect themselves in a male work culture, some women reinforce sexist norms against other women. Female hostility stems from women's mistrust of, dislike for, or prejudice against other women. Women may distance themselves from each other through competition, slights, and outright bullying.[79] One woman commented, "The majority of discrimination and unprofessional behavior I have experienced in the workplace has been done by other women. . . . I don't understand why we don't do more to raise each other up instead of pushing each other down." Female hostility is a consequence of discrimination that women have experienced and may therefore perpetuate.[80] When women aren't supported by other women, some in turn don't support women around them.[81]

Women on the receiving end of female hostility often feel that it is more severe than mistreatment from men.[82] While women may expect to be mistreated by men, they don't expect to be treated badly by other women; thus, it feels especially shocking and harsh when it happens. Female hostility may come from upper-level women (*queen bee behavior*) or peer and lower-level women (*mean girl behavior*).

Queen Bee Behavior

In 1974, a *Psychology Today* article identified "queen bee syndrome" and explained that when organizations start to admit previously excluded groups, like women, a few nonthreatening tokens are allowed in and well-rewarded with benefits, praise, and advancement. In return, tokens become supporters of the system that permitted them to advance. Having worked hard to get to their positions and being told that they are special and different, women leaders in such environments may see other women as competition and believe junior women should not have it any easier.[83] Pitting women against other women is an interesting trick of male leadership. They get the appearance of diversity, all the while reinforcing the status quo and keeping men in charge.

A half-century later, there are still upper-level women who mistreat, harass, or block opportunities for their lower-level counterparts. Queen bee behavior is usually driven by insecurity. When higher-level women worry that their positions are at risk, they may put subordinate women down. A corporate manager explained, "I received little support from other women who were in positions to mentor. . . . Women seem to view each other with suspicion. It was not unusual for women, feeling threatened, to backstab one another."

Television news journalist Katie Couric admitted to queen bee behaviors in her book *Going There*. She took female writers, researchers, and producers under her wing, but not female correspondents. She explained, "There were only a few coveted spots for women—I felt like I had to protect my turf." Couric recognized that the men in power could replace her with "someone younger and cuter" at any time.[84]

Queen bee behavior may be at play when women leaders actively favor men. A tech professional's manager greeted only the man if she walked past a man and a woman, reprimanded the women but not the men, and promoted the men but not the women. As this professional said, "It was the worst experience of my life. Several women on the team ended up in therapy during their time there."[85]

Sometimes higher-ranking women suppress the voices of subordinate women. One day a self-described "outspoken" woman questioned her female boss about perks. Taking offense, the boss told her that she should "not speak unless spoken to," to eliminate the tone in her speaking, and that her attitude was holding her back from promotions. A week later a man joined the team who "speaks out of turn, cusses, and just generally derails meetings," and has since been praised for being "outspoken." As this woman described, "Her 'discussion' with me only made me want to shut up completely and distance myself from the group. So, if that was her way of controlling the narrative, it worked."

Mean Girl Behavior

Other women experience hostility from peer or lower-level women, known as "mean girl" behavior. Socialized to express anger indirectly, women may undermine and judge each other.[86] Competition, insecurity, and gender stereotypes underlie mean girl behavior.

Many women have worked with peer or lower-level women who treat them disrespectfully. One woman described what happened when she spoke to an administrative assistant about a small error: "She repeatedly referred to me as being 'bitchy.' This is not the way she handles men giving their feedback." A professor hired into a department in which she was the second woman experienced mean girl behavior on her first day on the job. As she recounted, "I was told by the first woman that she didn't support my hiring and I could expect no help from her in any way."

Women in male-dominated roles often must go above and beyond to gain cooperation from women in closely aligned jobs, such as physicians with nurses and managers with administrative assistants, by being extra friendly and performing tasks outside their roles. This is known as "status-leveling burden," and can be time-consuming, emotionally difficult, and lead to burnout.[87] One surgeon befriended the nurses and baked cookies for them to prevent mistreatment: "Men never do that, but it works and helps grease the wheels."[88]

Women sometimes find ways to sabotage other women they are hired to assist. In one law firm, the female support staff "would say things that would get men in all but the worst organizations into hot water. Yet it's allowed for them to undermine female junior attorneys," as a lawyer described. Because the gender hierarchy places men above women, a woman may believe that women in higher positions violate their shared equality as women.[89] That, in turn, may lead the lower-level woman to undermine the woman who has broken gender norms by working in a high-status or male-stereotyped job.[90] Race can further complicate the equation. Another lawyer noted, "Other women who are not diverse have been much worse vis-a-vis race-based limiting of opportunities than have men, especially as I have gotten more senior."

Another variety of mean girl hostility can occur when women have the same professional status, such as physicians, lawyers, or professors, but one woman has an administrative leadership role, such as director or department chair. A status-equal but hierarchy-lower woman may exhibit "wannabee" behavior, in which she seeks to gain power by discrediting or bullying her colleague.[91] A lawyer described how women in her profession "give other women who are in a superior position to them a difficult time." In a previous role, Leanne worked with a colleague who exhibited wannabee hostility. This colleague was not an administrative leader but wanted to be in charge, so she actively undermined Leanne with lies and rumors. A woman acting as a wannabee knows there is limited space for women leaders in the organization and seeks to expand her own turf by taking her female colleague down.

Women in politics also experience mean girl behavior. A town mayor was mistreated in public meetings that she presided over: "No one speaks to the male mayors in our area the way some people speak to me. Interestingly, it has been women who have yelled at me . . . more frequently than men." Similarly, an attorney had difficulty obtaining endorsements from women when she ran for judicial office. She commented, "I have been surprised to learn some of the hyper-critical comments [from women] that were involved in the [endorsement] discussions. It is extremely disheartening." Female hostility is indeed disheartening, yet all too understandable in a world governed by gender hierarchy.

RETALIATION

Workplace retaliation occurs when an employer takes negative job action against an employee for legally protected activities such as making a harassment complaint or participating in workplace investigations.[92] Such actions can be overt (e.g., firing or demoting) or subtle (e.g., ostracizing or increased scrutiny).

RETALIATORY ACTIONS

- Firing or laying off
- Demoting
- Denying overtime or promotion
- Disciplining
- Denying benefits
- Reducing pay or hours
- Failing to hire or rehire
- Intimidation, harassment, or verbal or physical abuse
- Making threats
- Assigning to a less desirable position or affecting promotion prospects
- Blacklisting
- Spreading false rumors
- Making conditions intolerable so that the employee quits
- Subtle acts—isolating, ostracizing, mocking, false accusations of poor performance, increased scrutiny[93]

In the United States, several federal laws protect employees from retaliation: the Civil Rights Act, Equal Pay Act, Age Discrimination in Employment Act, and Americans with Disabilities Act.[94] Retaliation is the most frequently filed charge with the EEOC—56 percent of charges in 2021.[95] However, as with other types of hostility, just because retaliation is illegal doesn't keep it from happening.

Reporting workplace harassment often leads to retaliation, such as occurred to a restaurant host who found herself under excessive scrutiny after reporting that a chef groped her. Managers questioned her and suggested it had been an accident. Around the same time, several cooks told her that the chef had been making sexual comments about her. As the host explained, "He kept his job, and I was written up for very minor infractions. . . . [I was] fired shortly afterward."

Blacklisting is a retaliatory action effective in fields where networks and referrals are critical for obtaining the next job. Construction worker Concetta Defa explained, "You will run into the same people over and over again who will not want to work with you just because you reported harassment. In most cases, women become unemployable because of it."[96]

Sometimes HR departments may be of little help since they work for the organization and may place its needs first. A road construction worker stood up to her bully boss and was fired two days later. She lamented, "Did human resources care about how horrible he treated (still treats) people? It's only about the profit and the bottom line."

Fear of retaliation keeps women from speaking up. One long-serving lawyer described her conundrum in responding to her boss's verbal abuse of female attorneys: "I was afraid to report it or file a complaint because he would retaliate. I was afraid not to." At first, she chose not to report the behavior but eventually could no longer take it. After standing up to the boss, she was fired, which was "an unfortunate lesson for the other women in the office."[97] This attorney was ambivalent about whether to pursue a complaint with the state human relations commission. "I may do so but probably will not because I can't bear going through that," as she said.

Winning retaliation cases doesn't make up for the long-term aggravation, humiliation, and other losses from the experience. A male coworker sexually harassed machine operator Katy Degenhard, pressing his penis against her behind, rubbing his lips on her face, and touching her breasts. After Degenhard reported the behavior, she was disciplined for minor infractions and eventually fired. While the EEOC sued on her behalf and won a settlement, Degenhard questioned, "Why is it that we have to put up with all this in order to survive and have income for our family?"[98]

Other women experience subtle retaliation. Calling out sexist pet names to men comes with "some type of retribution/penance, especially if [the men] are more senior," as one woman noted. After reporting discrimination, a professor faced "efforts to force me to resign my (tenured) position," as she described. "There is no relief or remedy."

Closing this chapter, we are keenly aware of the disheartening nature of what we have described. Unfortunately, women are frequently the target of hostility at work. Hostility is emotional, anger- and resentment-based, aimed at hurting another person.[99] The goal is to punish women who break gendered social norms and to pressure them back into "approved" jobs in the workplace, those which support but don't compete with men's positions. Or to push them out of the paid workforce altogether—and back into the home.

SHATTERING HOSTILITY: A WELCOMING ORGANIZATION

Instead of a hostile environment, workplaces must create a welcoming organization that doesn't tolerate mistreatment. Solutions to shatter hostility are outlined below. Leaders must take the initiative, while allies—anyone who is supportive—can help promote a welcoming atmosphere. Individual women can also take steps to mitigate hostility if it happens to them.

Discrimination

LEADERS

- Establish a culture of zero tolerance for discrimination in hiring, pay, promotions, and firing.

- Provide anti-discrimination training tailored to supervisors and employees that addresses not just legal requirements but also the moral perspective of treating everyone fairly. Teach people to look out for intersectional discriminatory factors, such as race, ethnicity, age, motherhood, ability, and health.
- Provide confidential support to victims including external resources independent from the company reporting structure. Establish an ombuds office as an off-the-record resource for employees who are considering reporting discrimination. Create anonymous formal reporting channels and act on reports.[100]
- Publicize the process victims should use and their options if they suspect discrimination. Help them through the formal reporting process. Establish trust by maintaining confidentiality and being transparent through investigation and resolution processes. Ensure that victims are not harmed or retaliated against for reporting.
- Establish disciplinary consequences for those who perpetuate discrimination.

ALLIES

- Call out discriminatory behaviors: "It's not legal or relevant to ask if an applicant plans to have kids."
- If you are involved in hiring or promotions, speak up if discrimination creeps in: "Anita has more experience and better performance ratings than Eric. We should promote her."
- Let your colleagues know that you are a safe resource if they experience discrimination. Reach out to victims to help them and to direct them to safe sources of support. With your colleague's permission, speak to investigators or managers in support of your colleague.

SELF

- Take notes of discriminatory actions. Make copies of emails and other documents on your performance. Research pay for colleagues doing similar work. Retain documentation in personal file storage.

- Talk to trusted mentors and colleagues for support and an outsider perspective.
- Talk to other women in your organization to find out if they are victims of discrimination. If so, team up with these other victims to document it and present it to HR or senior leadership.
- Consider speaking to your organization's ombuds office (if it exists) for advice. Be sure to check that this resource is confidential.
- Discuss discriminatory behaviors with your boss or HR and provide your documentation. Ask them to guide you through the formal reporting process.
- If your leadership does not rectify the discrimination in a timely manner, talk to the U.S. federal or your state's equal opportunity employment commission about filing a gender discrimination claim. You may also wish to speak to an employment attorney for advice and consider your options for employment elsewhere.

Workplace Harassment

LEADERS

- Establish a culture of zero tolerance for harassment.
- Provide training for everyone on what constitutes harassment, how to support victims, and how victims can get help.
- Provide confidential support to harassment victims including external resources (e.g., employee assistance programs) independent from the company reporting structure. Establish an ombuds office as an off-the-record resource for employees who are considering reporting. Create anonymous formal reporting channels and act on reports.[101]
- Publicize the process victims should use and their options if they are harassed. Help them through the formal reporting process. Establish trust by maintaining confidentiality and being transparent through investigation and resolution processes. Ensure that victims are not harmed or retaliated against for reporting.

- Put alleged perpetrators—not the victims—on leave while investigating cases. Discipline perpetrators up to and including removal from their job.
- Establish policy for workplace romantic relationships. Consider disclosure requirements especially when a reporting relationship is involved. For dating relationships between managers and subordinates, move one of the employees to a different team or supervisor.[102]

ALLIES

- Call out harassing behaviors, such as "Steve, it's not okay to berate our colleagues. It makes them afraid to speak up and prevents them from doing their best work."
- Let your colleagues know that you are a safe resource if they experience mistreatment. Reach out to victims to help them and to direct them to safe sources of support. With your colleague's permission, speak to investigators or managers in support of your colleague.
- Don't pursue a coworker romantically unless you are serious about the relationship. Avoid pursuing anyone with whom you have a reporting relationship.[103]

SELF

- Take notes of harassing behaviors, including dates, times, and witnesses. Save in personal file storage.
- Consider talking to your organization's ombuds office or employee assistance program (if they exist) for advice and support. Be sure to check that these resources are confidential.
- Talk to trusted mentors or colleagues for an outsider perspective. Consider talking to a therapist or counselor not affiliated with your organization.
- Talk to other women in your organization to find out if they are victims of harassment. If so, team up with these other victims to

document the abusive behavior and present it to HR or senior leadership.

- If a colleague's behavior makes you uncomfortable, be direct: "Please don't touch me" or "Sexual remarks are not acceptable here." If the behavior continues, report it to your boss or HR. If the behavior consists of sexual advances or assault, report it to your boss or HR *and* law enforcement.
- If your leadership doesn't address the harassment, talk to the U.S. federal or your state's equal opportunity employment commission about filing a gender discrimination claim. You may also wish to speak to an employment attorney for advice and consider your options for employment elsewhere.
- Check company policy before dating a coworker. Don't date someone with whom you have a reporting relationship. If a superior pursues you, be direct: "It is unwise for us to date since I report to you. It could put the company in legal jeopardy." Keep notes and watch out for retaliatory behaviors. (See guidelines for retaliation.) If you want to date a superior or a direct report, request that one of you be moved to a different team.[104]

Female Hostility

LEADERS

- Incentivize women leaders to elevate junior women through recognition and rewards.
- Replace workplace competition with collaboration. Create safety for women with environments that establish room for multiple women.
- Create safe reporting mechanisms for women who have been the target of female hostility. (See guidelines for discrimination and workplace harassment.)
- Disincentivize female hostility through constructive feedback to women exhibiting queen bee or mean girl behaviors to allow for opportunity for growth, while also communicating that future hostile behaviors will result in formal investigation and disciplinary action.[105]

ALLIES

- If you are a woman, be thoughtful about how you treat female colleagues. Ensure that you are not blocking opportunities or mistreating them. If you feel threatened by other women, look for the root cause. If your organization limits the number of women in leadership, speak to your boss about the importance of inclusivity and creating opportunities for more women.
- Let your colleagues know that you are a safe resource if they experience female hostility. Reach out to victims to help them and direct them to safe sources of support. With your colleague's permission, speak to investigators or managers in support of your colleague.
- Advocate for more women in leadership and throughout the organization. Suggest specific women for promotional opportunities.

SELF

- Do not take female hostility personally. Recognize that women exhibiting these behaviors are likely insecure and feeling threatened.
- Start a conversation with women who have been hostile toward you and express your desire for a productive working relationship: "Mika, I recognize that our relationship has been strained. For the good of this company, let's discuss how we can work together in a productive way."
- Establish personal connections with women by asking about their families, vacations, pets, or hobbies and inviting them to coffee, lunch, or a virtual chat.
- Reach out to trusted mentors and colleagues for an outsider perspective and to strategize solutions.

Retaliation

LEADERS

- Establish a culture of zero tolerance for retaliation.
- Train managers how to avoid both overt and subtle retaliation.
- Put alleged retaliators—not the victims—on leave while investigating cases. Discipline retaliators up to and including removal from their job.
- Provide confidential support to retaliation victims including external resources (e.g., employee assistance programs) independent from the company reporting structure. Establish an ombuds office as an off-the-record resource for employees who are considering reporting. Create anonymous formal reporting channels and act on reports.[106]
- Publicize the process victims should use and options they have if they experience retaliation. Help them through the formal reporting process. Establish trust by maintaining confidentiality and being transparent through investigation and resolution processes. Ensure that victims are not harmed for reporting retaliation.

ALLIES

- Call out retaliatory behaviors: "It's not appropriate to treat Marina poorly." If you are in a position to do so, remind others of legal implications: "As you know, Marina filed a harassment report. It is not legal to treat her poorly."
- Let your colleagues know that you are a safe resource if they experience retaliation. Reach out to victims to help them and to direct them to safe sources of support. With your colleague's permission, speak to investigators or managers in support of your colleague.

SELF

- Take notes of retaliatory behaviors, including dates, times, and witnesses. Save in personal file storage.
- Consider talking to your organization's ombuds office or employee assistance program (if they exist) for advice and support. Be sure to check that these resources are confidential.
- Talk to trusted mentors or colleagues for an outsider perspective.
- Talk to other women in your organization to find out if they are victims of retaliation. If so, team up with these other victims to document the abusive behaviors and present them to HR or senior leadership.
- If your leadership doesn't address the retaliation or if you have been fired, talk to the U.S. federal or your state's equal opportunity employment commission about filing a retaliation claim. You may also wish to speak to an employment attorney for advice and consider your options for employment elsewhere.

6

ACQUIESCENCE

"You have your ambition drained out of you through a million different paper cuts."

—Self-employed professional

After Anna Coumou was hired as a brewer, her boss—twenty years her senior with a wife and two children—expressed feelings of affection for her. With support from a coworker, Coumou told her boss that he shouldn't speak to her romantically. When her boss's behavior didn't change, she quit. Although she found it challenging to explain to prospective employers why she left her previous position, she was eventually hired at a new company—as a bartender. This employer bought her former boss's beer, which meant Coumou had to continue to interact with him. She told few people of his bad behavior, since she didn't want to be perceived as "difficult to work with." As she said, "I want none of this to have ever come up—the same way it never comes up for [him]." Finally, Coumou moved on to work as a bartender at a third employer. One afternoon a male patron mansplained to her that women are not cut out for the beer industry since they "start drama" and "can't lift kegs." Coumou wrote, "It's easy to get stuck between a rock and a hard place. Say nothing, and he keeps coming back, staying longer, assuming you enjoy his idiotic rants. Say something, and risk being labeled as bitter or mean. . . . It is easier and safer to accept dehumanizing language than to stand up and defend myself. I am forced to choose between my dignity and my safety, and that's not a fight my dignity can win."[1] Her response was understandable; she gave up her job as a brewer and stayed silent on the harassment and sexism she experienced. She had no good choice.

When barriers are so prevalent, women internalize them, accept them as valid, and adapt to the limitations—they acquiesce. Acquiescence manifests in four ways. First, women accept that the *work-life conflict* they experience is their individual responsibility to solve. Yet, the problem occurs because male-normed workplaces assume that employees have someone at home—a wife—to take care of personal and family needs. Second, women may *self-blame* for sexism they encounter and take responsibility for organizational problems outside of their control. Third, to protect themselves, they may choose to *self-silence*. Like Anna Coumou, they may stay quiet about harassment and other inequities to avoid backlash and retaliation. And lastly, *self-limited aspirations* may be the outcome when women conclude that they are not capable of advancement, or they are unwilling to deal with pressures that men do not face. This final acquiescence to the pressure of gender bias is what researchers call "internalized oppression" occurring when women come to accept and incorporate society's prejudices against them.[2]

WORK-LIFE CONFLICT

With the COVID-19 pandemic and the closure of schools and daycares in 2020, society's assumption that women are *the* caretakers became stridently evident. As discussed in chapter 3, "Insufficient Support," the United States lacks communal resources like affordable childcare, legal requirements for paid family leave, and social expectations that men shoulder an equal share of child and family care, all of which would support women's ability to combine work and family. Workplaces have long been organized around the concept of an ideal worker—someone who can work eight hours or more without the interruption of family responsibilities. This type of worker has historically fit the male lifestyle, either unencumbered or having a spouse at home handling children and housework.[3]

For women in academia, the start of the pandemic reduced research output as they balanced university work with unpaid care responsibilities, including supervising children's schooling from home. According to one study, women scholars' output during the pandemic dropped by 19 percent from 2019 to 2020.[4] In response, universities offered time extensions to faculty to meet tenure criteria.[5] In most academic institutions, faculty promotion and tenure is competitive; published research is a heavily weighted requirement. When women are primarily responsible for caretaking and housework, men have the workplace advantage. A pre-pandemic study showed that tenure time extensions for having children benefits men because women spend more time bearing and taking care of children, thus men have more time for research.[6] Biologist Dr. Crystal Rogers balances her work running a lab with caring for her five-year-old son and her live-in immunocompromised mother. While Rogers believes she can keep her lab running, she is unsure if she can meet the requirements for tenure due to the pandemic. As she said, "You have to be excellent to continue moving [forward] in the field. But how do you maintain excellence while you're also trying to balance life?"[7]

Other women had to leave their jobs even though they could work from home during the pandemic. Mental health therapist Sharon Reetz explained that concentrating on clients "is hard when you have a child who is crying and you're trying to do something else." With her husband away for long stretches on a river barge, Reetz quit her job because she "couldn't find the balance" as the sole caregiver.[8]

Black and Hispanic women, mothers of young children, caregivers of parents, and women who could not work remotely shouldered the economic impact of the pandemic. These women disproportionately worked in industries that were shut down in early 2020, such as restaurants, salons, retail, daycare centers, and hotels.[9] An analysis of data from the American Time Use Survey and Current Population Survey found that women without a college degree left the workforce during the pandemic at twice the rate of those with a degree, largely because those with degrees were more likely to be able to work from home. "Black women who were not college graduates were hardest hit in terms of their employment and labor force participation," economist Dr. Claudia Goldin summarized.[10] Pandemic work-life conflict hurt many women, with the less-privileged suffering the most.

Motherhood

Work-life conflict has been an issue for women since long before the COVID-19 pandemic. Arguably the most prevalent conflict for women has been motherhood. While the term "working father" is rarely used, "working mother" is commonly used to describe women who have children and paid employment. The assumption remains that only women feel the effects of combining a career with parenthood. As a lawyer noted, "I never hear a male employee-parent asked how he manages to juggle his personal and professional life." One physician's workplace offered "women and medicine" meetings that focused on how to balance raising children and work. As she said, "Those issues are important, but they should be 'parents in medicine' problems!" Another physician described how even in her "egalitarian" marriage, "expectations from the kids' school, the doctor's office, the dentist, etc., are decidedly on me, not him. These societal expectations impact work and ability to advance."

The lack of societal and workplace supports for mothers can lead some women to delay having children or avoid it altogether, in favor of their career. Or women opt to not add to their families. A lawyer noted, "I am considering not having another child because I feel guilty for taking maternity leave. I wish men were forced to take paternity leave so the organization would have a better system for covering for people when they are out on family leave."[11]

Television news is one industry in which it is especially difficult to be a mother. When correspondent Julianna Goldman was offered a new three-year contract with CBS News—a role that would require travel on a moment's notice for breaking news—she turned it down. Having a husband with a demanding career and a small child, Goldman asked for schedule predictability but was told she wasn't "there yet"—even with fifteen years in the industry—and that she should be happy "to be offered a new contract at all." While her manager was a mother herself and said she was sympathetic, the offer was final. Goldman wondered "whether I was really made for TV news or whether institutional biases were forcing me out."[12]

As recently as 2018, not a single correspondent in NBC's Washington bureau was a mother. An NBC producer explained, "There's an unease. . . . No one wants to be the test case, because it hasn't been a common concern, and people are so committed to their jobs, they're worried about being able to juggle it all."[13] Most everyone in television news works contract to contract—only a few reach stardom with the ability to make family-friendly demands during contract negotiations. According to journalism professor Dr. Scott Reinardy, newsroom burnout rates are higher for women, and management forces women to choose between their careers and families due to a lack of interest in changing the work culture to support mothers.[14]

Work-life conflict can negatively impact health. During investor Ellen Pao's gender discrimination and retaliation lawsuit (discussed in chapter 1, "Male Privilege" and chapter 5, "Hostility"), she continued to work for her employer, Kleiner Perkins, to have a stronger case. But the company hired a public relations firm to defame her. During this time, Pao became pregnant but then miscarried. Her doctor told her, "When I saw all the horrible things being said about you, I was worried about you and the baby. Stress can be a factor." As Pao recalled, "Kleiner had taken everything from me."[15]

Maternity Leave

Many women in the United States lack paid leave, or sufficiently paid leave, to care for their newborns and themselves postpartum. Many organizations still do not provide paid maternity leave, let alone parental leave for fathers and partners. Of the world's forty-one richest countries, the United States is the only one that lacks mandated paid parental leave.[16] A lawyer explained that she and her wife had to use up their vacation and sick leave when their son was born. Neither had paid parental leave. Too many women are forced to make similar choices.

Even women with parental leave feel pressure to return to work quickly. As Jane Swift, former governor of Massachusetts, described, "The uproar around my need to take a few days off when I was on bed rest and my twins were born has to take the cake."[17] Nor is this pressure limited to executive women. When journalist Katherine Goldstein's son was born with serious health issues, she was back at her desk after a "too-short" maternity leave. She explained, "I was terrified that my colleagues would judge me as not committed to my job if I tried to take more time to be with my baby." Yet Goldstein lost her job anyway shortly after returning to work.[18]

In television news, maternity leave means time away from the camera, "out of sight . . . out of mind."[19] News anchor Trish Regan regretted not taking her full maternity leave but felt career success depended on returning to work quickly. She took six weeks of leave at CNBC when her twins were born and only three weeks with her son while at Bloomberg Television, even though both companies provided more paid leave, and twelve weeks unpaid leave is covered by the U.S. Family and Medical Leave Act.[20] Regan stated, "I was very aware that if I was gone for that amount of time, I was perhaps replaceable with either a man who could do the job or a woman who wasn't having a baby. These were very real concerns of mine, and there was no one in my environment at either of those networks [who] was encouraging me to think otherwise."[21]

Husband's Career Priority

Many heterosexual married women professionals find that their husband's career takes priority. A physician explained that many female colleagues have highly educated partners "who are far less willing to find flexibility in their occupations." And a lawyer noted, "The demands of parenting and keeping up a household fell largely on my shoulders because my schedule is generally more flexible than my husband's. That took time from my billables and has made me less profitable." In situations like these, the gender pay gap is self-reinforcing.

The priority taken by the husband's career is evident in a study of 6,643 dual-income heterosexual couples in which husbands averaged forty-three hours of paid work and seven hours of housework per week, compared to thirty-five hours of paid work and fourteen hours of housework for their wives. Astonishingly, when wives outearned their husbands and the couple had children, the wives did even more housework, rising to sixteen hours per week, while their husband's housework declined. Not only were parents likely falling into gender-specialized roles, but the women may have done more housework to alleviate their husband's psychological distress of bucking traditional gender stereotypes.[22]

Work Hours Expectations

Many fields have expectations that exacerbate work-life conflict. Law often expects around-the-clock availability and commitment. One attorney explained, "Lawyers do not have a workable lifestyle. . . . I am happy to lead and succeed, but from everything I see, succeeding means working at least 50 to 60 hours a week, and life is just too short for that."

Medicine is another field with extraordinary work hour requirements. After a health scare, physician Dr. Amy Chai wanted a lighter schedule to spend more time with her family. She found a position with fewer hours in an underserved area of her city but soon was told to go full time—fifty hours per week plus on-call expectations—or lose her job. With childcare centers closing at 6 p.m., she couldn't do it, and she blamed herself: "I was weak."[23] Organizations that have strict requirements and offer no assistance convey to women that work-life conflict is theirs alone to resolve.

Women may find that having a stay-at-home spouse is not enough to overcome challenges of long or inflexible work hours. A physician who works a hundred hours per week plus meetings and research feels fortunate to have a stay-at-home husband. But "he simply cannot be both mother and father to our three children," she noted. This physician is not the only woman who found that stay-at-home spouses are not the solution. A college president encouraged the finance director to apply for promotion to vice president. While the director's stay-at-home husband got the kids up, fed them, and sent them off to school, he didn't do the grocery shopping, cleaning, or pay the bills. Since the vice president position offered less flexibility, she turned it down: "I have never backed away from anything. To not go for that job was really, really hard for me."

Part-time Work Fallacy

Prior to serving as U.S. First Lady, when Michelle Obama had her first daughter, she negotiated with her employer to return to work part-time, figuring it would be a "win-win." Obama quickly learned that "a part-time job, especially when it's meant to be a scaled-down version of your previously full-time job, can be something of a trap."[24] She had all the same responsibilities and meetings as when she worked full-time. The only difference was that she had to fit it all into a twenty-hour work week and was paid only half her original salary. As Obama wrote, "Part time work was meant to give me more freedom, but mostly it left me feeling as if I were only half doing everything, that all the lines in my life had been blurred."[25]

There are many biases against part-time people—who are mainly women—as a physician delineated: "We are just 'extras.' We are not committed to our work. We can be asked to take on additional tasks or work since 'we have extra days off.' We should come to meetings on our non-work days. We should not complain when we are scheduled to work more days than what our part-time status calls for." When lawyers work "part-time," they are often still expected to put in long hours. One lawyer worked a reduced schedule when her second daughter was a baby, but only by negotiating "reduced billable hours . . . to devote more time to business development and not have to work 50 to 60-plus hours every week." Similarly, a commission-only attorney who works flexible part-time hours and cares for her daughter two days per week is still expected to be "available and working on my off-days," as she described.

Single Childless Women

While much discussion on work-life conflict focuses on mothers, this conflict also affects women without partners and children; they are expected to work more, perceived as having no other priorities. Amy found herself in this situation as a young IT staffer. Male colleagues used the excuse "I have kids" to leave the office by 4:30 p.m. every day, leaving her to stay late to fix system issues. A single physician without kids faced similar assumptions: "I am expected to take additional calls and cover more holidays than my colleagues with families." A divorced and childless university leader was "expected to work longer hours and neglect my family that does exist—four sisters and thirteen nieces and nephews." And a single higher education leader with no kids had to attend more evening and weekend events than colleagues—"because what else could I have to do?"

In the gender hierarchy, women are valued for their capacity to bear children. If they are single and childless, their societal value may be questioned. If they are not producing (literally) the next generation, their sole value is assumed to be their work. Yet the work demands may prevent time and opportunity to have a partner and children, such as a nonprofit leader who had to "choose between singleness with a career or marriage with no career."

Work alone is not the total of a person's life. Yet many organizations function as if it were, demanding long hours and perpetual availability from employees. Excessive work expectations disproportionately impact women, who also juggle societal expectations that they be primary care-givers for their families. This pressure exists for every woman, but with little communal support or value for caretaking work, individual women too often must choose between work and family.

SELF-BLAME

When Anita Hill (discussed in chapter 4, "Devaluation" and chapter 5, "Hostility") testified before the U.S. Senate Judiciary Committee in 1991, Senator Arlen Specter asked why she had not filed a sexual harass-ment complaint against Clarence Thomas, her boss at the U.S. Equal Employment Opportunity Commission (EEOC). Hill responded, "I may have shirked a duty. I am very sorry that I did not do something or say something." Specter's question was misleading; it disregarded the power imbalance between Hill and her boss and neglected to consider why the EEOC lacked a supportive human resources (HR) depart-ment.[26] Yet, Hill's response personalized her inaction. In fact, many sexual harassment victims blame themselves, which can prevent them from reporting.[27] Although the EEOC is the organization responsible for enforcement of federal harassment laws, Hill had little opportunity to safely report harassment if she wanted to keep her job.[28] While the harassment and non-reporting was not Hill's fault, she took the blame.

Victims of rape and sexual harassment self-blame partly because U.S. society often blames the victim. Psychotherapist Jennie Steinberg observed that judges talk about "lost potential" when sentencing young male rapists while the media focuses on what survivors were wearing and if they were drinking, implying victims are at fault for not being constantly on guard.[29] One study found media reports of sexual assault allegations on college campuses indicated doubt of the victims in almost 40 percent of the reports; yet fully 81 percent of the stories included information about the perpetrator's life, usually their athletic achievements. The stories described victims as using alcohol "nearly three times more often than the perpetrator."[30] Self-blame reflects internalized oppression, meaning that women have been socialized into the same system of oppression and believe the messages that they are at fault.

Like Anita Hill, many women personalize the problems they experience and feel guilt over inaction. Internalized oppression extends well beyond rape and harassment to include many arenas where women self-blame for things that are completely outside their control. A university vice president (discussed in chapter 1, "Male Privilege"), put on a glass cliff and made responsible for her predecessor's accounting errors, was still blaming herself *eight years later*: "It's still raw. I will carry it forever, as will my team. . . . I personalize and feel responsible for people who are loyal and are part of who we are. Some of the permanent damage that they suffered I can see in them as professionals. That bothers me the most."[31]

Appearance ideals for women entertainers can cause them to self-blame. When actor Debra Messing was hired in 1998 for the *Will & Grace* television show, she was a size 8 but had internalized Hollywood's "wildly skinny" beauty standards. The wardrobe clothing was too small, and she left fittings "just hating my body and hating myself," as she explained. Even though the costume designer told her not to worry, Messing still felt self-conscious. She dieted and lost weight yet felt "fat" and "ugly" compared to ultra-thin actors like Calista Flockhart and Portia de Rossi. Messing eventually dieted down to a size 2 when she could finally fit into "anything that was high fashion." But the weight loss made her sick and exhausted. She concluded, "I couldn't be healthy and a size two."[32] Hollywood's sexist standards—from glamourizing ultra-thin women to default clothing sizes—led Messing to believe she was at fault.

Women may be socialized to personalize bias and discrimination, as Leanne found when she interviewed faith-based leaders. One leader blamed herself for her boss's harassing behavior: "I grew up in a dysfunctional home and had therefore developed some tolerance for abuse, so maybe I had more ability to put up with it."[33] Another took the blame for working without recognition "because they wanted a man to have the title." As she said, "I've just learned these behaviors and so, on the one hand I think, well I have to expect it. On the other hand, I'm thinking, that's not right."[34]

Women may also feel regret for not doing enough to counter bias, discrimination, and harassment. A staffing agency employee pushed her boss away when he groped her and told him to never touch her again, but decided to stay in her job, which she needed because her husband had cancer. Yet she blamed herself: "I still carry guilt to this day that I was not strong enough at that time to take a stand for myself and future generations of women."

Other women experience shame. A manager pulled a newly hired woman aside, telling her she was "too ambitious" and should "be more quiet." The woman said, "I cried after he told me and felt horribly ashamed for weeks." A few weeks later she discovered the manager said the same thing to every new female team member.

Some women blame themselves when they don't realize that they are experiencing gender bias or discrimination. One woman was told that she spoke too intensely in meetings, and she rarely received affirmation while male colleagues doing the same hard work were openly praised. She said, "It took me years to realize it was tied to my being female. I used to take it as a personal failure."

Having to work harder than men can "cause even the most confident and competent women to doubt themselves," editor Sarah Green Carmichael wrote.[35] When media technology strategist Kathy-Anne McManus moved from Australia to the United States for an executive position, she quickly made her struggling 350-person division profitable. But she then learned that male peers were outearning her by as much as $100,000. When she attempted to renegotiate her salary, her boss said, "Let's see how you perform," as if he had forgotten that she had just turned around a failing unit. Then the boss added, "You're very aggressive." The incident caused McManus to "spiral" with self-doubt: "Why do I have to prove myself more than my peers?"[36]

Similarly, when journalist Katherine Goldstein (discussed in work-life conflict) lost her job, her self-confidence plummeted: "I was convinced everyone had this working mom thing figured out but me, that

I was personally a failure," as she said. No longer negotiating for leadership positions, Goldstein felt like she was just scraping by and surviving.[37] McManus and Goldstein's blame was misplaced. These weren't personal failures; the biased male-normed system was at fault.

SELF-SILENCING

In the face of bias and discrimination, many women are hesitant to speak up for themselves or for other women. And for good reason, considering the backlash that may follow. When an executive officer assigned a tech manager's female subordinate to work with an older, flirty male customer, the manager "was too scared of how my own position would be affected to call out such behavior," she said.[38] Similarly, a software engineer didn't question casual sexism and laughed along with uncomfortable jokes and gossip. But she blamed herself: "I just incorporated [the sexism] into my larger sense that I was out of place and not quite good enough."

In academia, untenured professors may be less inclined to call out bad behavior for fear of jeopardizing their tenure chances. Female academics—who are less likely to have tenure—sense they should not "make waves." Accusing anyone of using your work without authorization might "piss off the wrong person," as geopolitical consultant Dr. Ellen Wald explained.[39] Yet women faculty with tenure may also fear speaking out. One day history professor Dr. Joan Cashin heard a male scholar reading from her book "verbatim" on the radio. While she was shocked, Cashin never called the station to complain, deciding to "just let it go."[40]

These women's fears have merit. After one lawyer brought up the issue of sexism in her workplace, two male partners stopped talking to her unless necessary and were never alone with her in an office. Other women feared a loss of job opportunities. Photographer Daniella Zelcman noted, "If you are that irritating, harpy feminist, editors might not call you [because you're known] for calling them out for not hiring enough women." Photographer Andrea Bruce concurred: "If you start to complain, it just ruins your career."[41]

Women working in religious fields may also feel pressure to stay silent on women's issues. While one faith-based leader tends to speak up, she admitted, "I am cautious about fighting too much about opportunity for women because I don't want to be branded as a single-issue person who is focused only on feminist issues." Another faith-based leader explained that "we are 'branded' as 'over the top" when speaking up on issues of discrimination." She further noted, "Only men, at this time in history, have the opportunity to make changes about gender discrimination in Christian organizations."

Even harassment victims may not speak out, seeing it as "something they have to endure" as part of a career.[42] A male patient harassed Dr. Ersilia DeFilippis when she was a medical student, first by suggesting that he would "like to see [her] in a bikini" and later by inviting her to his pool "to wear such bikini." On his discharge day, the patient kissed De-Filippis on the cheek; she froze, hiding her embarrassment and disgust. She explained, "What I did was tell no one and go about my day. . . . In many situations, I internally debate between speaking or being silent. After I leave the room, I replay what I should or could have said. But in the moment, I opt for silence."[43] Surgeon Dr. Arghavan Salles noted that many female physicians struggle with what to say when mistreated and often let harassing comments go; one reason is that "medical students are taught always to put the patient first, this sometimes comes at our own risk."[44]

Blue-collar women may be fearful of reporting abuse, especially those in fields like construction where referrals for the next job are crucial. Employment attorney Megan Block explained, "They suffer in silence. They don't have the choice, they don't have the money, they don't have the time."[45] State trooper Mary McDaniel kept silent about four years of harassment before finally leaving her job. As she said, "Other women who reported were called sluts, given bad work assignments, and some male troopers refused to ride partner with them. They effectively drove me out."[46] Similarly a grocery store worker—who asked that her name be omitted from a newspaper story on this topic—was harassed yet told that nothing could be done unless she complained publicly, but she "was too frightened to do so."[47]

Economic and financial uncertainty can also lead women to self-silence. One woman visited a Starbucks with her boss. When asked if they needed a bag, her boss said, "No thanks, I'm with one." This woman explained, "It was during the recession, I had been without a job for a year, and I was new in my position, so I didn't report it to management."

In the field of journalism, women may be pressured to keep quiet about mistreatment—even though the industry's ethics include "giv[ing] voice to the voiceless."[48] When Brigid Schulte was a national news correspondent, an editor pinched her on the cheek in front of their publisher and said, "We love reporters like you. You're so insecure you'll do anything we say." The two men laughed. Schulte was embarrassed and ashamed and didn't speak up, feeling that she should be "the good girl." She explained, "I didn't want to make a fuss, cause trouble for anyone or be seen as someone who couldn't hack a little macho newsroom ribbing."[49]

The pressure for women to stay silent on bias, harassment, and discrimination is still all too common in many industries. When actor Mila Kunis refused a producer's request that she pose semi-nude on a men's magazine cover, he threatened her: "You'll never work in this town again." While Kunis had enough career success to say no, she explained, "What this producer may never realize is that he spoke aloud the exact fear every woman feels when confronted with gender bias in the workplace. It's what we are conditioned to believe—that if we speak up, our livelihoods will be threatened; that standing our ground will lead to our demise."[50]

Mantermediaries

One form of self-silencing is a workaround when women are consistently not heard. They may use what we have named a "mantermediary" to present their ideas because it is the only way to get them considered. One woman said, "Whenever a female member of our department had a new idea, we would ask one of our male colleagues to float it to supervisors knowing it would probably be approved coming from them and not from us." A faith-based leader knew her ideas would not be deemed credible if she presented them. So, she gave her solutions to certain men ahead of meetings for them to recommend. Amy often used this strategy working in IT, sometimes using male subordinates as mantermediaries.

Women use mantermediaries in many contexts. One woman used this workaround during parent-teacher conferences: "If I am in a meeting as a parent, I am better off giving a script to my husband ahead of time and let[ting] him speak for the two of us. If I speak the same words, I will not be taken as seriously." Even worse, female attorneys may have to let male attorneys take over a case if "her mere presence as counsel is a detriment to the client because of the bias of a judge," as one lawyer explained.

The problem with using a mantermediary is that women don't get appropriate credit for their ideas and work, further diminishing their chances for opportunities, promotions, and long-term success. The same can be said for women's self-silencing as a whole: whether done from self-protection or because it's the only way to get their ideas heard, women are the ones who lose because injustice continues unchallenged, and women's legitimate concerns and contributions remain unacknowledged.

SELF-LIMITED ASPIRATIONS

In 2018, after Oprah Winfrey gave a rousing award show speech, many people suggested that she run for United States president. Broadcast journalist Gayle King told her, "It wouldn't be good for you—it would be good for everyone else." But Oprah shut down the idea: "I've always felt very secure and confident with myself in knowing what I could do and what I could not. And so it's not something that interests me. I don't have the DNA for it."[51] Like Oprah, many women choose to limit their aspirations, either believing they are not capable of more responsibility or knowing that they are capable but don't want the hassle. Oprah expressed both in shutting down the notion of campaigning for U.S. president.

Psychological Glass Ceiling

When women believe they are not capable of doing more, they are affected by a psychological glass ceiling, an internal barrier that hinders them from advancing. It resembles impostor syndrome in which despite external recognition of success, women do not feel successful internally.[52] With impostor syndrome, women feel unqualified for their present role; with psychological glass ceiling, women feel they are not capable of advancement.

Bias, harassment, and discrimination may lead many women to step back. When Reah Bravo worked for *The Charlie Rose Show* as an intern and associate producer, host Charlie Rose "repeatedly groped her and exposed himself to her," which led her to take a less ambitious path. She noted, "After [the *Rose* show], I took a job as a speechwriter that took me far away. A mundane corporate job."[53] Similarly, throughout her career another woman was sexually harassed, told she was too aggressive for behaviors praised in men, and was interrupted, talked over, and hepeated. She explained, "Eventually I lost my confidence and ambition and ended up changing careers."

Some women overcome the psychological glass ceiling but only through the encouragement of others. Amy spoke with a woman who believed she was not cut out for university administration when she was a professor, even though she had served as the university ombudsperson. When asked to step into an interim provost role, this woman advocated against herself, telling her president, "You're bananas; that's stupid. There's other people that you should choose because I'm not big enough for this role."[54] It took the encouragement of her husband for this woman to step into the new role; she later went on to become a university president. Similarly, when she was a faculty member, Rev. Dr. Boyung Lee was asked to step into administrative leadership. Only after the loss of her husband did she become open to the idea, crediting "a spiritual director with helping her to see that she was being called to a new role." She is now serving in an executive administration role at a theology school.[55]

Other women don't recognize their abilities until getting away from toxic environments. One woman who spent two decades doubting herself under a "misogynistic, narcissistic boss" reluctantly went out on her own after being harassed and fired. As she said, "It was only then that I discovered what I should have known all along; not only am I good. I am very good." Understandably her advice to other women is "Stay off the corporate ladder, because where women are concerned, the rungs are broken. Believe in yourself—make your own life."

Retreating

Sometimes women choose not to advance to avoid hassles men don't have. They retreat. As a would-be chief executive officer described, "Many of the countries we were going into were so against women. I thought, 'I don't need that.'"[56] Similarly, a medical doctor believed she would "make good administration material," but others told her "not to try because it would be a hassle." A nonprofit leader expected to be offered her supervisor's position if he stepped down. While she was confident in her ability, she said, "I don't know if I would want the added personal stress that being in a director role brings." Another nonprofit leader was "so burnt by workplace bullying," she preferred "to not think about professional advancement at all."

Women with children may feel pressure to select less ambitious paths. One law firm partner felt she could not continue in the position after having two children. She was permitted to go part-time and was equally profitable to the company, but she was "not seen as being as much of a team player." She left to take a government job with "lower hours, expectations, and pay." Another attorney expects not to have movement in her career until her children are older. She said, "I cannot provide the necessary commitment when I have the primary role of dropping off and picking up kids and being home with them when they are off school or sick."

Other women lose the energy to fight discrimination. As one self-employed woman described, "The lack of women at the top of business is partly endemic sexism designed to keep women in their place however hard they try and partly that women [get] to a point when they simply can't take it anymore." Women are tired of being twice as good as men to succeed while earning less, fighting for recognition, and being expected to do office housework. She continued, "You have your ambition drained out of you through a million different paper cuts. You lose the will or energy to fight. You retreat. You find a place where your skills are underutilized, you are likely overqualified, but at least every day isn't a battle." This woman is considering going back into full-time employment but hesitates: "While I am sure I have a lot to offer, I just don't know if I have the energy to fight anymore."

There is nothing wrong with women's choices of less stressful or more fulfilling roles, but when multitudes of women feel they must make such choices, it's the system that is at fault. When woman after woman is kept from advancing in corporations and law firms and hospitals and nonprofits and universities and government, it serves to reinforce male control of those institutions. With their presence missing, women can't offer their talents to improve these institutions or to better society. A lawyer who gave up trial work due to the "million pinpricks of sexism" and now writes appeals from home said, "I feel unfulfilled and my talents are wasted." Her talents are wasted indeed.

The combined pressures of male privilege, disproportionate constraints, insufficient support, devaluation, and hostility too often lead women to acquiesce. They accept work-life conflict as a personal problem even though it exists across virtually all workplaces and cultures. They self-blame for problems they encounter, and they self-silence on injustice to themselves and others. Finally, and it's hardly surprising, under the combined weight of all the barriers, they may decide that the price tag for advancement is simply too high, and they retreat into less fulfilling but also less stressful roles.

SHATTERING ACQUIESCENCE: A MAXIMIZING ORGANIZATION

Workplaces must maximize everyone's contributions and participation, thus shattering acquiescence. Those serving as leaders must take the lead, while allies—anyone who is supportive—can help advance a maximizing organization. Individual women can also take steps to mitigate their own acquiescence.

Work-Life Conflict

LEADERS

- Establish and communicate the value of work-life balance for all employees. Eliminate cultures of overwork. Set reasonable expectations for full-time hours (e.g., forty hours maximum per week) and incentivize people to *not* work beyond their regular schedule. Set the expectation that staff disconnect from work communications (e.g., email, chat) after hours and when on leave. Measure success by goals and not by hours spent at work. Ensure that part-time employees have part-time workloads. Task supervisors with ensuring employee workloads are not excessive.
- Maximize employee autonomy to decide *where* work gets done. Offer remote work to reduce employee daily commutes and increase time for personal and family obligations. Rethink and reconfigure positions for a distributed workforce. Can processes or equipment be monitored remotely? Can manual work be completed at an employee's home with necessary materials? Consider hybrid schedules when full-time remote work is not possible. For example, a physician may see patients in person on certain days and do virtual visits and administrative work from home on other days.
- Maximize employee autonomy to decide *when* work gets done. Grant flexibility to attend to personal and family responsibilities during work hours. Allow employees to decide start and end times or swap shifts.
- Provide paid family leave, paid sick leave, and childcare to all employees. (See chapter 3, "Insufficient Support.")

ALLIES

- Advocate for policies to reduce work-life conflict, such as remote and flexible work, paid family leave, paid sick leave, and subsidized childcare.
- If you are a supervisor, check in with staff on their workloads, and help them to prioritize or reduce the workload if they are

overwhelmed. Provide flexibility on where and when work gets done. Allow staff to attend to personal and family obligations during work hours. Set the expectation that staff disconnect from work communications (e.g., email, chat) after hours and when on leave.

- If you send emails after hours, schedule emails to arrive during normal working hours.
- Support overworked colleagues. Help them with their responsibilities: "Eileen, I'll cover the phones while you take your son to the doctor."
- Advocate to leaders for reduced and equitable workloads. You can say, "Our staff are working sixty hours per week. Let's discuss ways to reduce their workloads before they burn out."

SELF

- Disconnect from work communications (e.g., email, chat) after hours and when on leave. Use an out-of-office autoreply to set expectations for your availability. Ask colleagues to contact you during off hours only in the event of an emergency.
- If your workload is excessive, solicit support from your supervisor. Frame it in terms of the impact to the company: "I am working fifty hours a week to keep up with my workload. I don't want to drop any balls or burn out. Can you help me prioritize and adjust my workload to ensure I'm focusing on the most important priorities for this company?"
- If your leadership fails to support your efforts to maintain work-life balance, consider your options for other employment.

Self-Blame

LEADERS

- Do not blame employees when they experience bias, harassment, discrimination, or organizational problems not in their control. Provide support and resources to address the issue.

ALLIES

- If colleagues blame themselves for bias, harassment, discrimination, or problems outside of their control, help them to understand that they are not at fault and provide them your support. You can say, "Aaliyah, don't blame yourself for being harassed. Let's discuss what to do next."

SELF

- Do not take bias personally. Recognize that often people act in ways in which they were socialized and that externalizing it will help you to address it. If a woman is hostile toward you, start a discussion with her: "Petra, we both experience many obstacles at work. Let's discuss how we can work together to overcome them."
- Do not blame yourself for discrimination or harassment. When reporting abuse, you can say, "Responsibility for the harassing behavior belongs with the harasser, not with me."
- Do not accept blame for problems outside of your control. Instead, you may say, "I inherited the financial challenges when I arrived. Let's discuss how to address them going forward."

Self-Silencing

LEADERS

- Establish a culture in which everyone has a voice, and which does not tolerate retaliation or backlash for speaking up. Discipline the retaliators, rather than people who report bias or mistreatment.
- Refer to chapter 5, "Hostility," for steps to create a safe culture for victims to report harassment, discrimination, and retaliation.

ALLIES

- Speak up in support of others when they experience bias, harassment, or discrimination.
- If a colleague is fearful of speaking up, talk to them to understand why and discuss whether it is safe to speak up.

SELF

- If you are fearful of speaking up about mistreatment, talk to a trusted colleague or mentor. Evaluate whether it is safe for you to speak up. If it is not safe for you to share your concerns with your boss or HR, consider your options for employment elsewhere.

Self-Limited Aspirations

LEADERS

- Recruit women in hiring and for promotions. Help them to see how they are capable of the role and address any concerns they have. Encourage them to take the role, explaining how you will support them.
- If a woman initially turns down a promotion, don't just accept her response. Ask why she said no and what it would take to get to "yes." Address her concerns and do what you can to enable her to say "yes."
- Ensure job advertisements are free of masculine bias including unnecessary minimum qualifications. Eliminate hiring and promotional criteria that can be exclusionary of women. (See chapter 1, "Male Privilege.")

ALLIES

- Suggest specific women for promotional opportunities.
- Encourage women to apply for new roles and promotions. Help them to see how they are capable of the role. Discuss their concerns and help them strategize how to overcome barriers. Offer advice on how to position themselves for success.

SELF

- Reach out to professionals inside and outside your workplace to learn about their career path, how they overcame barriers, and how you can position yourself for success.
- Do not assume that advancement is beyond your reach. If you are interested in a new role, discuss with trusted colleagues. Submit an application and use the interview process to assess if the role is a fit for you.
- Recognize it is also okay to be content in your current role. Prioritize your well-being and avoid roles and work cultures where more is expected than you can give.

7

GENDER BIAS

"We want what you aren't."

—University vice president

So far, we've presented the six glass walls of gender bias and the subcomponents in isolation, but women are rarely affected by just one type. Over the course of a day, a week, a month, a job, or a career, women may find themselves subjected to various aspects of bias in combination. The message they hear is that whatever they bring to the workplace, it's not right: "We want what you aren't."

In this chapter, we relate stories of women who have experienced a multitude of barriers and describe how those experiences have affected them. The combination of barriers leads to emotional and career damage and stops women from reaching their full potential. Not only does bias impact women and their families, but it also impacts organizations and humanity. When half of society is systemically held back, employers lose out on women's contributions, and society misses out on innovations and progress. In this chapter, we explain what happens when gender barriers combine and how to create equitable and inclusive organizations, which allow everyone to thrive.

WHEN BARRIERS COMBINE

Former Pinterest chief operating officer (COO) Francoise Brougher experienced all six walls of gender bias. Although 70 percent of Pinterest users are women, men run the company with little input from female executives (*male privilege: male gatekeeping*). When Pinterest was going public via an initial public offering (IPO) in 2019, Brougher and another female executive were given less favorable equity vesting schedules than male peers (*devaluation: salary inequality*). Shortly after the IPO, Brougher was excluded from board meetings but not told why. After speaking up about technical issues that resulted in declining ad revenue, she was suddenly disinvited from product meetings (*insufficient support: exclusion*). During her performance review, she was criticized for challenging her peers and not being collaborative: "If I were a man, I would have been considered bold and thoughtful. As a woman, I was 'misusing my energy and work ethic'" (*disproportionate constraints: muted voices*). By her own assessment, Brougher did not do enough to help other women, was not connected to a single diversity initiative, and was unsure that she could be an effective spokesperson for women since she was being told to "pipe down" (*acquiescence: self-silencing*). For her next performance review, the male chief financial officer (CFO) was asked to provide peer feedback, but Brougher was not asked to do likewise for him (*disproportionate constraints: unequal standards*). The CFO gave her a negative review, and when Brougher reached out to him, he became defensive, called her a liar, hung up on her, and later stopped talking to her entirely (*male privilege: shunning*). When she spoke to her male boss— the cofounder and chief executive officer (CEO)—about the incident, he trivialized her concerns (*insufficient support: unsupportive leadership*). While human resources promised to bring her and the CFO together to repair the relationship, it never happened (*insufficient support: unsupportive leadership*). Soon after, the CEO abruptly fired Brougher. Even though she had grown Pinterest revenue and expanded operations globally, Brougher was let go for speaking out about discrimination and the hostile work environment she faced (*hostility: discrimination*).[1] It didn't matter that Brougher was in a high-powered position and delivered results, she still experienced all the forms of gender bias and lost her job. As she stated, "Even as the COO of a major Silicon Valley company, I was expected to act a certain way and be deferential to men because I am a woman."[2]

While Brougher was a C-suite executive, women at lower levels also get the full brunt of gender bias. One woman counted the ways in which she experienced it:

1. After reporting several incidents of sexual harassment from a male colleague, [I] was repeatedly told that a male supervisor could not get involved with employee disagreements, and when the complaint moved up the chain, I was told by a male investigator that I was only out for retribution (*hostility: workplace harassment* and *insufficient support: unsupportive leadership*).

2. When instructed to collaborate with a male colleague who refused to comply, [I] was confronted by said male colleague who told me he was holding back from treating me worse "because you are a woman," and when I reported this to my male supervisor, he laughed in my face (*male privilege: shunning* and *insufficient support: unsupportive leadership*).

3. When running for a peer-elected position, [I] kept being told by male colleagues that they could never vote for a woman (*male privilege: male gatekeeping*).

4. Female department colleagues noticed that every year our assignments and locations were radically changed by our male supervisor, but our male colleagues stayed in the same place with the same duties (*male privilege: male gatekeeping*).

5. The countless times our female administrator openly voiced her preference for working with men (*hostility: female hostility*).

6. Whenever a female member of our department had a new idea, we would ask one of our male colleagues to float it to supervisors (*using a mantermediary*) knowing it would probably be approved coming from them and not from us (*acquiescence: self-silencing*).

7. When challenging the content and perspective of a key institutional document that failed to appropriately address women's issues, [I] received a rebuttal that questioned my intelligence, experience, and point of view and not the merits of my claim (*disproportionate constraints: scrutiny*).

8. While serving as the on-site manager for an organization, a supervisor came to review our location status and he spoke to everyone on site, including random customers, except for me. Never even asked my name (*male privilege: shunning*).

9. The countless times, in meetings or settings with male supervisors, where comments from women are met with smirks,

derisive comments, belittling put downs, or just outright dismis-
siveness (*devaluation: diminishment*).

These are just two stories of women who have encountered all six
walls of gender bias over the course of their employment. They are not
alone; countless women experience the combination of barriers, from
subtle to overt, on a daily or weekly basis. Bias is so pervasive that many
people never even question it. Yet the damage it causes can be immense.
First is the time and energy women spend in questioning themselves, defending themselves, and strategizing ways to get their jobs done despite
the obstacles. That lost time and energy is also a loss to the organization,
because the woman is less efficient and productive than she would be if
she could simply do her job without all the additional hurdles. Finally,
gender bias means a loss for society, because half the population is not
fully valued, and their contributions aren't maximized.

Emotional Damage

At the personal level, the impact of gender bias is that women
suffer emotional and self-esteem damage. When there is no satisfying
resolution, they are left with frustration and anger. A project manager
was often a token woman in meetings, subjected to office housework,
talked over, called pet names, and told to smile. While she learned to
use humor as her armor, she became exasperated: "It frustrates and sad-
dens me because for me and so many women, we feel trapped by our
gender and have been taught to have this mindset of overcoming our
'femaleness' in order to be taken seriously. Frankly, I'm sick of having to
formulate these strategies just to do my job. I want my experience and
capabilities to be enough."

Shame and regret are other outcomes. One woman who worked in
a male-dominated profession was cut off, dismissed, treated as less than,
and sexually demeaned in front of her teammates. She felt "ashamed and
embarrassed" but had little choice other than to self-silence: "Because
I was young and didn't want to 'rock the boat,' I didn't do anything.
I regret that I didn't." A band director also experienced regret. One
Saturday morning, the band students began rehearsal in an open gym.
Shortly after practice started, the football coach stormed up to the direc-

tor, demanding that she and her students "leave immediately because he had players coming in to practice." Refusing to hear that the director had permission to use the gym, the coach "threatened to take me outside and fight me," as she explained. At that point, her staff quickly moved the students out, while the athletic director (a woman) apologized for the scheduling confusion. As the band director described, "To this day, I hate that the coach himself never had to apologize, that my students had to lose out due to his rage, and that I never pressed charges."

Discouragement and anger are two more consequences. An administrative employee in a construction company discussed the countless times she was ignored, hepeated, and diminished with comments like "whether it was that time of the month." As she noted, "There are times when I get very discouraged, but then there are times where it infuriates me, and I keep going."

Emotional numbness is a further result of gender bias. A finance professional near retirement has been disrespected, paid less than male subordinates, humiliated, sexualized, mansplained, overlooked, and told to "just relax," "lower [her] voice," "smile," and "calm down." She taught herself to never cry as a response since "doing so would be the ultimate defeat and prove to everyone that I was less-than and a typical emotional woman," she said. "No matter how horrible the tragedy . . . I cannot cry. That is the permanent damage sexism in the workplace has done to me." YouTube CEO Susan Wojcicki has also suffered emotionally from a myriad of bias over her career. She's been interrupted and hepeated; her abilities and commitment have been questioned; she's been left out of key events; external leaders have shunned her by addressing junior male colleagues instead of her. As she explained, "No matter how often this all happened, it still hurt."[3]

Even when slights appear minor, they add up. A nonprofit professional was subjected to office housework and saw female colleagues be diminished, verbally harassed, and told to "smile more." She explained, "These are subtle, but mighty, expressions of bias. Bit by bit, they peck away at the morale of the female employee. Motivation, trust, and perceived value decline with every comment. Personally, they make me feel small and unimportant."[4]

Viewed at a surface level, women's emotional distress may seem to be a personal issue rather than a professional one. But that is a false view.

Organizations are so used to seeing everything from the male perspective that they neglect to consider what is lost when women deal with bias day after day after day. Each time a woman must pause to manage her emotions, control her thoughts, and reset her perspective, work is interrupted. She loses the flow of whatever she is doing, taking away valuable time and effort from the project at hand. The mistreatment may be so overwhelming that she spends inordinate time and energy fighting and recovering from it. Not only does it damage her emotional and physical health, it also stifles her spirit and will to work. Ultimately these losses pile up, hurting her career and causing lost productivity for the organization.

Career Damage

Gender bias also damages women's career potential and leads to less income during their working years and in retirement. A lawyer felt unfulfilled because even when she achieved a positive result for her client, her work was "never actually appreciated by them." She explained, "I do not see any incentive to continue to produce as I am not rewarded for my efforts by the firm with increased responsibilities or leadership roles. I am underpaid, I have little independence in my work, and my duties are more reminiscent of that of a paralegal rather than an attorney. This is not why I went to law school, so I do not know why I would continue on this path." Delayed development is a further outcome for some women, as much as half a lifetime, according to one professional: "I've been interrupted, talked over, belittled, ignored, but it only took me five decades to find my voice and my backbone."

Some women choose to leave destructive environments. One woman was interrupted, talked over, hepeated, told she was too aggressive for behaviors acceptable in men, and subjected to female hostility and sexual harassment. As she stated, "Eventually I lost my confidence and ambition and ended up changing careers." In another case, an engineer found she was treated differently than her male colleagues. She was told that her personality was abrasive and to bite her tongue even when asked a question by a client. She was characterized as having poor management skills in her performance review and passed over for even a cost-of-living raise. Her female managers did not support her even though they had attended a session on the pitfalls of implicit gender bias. This engineer said, "As a young woman in engineering, the slope is steep enough. Having to battle unfair perceptions of me being an uppity loudmouth with a flair for sticking her foot in her mouth was the cherry on top." She quit that job and moved to a woman-led firm: "Though it's not perfect, I'm never asked to shut my mouth."

Many women choose self-employment due to the lack of societal and workplace supports. The share of self-employed women has trended upward since 2010, sharply increasing in 2020 when the pandemic hit, likely a result of the burdens of in-home childcare.[5] Some women start their own businesses to avoid the sexism that comes with working for others. One woman who has been called "little lady," interrupted, mansplained, subjected to office housework, and passed over for a transfer in favor of a male colleague finally stopped working for others. She said, "I own my own business now, so I don't have to deal with it anymore."

Retiring early is the solution for some women. One woman was hepeated, criticized for attention to detail, and denied raises and promotions because her male counterpart "had a family to support." She said, "I retired early and I'm loving it!" But when women change careers or leave the workforce early, the result is often less income and a lower standard of living in retirement. An untenured professor dealt with a boys' club environment in which a male colleague posted nude art photos of women—but none of nude men—and told her that she was interviewed only because she was a woman. This professor was denied tenure for not being "collegial" enough, even though students had awarded her "Faculty of the Year." She said, "I never got a full-time job in my field, and my Social Security payment in retirement shows that."

Organizational Losses

It may seem like individual women are the only ones who pay the price for embedded gender bias, but that is not the case. Organizations also lose out. Leadership teams that are gender diverse yield better organizational performance overall, and perhaps even more in times of crisis.[6] A study of 21,980 firms from ninety-one countries showed that "the correlation between women at the C-suite level and firm profitability is demonstrated repeatedly," and the gains are substantial.[7] The survey found that "for profitable firms, a move from no female leaders to 30 percent representation is associated with a 15 percent increase in the net revenue margin."[8] A recent study showed fines imposed for misconduct were significantly lower—by $7.5 million in total annually—for banks with gender-diverse boards.[9] And, these banks perform better—financially, socially, and environmentally.[10] In healthcare, multiple studies have found that women surgeons have better outcomes—including lower patient death rates—than male counterparts.[11]

Replacing employees is also expensive financially. Each time a woman leaves for another position, to start her own business, or to retire early, the company must invest time and energy to replace her. In 2022, the average cost to replace a non-executive employee in the United States was over $4,400, and a new person typically needs three months to reach full productivity.[12] These costs are preventable. "There are multiple ways to reduce the cost of hiring an employee, but the best resource is to improve employee retention and keep turnover low," as *Business News Daily* writer Eduardo Vasconcellos noted.[13] Think tank director and author Brigid Schulte commented on the phenomenon of traditional work culture disadvantaging women, "Companies need to recognize their own failed imagination. It's costing them talent."[14]

As we have found in our own research, it is not enough to just "add women and stir" to eliminate gender bias; women must be fully accepted, supported, and promoted.[15] One study of 1,069 public companies in thirty-five countries found "the more that gender diversity has been normatively accepted in a country or industry, the more that gender-diverse firms experience positive market valuation and increased revenue."[16] With these kinds of benefits, including reduced fines, better safety, and greater profitability, the organizational losses for not embracing gender diversity are steep indeed.

SHATTERING GENDER BIAS: AN INCLUSIVE ORGANIZATION

For too long gender bias has been treated as an issue facing individual women. Over and over in our research women self-blamed, thinking the reason they had challenges was something to do with themselves—

their personality, upbringing, education, race, ethnicity, age, marital status, parental status, and on and on. We call it the "we want what you aren't" effect. There is always some seemingly rational reason told to any given woman to "explain" her challenges, such as having kids, or being too young or too old, or being outspoken or too quiet, or having too little education and experience or too much. Women internalize these messages because society and organizations treat gender barriers as if they are an individual woman's problem and if she were just somehow "enough," the problem would go away.

Many people take a "blame-the-woman" mentality and argue that if women can't take the heat, they should get out. But such an attitude is both ignorant and harmful. Throughout this book, we have shown that the heat is immensely higher for women than for men. Women encounter all the regular challenges of work, and then have a mountain of additional hindrances piled on through the gender-biased systems that pervade the workplace. It is a system in which everyone loses. Women lose, organizations lose, and society loses. It's lose-lose all around. Women miss out on good health, career choices, meaningful work, and living into their passions. They also lose earnings, a sense of fulfillment and meaning, and the opportunity to change the world for the better. But what organizations lose is rarely counted and very costly: they squander the ideas, the brilliance, the contributions, and the input of women who would, if treated well, be superb leaders and team members helping the organization achieve its goals. Society misses out on innovations and advancement that would support better health, safety, quality of life, and conveniences for us all.

For years, study after study has shown that more diverse organizations have better outcomes on every level. Yet somehow, despite that knowledge, organizational leaders are all too often willing to settle for less: less profit, less value, less progress, less healthy workplaces, just less all around, because they'd rather stick to the usual ways. They accept the ongoing loss of talented women and the costs associated with recruiting new talent, because it seems simpler than changing to meet the needs of a diverse, twenty-first-century workforce. While it may seem easier to stick to the familiar, doing so will eventually kill every organization. Companies that don't grow and adapt die.[17] In the turbulent times that characterize the 2020s, no business can afford to be stagnant. The pandemic brought disruptive change to virtually every industry. And disruptive change can't be addressed with incremental steps. Too many systems still work well only for men. The time to overhaul them is now, for the good of women, all people, organizations, and society. That's our only hope for a better future.

On a practical level, what needs to be done? To shatter gender bias, the primary responsibility lies with organizational leaders. Successful change starts at the top. Unless top leadership is on board, lasting change is unlikely. In each chapter we've given specific, concrete recommendations for leaders to ensure that their organization is diverse, equitable, supportive, valuing, welcoming, and maximizing. But to create full gender equity and inclusion, the problem must be tackled holistically and strategically as well.

Gender Equity and Inclusion Roadmap

Before starting any journey, it's important to know the destination. In this book we advocate for the development of an inclusive organization that embraces diversity by welcoming and supporting every employee, for the good of people and the company. This type of organization looks a bit different from one that only values equality, or even equity. Equality means giving every person the same resources. While equality sounds like a good goal, it will not yield optimal results for all individuals and organizations. Equity is more than equality of resources; it means realizing that people start from different points and therefore need different resources to achieve an equal outcome. Equity will yield better results for individuals and organizations. But because it doesn't remove the barriers to full inclusion, equity requires an ongoing investment of supports and resources to ensure continued positive outcomes. In the long run, it's more strategic to aim for inclusion, which means removing the barriers altogether such that everyone belongs, feels accepted, and is valued.[18] An inclusive organization eliminates obstacles to people's full engagement and then ensures they don't creep back in, maintaining a culture where everyone's contributions are maximized and the organization flourishes in every way. The goal we present is an inclusive organization, which incorporates gender equity along the way to the final destination. Figure 7.1 illustrates the differences between equality, equity, and inclusion.

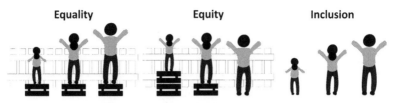

Figure 7.1. **The difference between equality, equity, and inclusion. Equality gives everyone the same supports but has differing outcomes. Equity gives different supports for equitable outcomes. Inclusion eliminates barriers in the first place.** *Image credit*: **Amy Diehl adapted from Iam2mai**

All organizations can be characterized on a gender equity and inclusion continuum, shown in figure 7.2. Getting to full inclusion is a journey. Leaders can use this roadmap to assess where their company currently sits and strategically plan to move toward an equitable and inclusive culture.[19]

Progressing from a gender-blind organization to a fully sustainable equitable and inclusive organization takes time and effort and culture change. But it's worth the work for two reasons. First, it's just the right thing to do. The gender bias stories we've presented range from irritating experiences to truly horrific ones. Treating women as less than has no place in a healthy organization or society. Second, as we have shown, it makes better business sense. Evidence continues to mount that diverse and inclusive organizations simply perform better. Gender equity and inclusion are win–win.

Gender Equity and Inclusion Roadmap

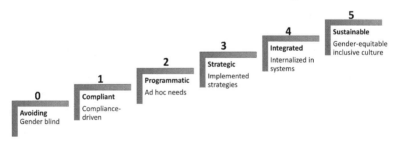

Figure 7.2. **Roadmap toward a gender-equitable and inclusive organization.** *Image credit*: **Amy Diehl**

Level 0: Avoidant

An avoidant organization is gender blind, not even recognizing that gender equity issues exist. Exclusionary behavior toward women is normalized, and there are no resources put to gender equity initiatives. Any leader who realizes the organization is at this stage can start by learning. Reading this book is a good start. There are also plenty of online resources easily available for anyone who is willing to learn.[20] Be sure to look for sources that address the organization's culture instead of trying to "fix the women."[21] In the Information Age with the Internet at one's fingertips, ignorance is not an excuse.

Level 1: Compliant

At the first level is a compliant organization that follows the minimum legal requirements. To get to this level, leaders can meet with HR to begin the process toward compliance. Each country, state, and region has specific laws, and it is HR's responsibility to know the rules and ensure compliance. If the company lacks an HR person, the owner should take on this responsibility and consider adding a dedicated HR professional when there are about ten employees.[22] Larger organizations can also establish an ombudsperson to receive complaints and establish investigations into lack of compliance. But while compliance may satisfy legal requirements and prevent lawsuits, it won't do much to improve company performance outcomes. For that to happen, the journey must continue.

Level 2: Programmatic

The second level is an organization that has programs geared for specific gender equity needs. There are several actions that can be taken to create such programs. Gender bias training is an important starting point to help employees learn to identify biased behaviors and how to respond. Sessions should include time for participants to process what they have learned and develop strategies to combat bias.

Initiatives aimed specifically at supporting women, like a women's resource group, also fit in this stage. Going further, creation of mentoring and professional development programs for women at every level are beneficial programmatic actions. Developing women's leadership capacity and moving them into the pipeline for leadership roles can begin to propel the organization forward. Organizational leaders could also host a "listening tour" to meet with women employees to learn specific issues that need to be addressed. Companies should also ensure pay equity via a study of pay rates and promotion policies. Each of these recommendations can help address specific pain points women may be experiencing. However, this piecemeal approach to gender equity won't enable full inclusivity. The next step is to work toward a gender equity strategy.

Level 3: Strategic

The third level is an organization that has implemented strategies to improve gender equity. The leadership of a strategic organization recognizes the full value of gender diversity and equity. They know the business case and the moral case for having gender equity woven into company strategy rather than tacked on as *ad hoc* programs. To make this step, leaders must first believe in the value before they can imbue it into the organization. They should familiarize themselves thoroughly with the abundant resources showing that diverse and inclusive organizations perform better. Additionally, leaders should attend to their own education via professional development programs on gender equity and inclusive leadership.[23] It is also vital that leaders establish a plan to communicate the value of gender equity and that non-inclusive behaviors will not be tolerated.

In this stage, leaders can create a network of champions who can carry the gender equity message forward by meeting regularly to share knowledge and develop strategies to deal with resistance to equity advancements. Champions may be existing employees who are already knowledgeable about and working toward equity and inclusion, and they can include people who want to learn how to take strategic action to support women. Bringing these people together to support each other's work will continue the process of strategic change.[24]

Another step is to put women on the board and ensure their voices are heard. A recent global survey of almost twenty-two thousand firms found that "the presence of a female CEO, the size of the board, and the size of the firm as measured by revenue are all positively correlated with the share of women on the board."[25] A woman as board chair is also strategically useful, along with having multiple other women board members.[26] The board should institute governance and reporting mechanisms to ensure leadership oversight of gender equity initiatives.

Organizational leaders should evaluate gender equity throughout all divisions and departments. Diagnosis may be done using the Gender Bias Scale for Women Leaders to measure women's experiences of bias. The scale results will be broken down by the six primary barriers covered in this book (*male privilege*, *disproportionate constraints*, *insufficient support*, *devaluation*, *hostility*, and *acquiescence*) plus fifteen sub-factors.[27] Careful use of the survey and analysis of results will point out areas in which women experience the most bias. Depending on which barriers are most problematic, action plans using the strategies for leaders described in chapters 1 to 6 of this book can be created and deployed. The scale should be used to reassess gender bias at regular intervals and after specific interventions to guide priorities for areas to improve. Eliminating gender bias is like pulling back the layers of an onion. Once outer layers are addressed, keep peeling to reveal the inner layers working toward a gender-equitable workplace.[28] Be sure to call attention to successes and celebrate wins along the way to build enthusiasm and confidence about changes as they happen.[29]

Level 4: Integrated

The fourth level is an integrated organization where systems and processes have been assessed and adjusted to ensure equity at every level. Leaders are convinced that gender equity is better for business in all respects—the bottom line, corporate social responsibility, societal impact—and they ensure that gender equity is woven into every facet of the company. Change at this stage is culture change rather than just program change, pay equity revisions, or other interventions targeting individual barriers. Leaders should do a complete audit to ensure gender equity is integrated into every policy, practice, and value embraced by the organization. A programmatic organization might have a maternity leave policy, but an integrated organization will have a fully developed parental leave policy available to parents of any gender covering birth, adoption, fostering, and guardianship and will incentivize or even require men to take the leave. A global survey of almost twenty-two thousand firms found that parental leave, not just maternity leave, increased gender equity by eliminating employer's expectations "that young men will necessarily provide greater returns to training and mentoring than young women."[30] Thus an incentivized parental leave policy cares for individual families and changes the workplace culture, thereby moving toward a healthier and more profitable business.

An integrated organization shifts to a culture of cooperation rather than competition. Competition disincentivizes people in the long run, while collaboration brings out better performance. Similarly, leaders should create pay structures that recognize and reward all types of work, especially collaborative work. An integrated organization evaluates employees based on goals rather than time at work to ensure that what's being measured counts toward organizational performance. Remote and flexible work policies should also be created to help employees accomplish their best work and have work-life balance.[31]

An integrated organization ensures that women are well represented at all levels, from the board down, and that all barriers to women's career progression are addressed. An integrated organization needs a strong "pipeline" of women. The same global survey found that "the largest gains [in organizational performance] are for the proportion of female executives, followed by the proportion of female board members."[32] Their finding "underscores the importance of creating a pipeline of female managers and not simply getting women to the very top."[33] Company management can assess if there is a clear pipeline of women moving up through the ranks and into leadership and make sure that it does not "leak" with women dropping out. If necessary, determine which changes are needed to create that pipeline and support women throughout the organization. The actions we've recommended at the "programmatic" and "strategic" steps help with recruiting and retaining talented women. And although the pipeline alone won't guarantee equity, it's part of an overall strategy to make progress toward an inclusive organization.

Level 5: Sustainable

Finally, on the fifth level is a sustainable organization, where gender equity has become so embedded into the organizational systems, structures, and processes that the entire culture is characterized as inclusive. Leaders are role models who hold themselves and their employees accountable for gender-equitable solutions and gender-equal outcomes. They use data from tools such as the Gender Bias Scale to show if equity and inclusion are being enhanced. They demonstrate other outcomes including strengths and weaknesses of initiatives and cost-benefit ratios for improving equity and inclusion. Decision making is completely transparent and inclusive, making sure every stakeholder has input—thereby increasing trust as well as innovation.[34]

At the sustainable stage, leaders make promotion of gender equity part of their public image. Leaders themselves are not only well educated about the benefits of and challenges to gender equity and inclusion; they are also active in promoting it both inside and outside the organization. They present diversity as an inherent value, not up for discussion, knowing that no justification is needed for the presence of underrepresented groups just as none is needed for well-represented groups.[35]

Leaders may choose to invest in girls' schooling and organizations that help girls and young women develop technical and leadership skills, for example, to help ensure the future. It's been shown that societies where girls do better in math are also societies where there are more women on boards and in C-suite roles.[36] Investing in girls and young women is an investment in society's and the organization's future.

Further, gender equity and inclusion are now such an ingrained part of company culture that even when leaders change, the culture stays the same. To minimize the effects of change, sustainable organizations do the following:

- Revise job descriptions to include equity and inclusion responsibilities
- Evaluate equity and inclusion work during performance reviews
- Ensure multiple people carry responsibility for equity and inclusion initiatives
- Create succession plans that incorporate equity and inclusion work[37]

Those who are hired or promoted to lead are committed to inclusivity, and the culture will not tolerate a non-supportive leader. Business practices themselves will also reflect gender equity. Women—whether employees, customers, shareholders, or the general public—will be seen and valued as vital members of society and treated as such. There will be no space for bias, discrimination, hostility, or sexism of any kind. Instead, the values of equalism will prevail, where every person regardless of any socially defined identity category is seen and treated as having equal value and worth and is fully included. Nothing less will be accepted.

———————

Recently, Leanne chatted with a young girl at an outdoor concert. The girl explained that she loved playing soccer and was, as she put it, "pretty good, for a girl." When Leanne asked about the comment, the girl explained that her older brother was a better soccer player. Leanne suggested that maybe he was better because he is older and has been playing longer, rather than because he's a boy. The girl seemed surprised by this idea—perhaps she hadn't heard it before. Girls and women need to hear that they are good, period, not that they are "good, for a girl." Instead of hearing "we want what you aren't," they need to hear "*we want what you are.*" If everyone reading this book commits to changing the narrative, improvement will happen. Society has successfully changed the narrative on many things, such as women's suffrage, seatbelts, child car seats, smoking, forest fires, and drunk driving. Gender equity and inclusion can be the next social change if we all work together. The glass walls will be shattered.

8

TAKING CHARGE OF
YOUR OWN SUCCESS

After reading this book you may still wonder, "What should I do if I experience gender bias?" We are going to leave you with some personal strategies. These strategies are not meant to tell you how to change yourself to fit into a male-normed workplace. We won't tell you how to dress or how to speak or how to change what's unique about you. Instead, we offer research-based strategies for women on how to navigate adversity.[1]

PREPARATION

Being prepared means anticipating obstacles. As a higher education leader told Amy, "I had to, at all times, realize that I had to be über-prepared because the environment didn't anticipate that I was up to the challenge."[2] By reading this book, you are taking the most important first step. You are learning to recognize and name gender bias in all its insidious forms.

It's also worthwhile to do some personal preparation. Spend some time thinking through what you've learned in this book. Reflect on how intensely you have been socialized into gender stereotypes that permeate society. And think about how that socialization may be affecting you, even unconsciously. Women may compensate for breaking some gender norms by performing other ones, like the physician who baked cookies for her support staff or the women who outearned their husbands but did more family care to uphold gender norms. Maybe the cookies and the housework seem like a good trade-off to smooth work and home life. But maybe those tasks are eating up your limited time and energy in ways that are counterproductive. Different choices have consequences, and it's good to think about which consequences maximize your definition of success. No choice is wrong. Make your choices mindfully and with full awareness rather than following old habits or social pressure.

Don't be afraid to think or talk about bias. Some women want to pretend it doesn't exist or doesn't affect them—a strategy that won't work well in the long run. And it's not likely to lead to improvement. Instead, think about your context and identify what is going on. This book has given names and definitions for all kinds of gender barriers that may impact you in the workplace. Then, decide for yourself what you are and are not willing to accept, and how you may respond.

SPEAK UP

Voice your concerns and explain the consequences of bias. Use the model of one higher education vice president: "I was the one who was brave enough to say . . . 'We feel mistreated. We'll work as hard as you want us to, but you can't . . . mistreat people and expect them to perform at their optimal performance.'"[3] Some women may be comfortable directly confronting bias and sexism, such as a nonprofit leader who described herself as a "boat rocker" who asks questions and a physician who explained, "[I] power through and insist on what I need." If you like to tackle challenges and call out injustice, do so. As we have shown in this book, some people may try to stop you or prevent you from achieving your goals. But others will be grateful. One woman benefited from a female predecessor "with a dominant personality" who paved the way for her. Today's women stand on the work of foremothers like Elizabeth Cady Stanton and Sojourner Truth and Ruth Bader Ginsburg and bell hooks and more recent activists like Gloria Steinem and Hillary Clinton and Alexandria Ocasio-Cortez and Malala Yousafzai. Each generation needs women who will confront all forms of gender bias in every setting in which we live and work. Any woman or ally can play a part in bringing change by speaking up and speaking out against bias.

Other women may prefer behind the scenes advocacy or talking to trusted colleagues in private settings. One woman created a "safe zone" where colleagues could discuss issues with one another. Sometimes the right approach for you will vary based on the day or the setting. That's okay. It may change over time, too. As one woman described, "The older I get, the easier it is to say, 'Back off, buster!'" Take each day as it comes and do what you can that day.

No matter your usual approach, try calling out bias directly when you see it. It may work. One woman called out mansplaining and he-peating and found that the behaviors "subsided." If you don't feel safe or comfortable speaking up in the moment, reflect on the situation and the power structures involved. Assume good intent and start a private conversation with the person by saying, "I know you didn't mean it this way, but your comment didn't sit well with me."[4] Document the incident not only to help you process it but also to create a paper trail that is so important when reporting bias and discrimination. Name the behaviors and situations with specific labels described in this book to further add credence to your experiences. Identifying and exposing bias is the first step to eliminating it.

Going a step further, teach others what you have learned. You could help others learn about bias by leading a workshop or discussion group at your workplace, using this book as a resource. You can also help others learn about bias in informal ways by sharing your experiences. If you notice that people often call women pet names or untitle them, talk to your coworkers about it. You can say, "I've noticed that our female colleagues are sometimes called by their first names while our male colleagues are almost always called Dr. So-and-So. That's called 'untitling' and it is a form of gender bias." You can also discuss ways to work together to eradicate biased behaviors.

DEPERSONALIZE

If you experience bias, do not take it personally. You are not alone in your experiences. Prominent and wealthy women experience bias, as do everyday women. The person exhibiting the bias may not even realize it, as they are often just acting in a way in which they were socialized. A university vice president commented, "I don't really make it personal to me. If anything, it's unfortunate that that person feels and behaves that way." That doesn't make bias or discrimination right or okay, but it does help to realize that the problem is not you and is not unique to you. Not taking it personally will help you to externalize the behavior and minimize self-blame—which can make it easier for you to address the person who is mistreating you or exhibiting bias. When women exhibit queen bee or mean girl behaviors, they are operating out of their own insecurities. It may help you to directly confront the person and have a conversation if you remember she is feeling afraid of losing her position or status or other hard-earned gains. It doesn't mean that such a conversation will be easy, but keep in mind that it isn't about you. The woman herself has had to learn to survive in a sexist system. Indicate your support, try to get to know her, and communicate your willingness to establish a relationship to work toward mutual organizational goals. Or if a man is exhibiting benevolent sexism, thinking he's protecting you, talk about it with him. Help him see that limiting your travel or your work choices isn't doing you a favor but is hindering your career. If he has your best interests at heart, he may be willing to listen and change his thinking. We can't promise that these strategies will work with every unsupportive person, but they will work with many.

BUILD YOUR SUPPORT NETWORK

When Amy interviewed women higher education executives, many mentioned that support networks aided their success. One commented, "No one does it on their own. . . . It's really important that you have a group of people that you can talk to, get advice from, believe in, understand, and who understand you."[5] Building your own network is a key to navigating gender bias. Find allies—anyone who is supportive—inside and outside of the organization. Reaching out to others will help you to realize that your problems are not unique and help is available.

To build your network, start with the people on your team or in your department. Get to know them on a personal level. These questions are an easy way to start: "What do you like to do in your free time?" or "How did you get interested in this career?" Later as you grow in your level of trust, you can ask about how they have overcome obstacles and discuss ways you can support each other.

Not all connections should be in your own department. As one higher education leader said, "You have to gather around you a community of supportive people, who don't necessarily have to be the people that are in your hallway." To get to know people outside your department, join committees and attend work events, which research shows can reduce experiences of bias by helping colleagues see each other as individuals rather than their gender.[6] Think strategically about which committees and events to join to maximize your visibility and connections to others while not overextending yourself. You can also invite individual colleagues to an in-person or virtual coffee break or lunch to get to know them.

To connect with people outside of your workplace, attend professional conferences, join professional organizations, and sign up for volunteer roles. Attend affiliation events or offer to coordinate such events if doing so appeals to you. Such meetups can be in person or through web conferencing. Carefully consider which organizations to join and volunteer roles to take so as not to overburden yourself. And don't be afraid to discontinue such roles when they are no longer rewarding to you.

If you work remotely, you can still build relationships inside and outside of your organization. Make a list of people you would like to get to know in your organization and invite them to a short video or phone call. You can do the same thing for people not in your workplace. Find people through social media, such as LinkedIn and Twitter, or virtual conference attendees. Send them an invite to chat via web conference. You will be surprised at how many will say yes. Be sure to explain your goals for talking to them, such as to learn more about what they do. Avoid any inference that you are trying to sell them a product or a service. You're wanting to make connections in your field.

Look for people who can serve as your mentors. Within your organization, ask colleagues, your supervisor, and human resources for recommendations and connections to potential mentors. It can sometimes be a challenge to find a compatible mentor, but don't let that dissuade your search. Stay in touch with supportive former bosses who can act as sounding boards. Not all mentors need to be senior to you. There is much value in peer mentoring where you and a colleague listen to the other's concerns and provide advice to each other.

Be on the lookout for someone who might become a sponsor. While asking a leader directly to be your sponsor might not be the best approach, especially if that person doesn't know you well, cultivating connections with higher-level leaders can work. When approaching a senior leader, have a specific plan and a clear ask. You could say, "I really appreciated how you handled the conflict that happened in yesterday's meeting. Could we get a coffee and talk about how you learned to have hard conversations?" Leanne's interviews with leaders in faith-based organizations showed that having even one or two senior leaders who believe in you and support you can make a difference.[7] Such a sponsor can affirm your abilities and recommend you for additional roles. They can also offer perspective when you encounter barriers.

Build your personal support network. Lean on your friends, partners, parents, siblings, and other supportive family members. Build friendships outside of work. Join groups with common interests, like fitness groups, travel tours, arts and crafts nights, religious or spiritual organizations, and make connections with people there. Finding and cultivating relationships inside and outside of work will help you know that you are not alone. Connect with these people on a regular basis, and don't be afraid to reach out when you need help. Maintain these supportive relationships so that you have people to vent to, strategize with, help you to navigate bias, grow in your career, and live life with.

PERSISTENCE

Being persistent means to keep moving and to have patience. One higher education leader found success with this strategy: "[I] just keep going at obstacles in my way again and again, and I nearly always break through, if I really want whatever it is. I find that most people are not motivated to outlast me." Most things worth accomplishing take effort. Roadblocks are common and should be expected. Succeeding in a system or workplace that was not built for you is no different. Recognize that as individuals, we cannot—nor should we be expected to—address systemic bias on our own. Yet you can use the strategies in this book to minimize the impact of bias, while also recognizing that change takes time and celebrating the wins along the way. Amy recently gave feedback to a new parental leave policy in her workplace that resulted in more weeks of leave for newer employees, and she advocated to include miscarriage and stillbirth in a new bereavement leave policy. Both ideas were heard and incorporated into policy. And Leanne's advocacy in her workplace helped establish lactation rooms as well as a review of promotion policies. Even when the win seems small, remember that is how culture changes—one person, one policy, one process at a time.

SELF-CARE

Self-care involves making time for personal needs and interests. Control what you can and don't sweat the small stuff. A college chief of staff noted, "I can't control what's happened to me, but what can I do?" Most important is to maintain your perspective—life is not all about work. Make sure you have hobbies and friendships outside of work. Make time for exercise and be sure to get enough sleep. Prioritize time for yourself and with your family. Take vacations and really unplug while you are away. Use your out-of-office email reply to let people know that you are away and how to get help or when they can expect an answer from you. When you are home, be home, instead of constantly connecting to your work email or chat. Encourage your coworkers to call or text you after hours only in cases of an emergency where a solution really can't wait until the next working day. Taking care of yourself first is a win-win-win. It will help you to feel refreshed, give you energy for your work, and allow you to support others.

ALTERNATIVES

Finally, find alternatives and be willing to use them. You may find yourself in a situation that is untenable. Some workplaces and some bosses are not supportive and never will be. As a college provost told Amy, "Some of our greatest adversities come from our own narrow visions of ourselves and our opportunities." She described how to overcome people who mistreat you: "Step around them. Find a different place. Make clear if someone's broken the law, you're going to report them. But then you just step away. Life is way too short to go head-to-head with someone that's as narrow-minded as that. Step away. Step around. Move ahead."

To step away from a discriminatory environment, first consider your options. Could you apply for other positions? Do you have skills in which you could work for yourself or start a small business? Are you in a job that lends itself to telecommuting such that you could expand the region of your job search? Many organizations are now more open to remote work. Could you go back to school to develop new skills? If you can't leave your current position immediately but would like a career change, you could attend school while in the current role. There are lots of jobs, lots of organizations, and lots of opportunities to use your skills in a place where you will be valued. Don't let one job, one organization, or one person block your personal fulfillment and advancement. You can and should try to rectify the problem within your current workplace, but if you keep hitting roadblocks, realize that there are many paths to opportunity and success, and you can find them.

———————

In this chapter and throughout this book, we've offered various steps to improve your situation. Gender bias is pervasive; you're highly likely to encounter it in your work life. When you do, it is difficult to shatter the glass walls all by yourself. But the message of this chapter is simple: don't be a passive victim. Instead, when you are confronted with bias, see yourself as someone with agency, who can and should make her own decisions and choices. Different women will make different choices, and you may make different choices at different stages in your career. All of that is okay! Don't measure yourself or judge yourself by anyone else. Instead, take charge of your own success, recognizing that at the end of it all, you are the one who knows what is best for you.

ACKNOWLEDGMENTS

While writing a book can feel daunting, there are many people in our lives who have enabled our journey.
We both wish to thank the following:

- Our literary attorney, Tim Brandhorst, who saw our vision and helped us to enhance our proposal and find a publisher.
- Susan Spilka and Debra Englander who enabled our connection to Tim.
- Suzanne Staszak-Silva, our editor, for taking this project and giving us pertinent, actionable feedback to our draft. We have become better writers because of her advice.
- Gretchen Crary, our publicist, for book title and cover inspiration as well as handling promotion.
- Dr. Amber Stephenson, who took on the gargantuan effort to partner with us to create a scale to measure gender bias. While none of us anticipated the far-reaching results of this painstaking work, the outcome has been not only the scale, but also discovery of a factor model undergirding workplace gender bias and forming the basis for this book. In addition, we have gained another research partner in our efforts to understand gender bias and create gender-equitable workplaces.
- Dr. David Wang, who helped us through confirmatory factor analysis for our gender bias scale development and responded to round after round of journal review feedback.
- Dr. Susan Madsen for putting the two of us in the same workgroup at the 2014 research colloquium and for encouraging Amy

to attend, even though Amy couldn't speak due to laryngitis at the start of the conference.

- Our study participants from our respective dissertations and scale development, and all the women who told their stories through public posts or articles. This book is dedicated to you. By using your voice and sharing your experiences, you contribute to understanding gender bias and creating a more gender-equitable world.
- You, our readers, for caring about this topic. It is our hope that you will be able to identify and call out gender bias as it happens and use the strategies in this book to make your workplace gender equitable and inclusive.

Amy wishes to thank:

- My mother, for going through the working world ahead of me. The first and only in her family to attend college, she studied teacher education because that's what most women did, and she wasn't familiar with other professions. Upon discovering that being an elementary school teacher was not her passion, she left that role and imparted her knowledge and love of learning to me as a young child. Later when she reentered the workforce, she transformed a clerical role into an adult education career, working while also mothering three children. She is truly my inspiration and my go-to person for "life" answers.
- My father for always supporting me and instilling in me the principle of self-sufficiency.
- My former boss, Rick, for encouraging my professional development in both information technology and research, for "getting it" when it comes to how women are treated in the workplace, and for listening to my ideas and encouraging me to write this book when it was still just an idea in my head.
- Leanne, my research partner and friend, for her willingness to connect with me when we first met even though I had lost my voice. I still remember the day of our departure at the airport, after we had talked, when I said, "I feel like we're best friends." That was how much immediate kinship I perceived in our

backgrounds and mutual interest in women's equity. Who could have imagined that nine years later we would have written this manifest, this treatise on gender bias and how to eliminate it? It's been a journey, and we have truly accomplished more together than either of us could have accomplished alone. Onward we go to continue this fight for women's inclusion.

- My husband, Sam, for always being there for me. For giving early feedback to the first drafted book chapter. For understanding when I was too engrossed in writing or editing to do anything else. For being an equal partner and encouraging and supporting my professional goals. I love you.

Leanne wishes to thank:

- My mother, who pursued higher education as the first woman in her family. She had to wait until winter quarter for a man to drop out of the program to be admitted. She persevered through bachelor's and master's degrees, set the pace for all her daughters, and worked her entire adult life modeling being a professional and a mother. She has also told stories of the strong women in our family line who are a cloud of witnesses to my work today.
- My father, who always encouraged me and never told me anything was unsuitable for me.
- My mother-in-law, who studied biology in the late 1950s. After graduation she worked in a hospital. When she married, she accepted the expectation to stay home with her children. Soon she created businesses out of her home, first decoupage and later a successful homemade candy business.
- My grandmother Sara who, despite not completing her education, worked her way up the corporate ladder. And my grandmother Ruby who invested in her community through church volunteer work her entire life.
- My sisters, sisters-in-law, daughters, and nieces, all of whom model being strong competent women despite the plethora of bias they encounter.

- Dr. Karen Longman, Dr. Rich Starcher, and Dr. Liz Hall who all have encouraged me to write. And have read multiple drafts of various works and given invaluable feedback.
- Amy, friend and collaborator for many years now. Together we've studied, written, consulted, traveled domestically and internationally, visited each other's homes—everything a friend-ship and research partner should be! Two are stronger than one, and we will continue the journey to support and advocate for women, together.
- Paul Dzubinski for believing in me and supporting me every step of the way. When we started this life journey together, we had no idea what we'd find along the way, or that advocacy for women would be part of our story. Thank you for being my partner and best friend.

NOTES

PREFACE

1. Amy B. Diehl et al., "Measuring the Invisible: Development and Multi-Industry Validation of the Gender Bias Scale for Women Leaders," *Human Resource Development Quarterly* 31, no. 3 (2020): 268, https://doi.org/10.1002/hrdq.21389.

2. Amy B. Diehl and Leanne M. Dzubinski, "Making the Invisible Visible: A Cross-Sector Analysis of Gender-Based Leadership Barriers," *Human Resource Development Quarterly* 27, no. 2 (2016): 185, https://doi.org/10.1002/hrdq.21248.

3. For more on intersectionality see the work of Kimberle Crenshaw, "Demarginalizing the Intersection of Race and Sex: A Black Feminist Critique of Antidiscrimination Doctrine, Feminist Theory and Antiracist Politics," *University of Chicago Legal Forum* 1989, no. 1 (1989): 139–67, https://chicagounbound.uchicago.edu/uclf/vol1989/iss1/8/.

4. Diehl et al., "Measuring the Invisible: Development and Multi-Industry Validation of the Gender Bias Scale for Women Leaders," 268–69.

5. Amber L. Stephenson, Leanne M. Dzubinski, and Amy B. Diehl, "A Cross-Industry Comparison of How Women Leaders Experience Gender Bias," *Personnel Review* (2022), https://doi.org/10.1108/PR-02-2021-0091; Amy B. Diehl, "Making Meaning of Adversity: Experiences of Women Leaders in Higher Education" (PhD diss., Indiana University of Pennsylvania, 2013), Proquest (3589972); Leanne M. Dzubinski, "Playing by the Rules: How Women Lead in Evangelical Mission Organizations" (PhD diss., University of Georgia, 2013), http://getd.libs.uga.edu/pdfs/dzubinski_leanne_b_201305_phd.pdf.

INTRODUCTION

1. Herminia Ibarra, Robin Ely, and Deborah Kolb, "Women Rising: The Unseen Barriers," *Harvard Business Review*, September, 2013, 64, https://hbr.org/2013/09/women-rising-the-unseen-barriers.

2. Carolyn Y. Johnson, "A One-Way Ticket. A Cash-Stuffed Teddy Bear. A Dream Decades in the Making," *The Washington Post*, October 1, 2021, https://www.washingtonpost.com/health/2021/10/01/katalin-kariko-covid-vaccines/.

3. David Cox, "How mRNA Went from a Scientific Backwater to a Pandemic Crusher," *Wired*, December 2, 2020, https://www.wired.co.uk/article/mrna-coronavirus-vaccine-pfizer-biontech; Damian Garde and Jonathan Saltzman, "The Story of mRNA: How a Once-Dismissed Idea Became a Leading Technology in the Covid Vaccine Race," *STAT*, November 10, 2022, https://www.statnews.com/2020/11/10/the-story-of-mrna-how-a-once-dismissed-idea-became-a-leading-technology-in-the-covid-vaccine-race/.

4. Garde and Saltzman, "The Story of mRNA: How a Once-Dismissed Idea Became a Leading Technology in the Covid Vaccine Race."

5. Johnson, "A One-Way Ticket. A Cash-Stuffed Teddy Bear. A Dream Decades in the Making."

6. Garde and Saltzman, "The Story of mRNA: How a Once-Dismissed Idea Became a Leading Technology in the Covid Vaccine Race."

7. Cox, "How mRNA Went from a Scientific Backwater to a Pandemic Crusher."

8. Adapted from Amy B. Diehl, "How Gender Bias Inhibits Progress and What Leaders Can Do about It," *Ms. Magazine*, August 18, 2021, https://msmagazine.com/2021/08/18/gender-bias-covid-vaccine-katalin-kariko/.

9. Genevieve Carlton, "A History of Women in Higher Education," Best Colleges, last modified February 22, 2022, https://www.bestcolleges.com/news/analysis/2021/03/21/history-women-higher-education/.

10. Kim Parker and Cary Funk, "Gender Discrimination Comes in Many Forms for Today's Working Women," Pew Research Center, December 14, 2017, https://www.pewresearch.org/fact-tank/2017/12/14/gender-discrimination-comes-in-many-forms-for-todays-working-women/.

11. C. Haerpfer et al., "World Values Survey Wave 7: 2017–2020," D Systems Institute & WVSA Secretariat, 2020, accessed June 21, 2022, https://www.worldvaluessurvey.org/WVSOnline.jsp. The data in this survey was intended to be collected from 2017 to 2020 but was extended due to the pandemic. Some countries' data were collected in 2021 and 2022.

12. Amy B. Diehl and Leanne M. Dzubinski, "Making the Invisible Visible: A Cross-Sector Analysis of Gender-Based Leadership Barriers," *Human Resource Development Quarterly* 27, no. 2 (2016): 181–206, https://doi.org/10.1002/hrdq.21248.

13. Amy B. Diehl et al., "Measuring the Invisible: Development and Multi-Industry Validation of the Gender Bias Scale for Women Leaders," *Human Resource Development Quarterly* 31, no. 3 (2020): 249–80, https://doi.org/10.1002/hrdq.21389. The scale was validated with women leaders in higher education, faith-based organizations, healthcare, and law.

14. Diehl et al., "Measuring the Invisible: Development and Multi-Industry Validation of the Gender Bias Scale for Women Leaders," 256–59.

15. Diehl et al., "Measuring the Invisible: Development and Multi-Industry Validation of the Gender Bias Scale for Women Leaders," 259.

16. The "queen bee behavior" label is included in this list for completeness in describing female hostility. This label was tweaked from "queen bee syndrome" first identified by Graham L. Staines, C. Tavris, and T. E. Jayaratne, "The Queen Bee Syndrome," *Psychology Today* 7, no. 8 (January 1974): 55–60, https://doi.org/10.1037/e400562009-003.

17. Diehl and Dzubinski, "Making the Invisible Visible: A Cross-Sector Analysis of Gender-Based Leadership Barriers," 185.

CHAPTER 1

1. Elaine Moore, "How Ellen Pao Lost a Lawsuit, but Won a Hearing," *Financial Times*, March 7, 2019, https://www.ft.com/content/9fc459da-2f7a-11e9-80d2-7b637a9e1ba1.

2. Ellen K. Pao, *Reset: My Fight for Inclusion and Lasting Change* (New York, NY: Spiegel & Grau, 2017), 133–34.

3. Laura L. Bierema, "Critiquing Human Resource Development's Dominant Masculine Rationality and Evaluating Its Impact," *Human Resource Development Review* 8, no. 1 (2009): 69–70, https://doi.org/10.1177/1534484308330020.

4. Leanne M. Dzubinski, *Playing by the Rules: How Women Lead in Evangelical Mission Organizations*, vol. 52 (Eugene, OR: Pickwick Publications, 2021), 26.

5. Patsy Parker, "The Historical Role of Women in Higher Education," *Administrative Issues Journal* 5, no. 1 (2015): 6, https://doi.org/10.5929/2015.5.1.1.

6. Parker, "The Historical Role of Women in Higher Education," 3.

7. Dzubinski, *Playing by the Rules: How Women Lead in Evangelical Mission Organizations*, 52, 26.

8. Stephen J. Dubner, "Extra: Carol Bartz Full Interview," March 25, 2018, in *The Secret Life of a C.E.O.*, produced by Freakonomics Radio, podcast audio, http://freakonomics.com/podcast/carol-bartz/.

9. Cammy Pedroja, "Celebs Who Have Spoken Out Publicly about Sexism in Hollywood," The List, 2019, accessed September 8, 2019, https://www.thelist.com/79855/celebs-spoken-publicly-sexism-hollywood/.

10. M. Elizabeth Lewis Hall, Brad Christerson, and Shelly Cunningham, "Sanctified Sexism: Religious Beliefs and the Gender Harassment of Academic Women," *Psychology of Women Quarterly* 34, no. 2 (2010): 182, https://doi.org/10.1111/j.1471-6402.2010.01560.x.

11. Amy B. Diehl and Leanne M. Dzubinski, "An Overview of Gender-Based Leadership Barriers," in *Handbook of Research on Gender and Leadership*, ed. Susan R. Madsen (Northampton, MA: Edward Elgar Publishing, 2017), 277–78.

12. "What Are the Biggest Challenges You've Faced as a Female Leader?," *Chronicle of Higher Education*, November 25, 2018, https://www.chronicle.com/article/What-Are-the-Biggest/245151.

13. Jennifer R. Grandis, "Fishing, Strip Clubs and Golf: How Male-Focused Networking in Medicine Blocks Female Colleagues from Top Jobs," *The Conversation*, April 8, 2022, https://theconversation.com/fishing-strip-clubs-and-golf-how-male-focused-networking-in-medicine-blocks-female-colleagues-from-top-jobs-179931.

14. Callum Borchers, "Your Office Is Open and the Liquor Is Flowing," *The Wall Street Journal*, April 14, 2022, https://www.wsj.com/articles/your-office-is-open-and-the-liquor-is-flowing-hybrid-work-beer-wine-booze-11649871713.

15. Sarah Green Carmichael, "Boston Has Eliminated Sexism in the Workplace. Right?," *Boston*, July 23, 2017, https://www.bostonmagazine.com/news/2017/07/23/sexism-workplace/.

16. Adapted from Patrick Allan, "10 Sports Metaphors Used in Business, and Where They Really Came From," Lifehacker, June 21, 2016, https://lifehacker.com/10-sports-metaphors-used-in-business-and-where-they-re-1782325688; Matthew Zeitlin, "The Business World's 9 Favorite Sports Metaphors," BuzzFeed News, August 9, 2013, https://www.buzzfeednews.com/article/matthewzeitlin/the-business-worlds-9-favorite-sports-metaphors.

17. Sasha Shillcutt, "Battling Built-in Bias," Brave Enough (blog), January 4, 2018, accessed February 26, 2018, https://www.becomebraveenough.com/blog/2018/1/4/battling-built-in-bias.

18. Tamar Lewin, "Nude Pictures Are Ruled Sexual Harassment," *The New York Times*, January 23, 1991, 14, https://www.nytimes.com/1991/01/23/us/nude-pictures-are-ruled-sexual-harassment.html.

19. Deborah Ann Campbell, *The Evolution of Sexual Harassment Case Law in Canada* (Kingston, ON: Queens University Industrial Relations Centre, 1992), 10, https://irc.queensu.ca/the-evolution-of-sexual-harassment-case-law-in-canada/.

20. Elizabeth Rollins Epperly, "Power and the Woman President," *University Affairs*, September 11, 2017, http://www.universityaffairs.ca/features/feature-article/power-woman-president/.

21. Suzannah Weiss, "16 Women in Tech on Their Experiences with Workplace Sexism," Bustle, January 8, 2019, https://www.bustle.com/p/16-women-in-tech-on-their-experiences-with-workplace-sexism-15568057.

22. Kara Noreika, "Yep. I Cried in the Bathroom," Medium, December 26, 2017, https://medium.com/@karamelg1/yep-i-cried-in-the-bathroom-920 31c2e08b3.

23. Amy B. Diehl and Leanne M. Dzubinski, "When People Assume You're Not in Charge Because You're a Woman," *Harvard Business Review*, December 22, 2021, https://hbr.org/2021/12/when-people-assume-youre-not-in-charge-because-youre-a-woman.

24. Tina Mickelson, "My Perspective on Gender Bias," *Southern California Golf Association FORE Her*, August 2, 2019, http://www.scga.org/fore-her/Content/my-perspective-on-gender-bias.

25. Diehl and Dzubinski, "When People Assume You're Not in Charge Because You're a Woman."

26. Diehl and Dzubinski, "When People Assume You're Not in Charge Because You're a Woman."

27. Diehl and Dzubinski, "When People Assume You're Not in Charge Because You're a Woman."

28. Diehl and Dzubinski, "An Overview of Gender-Based Leadership Barriers," 277; Dzubinski, *Playing by the Rules: How Women Lead in Evangelical Mission Organizations*, 52, 175.

29. Laura Turner, "The Religious Reasons Mike Pence Won't Eat Alone with Women Don't Add Up," *The Washington Post*, March 30, 2017, https://www.washingtonpost.com/news/acts-of-faith/wp/2017/03/30/the-religious-reasons-mike-pence-wont-eat-alone-with-women-dont-add-up/.

30. Rebecca Korzec, "The Glass Ceiling in Law Firms: A Form of Sex-Based Discrimination," *Journal of Employment Discrimination Law* 2, no. 3 (2000): 253, https://ssrn.com/abstract=1418046.

31. Kim Elsesser and Letitia Anne Peplau, "The Glass Partition: Obstacles to Cross-Sex Friendships at Work," *Human Relations* 59, no. 8 (2006): 1094, https://doi.org/10.1177/0018726706068783.

32. Susan Chira, "Why Women Aren't C.E.O.s, According to Women Who Almost Were," *The New York Times*, July 21, 2017, https://www.nytimes.com/2017/07/21/sunday-review/women-ceos-glass-ceiling.html.

33. Mary Kathryn Paynter, "I Spoke up Like This," li.st, 2017, accessed December 30, 2019, https://li.st/marykathryn/i-spoke-up-like-this-4fp0VvdqneQjbc69J6ZhxU.

34. Leanne M. Dzubinski, M. Elizabeth Lewis Hall, and Richard L. Starcher, "The Stained-Glass Partition: Cross-Sex Collegial Relationships in Christian Academia," *Christian Higher Education* 20, no. 3 (2021): 184, https://doi.org/10.1080/15363759.2020.1756532.

35. Dzubinski, Hall, and Starcher, "The Stained-Glass Partition: Cross-Sex Collegial Relationships in Christian Academia," 193.

36. Weiss, "16 Women in Tech on Their Experiences with Workplace Sexism."

37. Rosabeth Moss Kanter, "Some Effects of Proportions on Group Life: Skewed Sex Ratios and Responses to Token Women," *American Journal of Sociology* 82, no. 5 (1977): 966, 70–71, https://doi.org/10.1086/226425

38. Amy B. Diehl and Leanne M. Dzubinski, "Making the Invisible Visible: A Cross-Sector Analysis of Gender-Based Leadership Barriers," *Human Resource Development Quarterly* 27, no. 2 (2016): 195, https://doi.org/10.1002/hrdq.21248.

39. Amit Chowdhry, "Microsoft CEO Satya Nadella Apologizes for Comments on Women's Pay," *Newsweek*, October 10, 2014, https://www.forbes.com/sites/amitchowdhry/2014/10/10/microsoft-ceo-satya-nadella-apologizes-for-comments-on-womens-pay/#b1c3d0c6d2b2. After the backlash, Nadella apologized for his comment.

40. Tara Sophia Mohr, "Why Women Don't Apply for Jobs Unless They're 100% Qualified," *Harvard Business Review*, August 25, 2014, https://hbr.org/2014/08/why-women-dont-apply-for-jobs-unless-theyre-100-qualified.

41. Maria Ignatova, "New Report: Women Apply to Fewer Jobs Than Men, but Are More Likely to Get Hired," *LinkedIn Talent Blog*, March 5, 2019, https://www.linkedin.com/business/talent/blog/talent-acquisition/how-women-find-jobs-gender-report.

42. Danielle Gaucher, Justin Friesen, and Aaron C. Key, "Evidence That Gendered Wording in Job Advertisements Exists and Sustains Gender Inequality," *Journal of Personality and Social Psychology* 101, no. 1 (2011): 109, 25, https://doi.org/10.1037/a0022530.

43. PushPros, "Join the Team," 2020, accessed April 30, 2022, https://pushpros.com/join-the-team/.

44. Diehl and Dzubinski, "An Overview of Gender-Based Leadership Barriers," 280.

45. Cosimo Giovine (@beerandcandy), "I learned to address a classroom of students with gender neutral words during my first day teaching. I said, 'Hey guys' and one student said 'I'm a girl' and rolled her eyes so hard I gasped." Twitter, January 29, 2022, https://twitter.com/beerandcandy/status/1487444211481808899.

46. Lila Ralston (@epicdemiologist), "One of my co-workers calls all co-workers of any gender 'dude.' He's in his 30s." Twitter, March 7, 2021, https://twitter.com/epicdemiologist/status/1368582829148344321.

47. MD (@YourVoiceMD) Ronda Alexander, "It hurts most when it's an organization/group composed entirely of women. I'd like to add to your list a fave from the Pittsburgh, PA region- Yinz." Twitter, March 5, 2021, https://twitter.com/YourVoiceMD/status/1368055671124557824.

48. Jane G. Stout and Nilanjana Dasgupta, "When He Doesn't Mean You: Gender-Exclusive Language as Ostracism," *Personality and Social Psychology Bulletin* 37, no. 6 (2011): 757, https://doi.org/10.1177/0146167211406434.

49. Amy B. Diehl, "'Guys' Is Not Gender-Neutral—Let's Stop Using It Like It Is," *Fast Company*, April 27, 2021, https://www.fastcompany.com/90629391/guys-is-not-gender-neutral-lets-stop-using-it-like-it-is.

50. Wing-Sum Lao (@WingSum_Lao), "#UnconsciousBias episode 502: This morning an anaesthetist walks into the neurosurgery handover meeting and addresses the room with 'Hello Gents.' I'm sure it wasn't intentional, but as the only female neurosurgery reg present I can't help but feel a little excluded." Twitter, January 28, 2022, https://twitter.com/WingSum_Lao/status/1487000404563046401.

51. Hanna Papanek, "Men, Women, and Work: Reflections on the Two-Person Career," *American Journal of Sociology* 78, no. 4 (1973): 852, https://doi.org/10.1086/225406.

52. Michelle Obama, *Becoming* (New York, NY: Crown Publishing Group, 2018), 326.

53. "A Call to Service, a Decision to Lead," *Shippensburg University Magazine*, Fall 2021, 31.

54. Sarah Rumpf, "VP-Elect Harris Confirms 'Second Gentleman' Will Be Her Husband's Official Moniker: 'But I'll Call Him Honey,'" *Mediaite*, December 3, 2020, https://www.mediaite.com/tv/vp-elect-harris-confirms-second-gentleman-will-be-her-husbands-official-moniker-but-ill-call-him-honey/.

55. Darlene Superville, "Jill Biden Heads Back to Classroom as a Working First Lady," AP News, September 7, 2021, https://apnews.com/article/business-jill-biden-6a025ecc48cd6efed9c99ce578fb7fb4; Michelle Garcia,

"The First Lady Has a Huge Job. It's Time She Had a Salary to Match," *Glamour*, April 3, 2019, https://www.glamour.com/story/the-first-lady-should-be-paid.

56. Danielle Kurtzleben, "What Happened to Jill Abramson Shows Everything That Sucks about Being a Woman Leader," Vox, May 14, 2014, https://www.vox.com/2014/5/14/5717926/the-jill-abramson-story-highlights-everything-thats-bad-about-being-a.

57. David Carr and Ravi Somiaya, "*Times* Ousts Its Executive Editor, Elevating Second in Command," *New York Times*, May 15, 2014, https://www.nytimes.com/2014/05/15/business/media/jill-abramson-being-replaced-as-top-editor-at-times.html. Kurtzleben, "What Happened to Jill Abramson Shows Everything That Sucks about Being a Woman Leader."

58. Carr and Somiaya, "*Times* Ousts Its Executive Editor, Elevating Second in Command." Rebecca Traister, "I Sort of Hope We Find Out That Jill Abramson Was Robbing the Cash Register," *The New Republic*, May 14, 2014, https://newrepublic.com/article/117767/jill-abramsons-firing-was-singularly-humiliating.

59. Carr and Somiaya, "*Times* Ousts Its Executive Editor, Elevating Second in Command."

60. Traister, "I Sort of Hope We Find Out That Jill Abramson Was Robbing the Cash Register." A version of this paragraph appeared in Leanne M. Dzubinski, Amy B. Diehl, and Michelle O. Taylor, "Women's Ways of Leading: The Environmental Effect," *Gender in Management: An International Journal* 34, no. 3 (2019): 242, https://doi.org/10.1108/GM-11-2017-0150.

61. Traister, "I Sort of Hope We Find Out That Jill Abramson Was Robbing the Cash Register."

62. Emily Stewart, "Why Struggling Companies Promote Women: The Glass Cliff, Explained," Vox, October 31, 2018, https://www.vox.com/2018/10/31/17960156/what-is-the-glass-cliff-women-ceos.

63. Stephen J. Dubner, "After the Glass Ceiling, a Glass Cliff," February 14, 2018, in *The Secret Life of a C.E.O.*, produced by Freakonomics Radio, podcast audio, http://freakonomics.com/podcast/glass-cliff/.

64. Stewart, "Why Struggling Companies Promote Women: The Glass Cliff, Explained"; Robert Hof, "Yahoo Fires CEO Carol Bartz, Here's Why," *Forbes*, September 6, 2011, https://www.forbes.com/sites/roberthof/2011/09/06/report-yahoo-cans-ceo-carol-bartz-heres-what-went-wrong/.

65. Dubner, *Extra: Carol Bartz Full Interview.*

66. Christy Glass and Alison Cook, "Leading at the Top: Understanding Women's Challenges above the Glass Ceiling," *The Leadership Quarterly* 27, no. 1 (2016): 60, https://doi.org/10.1016/j.leaqua.2015.09.003.

67. Dzubinski, *Playing by the Rules: How Women Lead in Evangelical Mission Organizations*, 52, 138.

68. Diehl and Dzubinski, "An Overview of Gender-Based Leadership Barriers," 277.

69. Solutions adapted from Diehl and Dzubinski, "When People Assume You're Not in Charge Because You're a Woman."

70. Solutions adapted from Diehl, "'Guys' Is Not Gender-Neutral—Let's Stop Using It Like It Is."

CHAPTER 2

1. Michelle Obama, *Becoming* (New York, NY: Crown Publishing Group, 2018), 312.

2. Obama, *Becoming*, 380.

3. Valentina Cartei et al., "'This Is What a Mechanic Sounds Like': Children's Vocal Control Reveals Implicit Occupational Stereotypes," *Psychological Science* 31, no. 8 (2020): 957–58, https://doi.org/10.1177/0956797620929297.

4. University of Sussex, "Jobs for the Boys: How Children Give Voice to Gender Stereotyped Job Roles," *Phys.org*, July 27, 2020, https://phys.org/news/2020-07-jobs-boys-children-voice-gender.html.

5. Rebecca Papin (@RebeccaPapin), "Pilot (to my 5-year-old daughter a few days ago): Do you know you could be a flight attendant when you grow up? 5: I could also own the plane." Twitter, April 12, 2022, https://twitter.com/RebeccaPapin/status/1514033051617009674.

6. Amy B. Diehl and Leanne M. Dzubinski, "An Overview of Gender-Based Leadership Barriers," in *Handbook of Research on Gender and Leadership*, ed. Susan R. Madsen (Northampton, MA: Edward Elgar Publishing, 2017), 274.

7. Susan D'Agostino, "The Architect of Modern Algorithms," *Quanta Magazine*, November 20, 2019, https://www.quantamagazine.org/barbara-liskov-is-the-architect-of-modern-algorithms-20191120/.

8. D'Agostino, "The Architect of Modern Algorithms."

9. Luba Chliwniak, *Higher Education Leadership: Analyzing the Gender Gap*, George Washington University (Washington, DC: ASHE-ERIC Higher Education Report, 1997), 22, https://eric.ed.gov/?id=ED410847.

10. Barbara Miller Solomon, *In the Company of Educated Women: A History of Women and Higher Education in America* (New Haven, CT: Yale University Press, 1985), 47–48.

11. Solomon, *In the Company of Educated Women: A History of Women and Higher Education in America*, 56.

12. Solomon, *In the Company of Educated Women: A History of Women and Higher Education in America*, 56; Genevieve Carlton, "A History of Women in Higher Education," Best Colleges, last modified February 22, 2022, https://www.bestcolleges.com/news/analysis/2021/03/21/history-women-higher-education/.

13. U.S. Department of Education, "Digest of Education Statistics, Table 318.10. Degrees Conferred by Postsecondary Institutions, by Level of Degree and Sex of Student: Selected Years, 1869–70 through 2030–31," National Center for Education Statistics, 2021, accessed July 8, 2022, https://nces.ed.gov/programs/digest/d21/tables/dt21_318.10.asp.

14. Myra Sadker and David Miller Sadker, *Failing at Fairness: How America's Schools Cheat Girls* (New York, NY: Scribner, 2010), 33.

15. U.S. Department of Education, "Digest of Education Statistics, Table 318.10. Degrees Conferred by Postsecondary Institutions, by Level of Degree and Sex of Student: Selected Years, 1869–70 through 2030–31."

16. U.S. Department of Education, "Digest of Education Statistics, Table 322.50. Bachelor's Degrees Conferred to Females by Postsecondary Institutions, by Race/Ethnicity and Field of Study: 2018–19 and 2019–20," National Center for Education Statistics, last modified August 2021, https://nces.ed.gov/programs/digest/d21/tables/dt21_322.50.asp; U.S. Department of Education, "Digest of Education Statistics, Table 322.40. Bachelor's Degrees Conferred to Males by Postsecondary Institutions, by Race/Ethnicity and Field of Study: 2018–19 and 2019–20," National Center for Education Statistics, last modified August 2021, https://nces.ed.gov/programs/digest/d21/tables/dt21_322.40.asp.

17. Tracy Chou, "'I Had So Many Advantages, and I Barely Made It': Pinterest Engineer on Silicon Valley Sexism," Quartz, April 12, 2016, https://qz.com/659196/i-had-so-many-advantages-and-i-barely-made-it-pinterests-tracy-chou-on-sexism-in-tech/.

18. The Triketora Press, "About," 2020, accessed August 22, 2022, https://triketora.com/about/.

19. Nancy L. Cohen, "How to Talk about Feminism in Politics When No One's Asking," *Ms. Magazine*, September 13, 2019, https://msmagazine.com/2019/09/13/how-to-talk-about-feminism-in-politics-when-no-ones-asking/.

20. @NoisyAstronomer, "My friends coined a word: hepeated. For when a woman suggests an idea and it's ignored, but then a guy says the same thing and everyone loves it" Twitter, September 22, 2017, https://twitter.com/NoisyAstronomer/status/911213826527436800.

21. Devon Ivie, "Lena Headey Says She Lost Roles for Not Flirting with Casting Directors," *Glamour*, July 6, 2017, https://www.glamour.com/story /lena-headey-says-she-lost-roles-for-not-flirting-with-casting-directors.

22. Jessica Bennett, "How Not to Be 'Manterrupted' in Meetings," *Time*, January 20, 2015, https://time.com/3666135/sheryl-sandberg-talking-while -female-manterruptions/.

23. *Merriam-Webster*, s.v. "Mansplain," accessed July 16, 2022, https://www .merriam-webster.com/dictionary/mansplain; Merriam-Webster, "Mansplaining," 2020, accessed February 2, 2020, https://www.merriam-webster.com /words-at-play/mansplaining-definition-history.

24. Merriam-Webster, "Mansplaining."

25. Kimberly Weisul, "Why Even a Big Wall Street Career Wasn't Enough for Some Venture Capitalists to Take This," *Inc.*, October 30, 2018, https:// www.inc.com/kimberly-weisul/wall-street-veteran-turned-entrepreneur-sallie -krawcheck-on-raising-money-female.html.

26. Sallie Krawcheck, "The Cost of Devaluing Women," *The New York Times*, December 2, 2017, https://www.nytimes.com/2017/12/02/opinion /sunday/the-cost-of-devaluing-women.html.

27. Ada McVean, "The History of Hysteria," McGill Office for Science and Society, July 31, 2017, https://www.mcgill.ca/oss/article/history-quackery /history-hysteria.

28. Katie Mettler, "As a Prosecutor, Kamala Harris's Doggedness Was Praised. As a Senator, She's Deemed 'Hysterical,'" *The Washington Post*, June 14, 2017, https://www.washingtonpost.com/news/morning-mix/wp/2017/06/14/as-a -prosecutor-kamala-d-harris-doggedness-was-praised-now-shes-hysterical/.

29. Mike Lillis, "Ocasio-Cortez Accosted by GOP Lawmaker over Remarks: 'That Kind of Confrontation Hasn't Ever Happened to Me,'" *The Hill*, July 21, 2020, https://thehill.com/homenews/house/508259-ocaasio-cortez -accosted-by-gop-lawmaker-over-remarks-that-kind-of.

30. David Freedlander, "Kirsten Gillibrand's Moment Has Arrived," *Politico*, December 7, 2017, https://www.politico.com/magazine/story/2017/12/07 /kirsten-gillibrand-profile-feature-sexual-assault-2017-216053.

31. Michael G. Miller and Joseph L. Sutherland, "The Effect of Gender on Interruptions at Congressional Hearings," *American Political Science Review* (2022): 1, https://doi.org/10.1017/S0003055422000260.

32. Li Zhou, "'Mr. Vice President, I'm Speaking': Kamala Harris Repeatedly Shut Down Mike Pence's Interruptions at the Debate," Vox, October 8, 2020, https://www.vox.com/2020/10/8/21507194/mike-pence-interruptions -kamala-harris-vice-presidential-debate.

33. Molly Callahan, "Is There Implicit Gender Bias in the Field of Economics?," *Phys.org*, January 15, 2020, https://phys.org/news/2020-01-implicit-gender-bias-field-economics.html.

34. Callahan, "Is There Implicit Gender Bias in the Field of Economics?"

35. 1 Cor. 14:34–35; 1 Tim. 2:11–12; Armin D. Baum, "Paul's Conflicting Statements on Female Public Speaking (1 Cor. 11:5) and Silence (1 Cor. 14:34–35): A New Suggestion," *Tyndale Bulletin* 65, no. 2 (2014): 253–55, 61–62, 73, https://doi.org/10.53751/001c.29377.

36. Johannes Mirkus, *Mirk's Festial: A Collection of Homilies*, ed. Theodor Erbe (London, UK: Kegan Paul, Trench, Trübner & Co, 1905), 230.

37. Anderson Sumarli, "Op-Ed: Want to See Silicon Valley's Sexism in Action? Just Sit through a Pitch Meeting," *Los Angeles Times*, May 29, 2019, https://www.latimes.com/opinion/op-ed/la-oe-sumarli-sexism-silicon-valley-startups-20190529-story.html.

38. Lydia Price, "Serena Williams, Jennifer Lawrence and 22 More Stars Share Powerful Stories about Sexism in Hollywood," *People*, September 10, 2018, https://people.com/celebrity/sexism-in-hollywood-10-powerful-stories/.

39. Julie Beck, "The Concept Creep of 'Emotional Labor,'" *The Atlantic*, November 26, 2018, https://www.theatlantic.com/family/archive/2018/11/arlie-hochschild-housework-isnt-emotional-labor/576637/.

40. Catie Edmondson, "State Dept. Inquiry into Clinton Emails Finds No Deliberate Mishandling of Classified Information," *The New York Times*, October 18, 2019, https://www.nytimes.com/2019/10/18/us/politics/state-dept-inquiry-clinton-emails.html.

41. Lorraine Ali, "Sundance 2020: 'Hillary' Film Takes on Scandal Allegations, Bias and, Yes, Bernie Too," *Los Angeles Times*, January 25, 2020, https://www.latimes.com/entertainment-arts/tv/story/2020-01-25/review-sundance-2020-hillary-documentary-review.

42. Hillary Rodham Clinton, *What Happened* (New York, NY: Simon & Schuster, 2017), 87–88.

43. Eli Rosenberg, "Alexandria Ocasio-Cortez Wore Clothing, a Journalist Tweeted a Photo, and the Internet Pounced," *The Washington Post*, November 15, 2018, https://www.washingtonpost.com/nation/2018/11/16/eddie-scarry-tweet-about-alexandria-ocasio-cortezs-clothing-is-latest-critique-about-class/.

44. Alex Swoyer, "Exclusive: Self-Declared Socialist AOC Splurges on High-Dollar Hairdo," *The Washington Times*, October 9, 2019, https://www.washingtontimes.com/news/2019/oct/9/alexandria-ocasio-cortez-spends-300-hairdo-last-ta/; Monica Iati, "The Backlash over Ocasio-Cortez's Haircut Shows Women Can't Win When It Comes to Their Appearance, Experts Say,"

The Washington Post, October 11, 2019, https://www.washingtonpost.com/life style/2019/10/11/backlash-over-ocasio-cortezs-haircut-shows-women-cant -win-when-it-comes-their-appearance-experts-say/.

45. Iati, "The Backlash over Ocasio-Cortez's Haircut Shows Women Can't Win When It Comes to Their Appearance, Experts Say."

46. Michele Corriston, "Before Friends, Jennifer Aniston Was Told She Had to Lose 30 Lbs. To Make It in Hollywood," *People*, September 18, 2019, https://people.com/tv/before-friends-jennifer-aniston-was-told-lose-30-lbs/.

47. Price, "Serena Williams, Jennifer Lawrence and 22 More Stars Share Powerful Stories About Sexism in Hollywood."

48. Price, "Serena Williams, Jennifer Lawrence and 22 More Stars Share Powerful Stories About Sexism in Hollywood."

49. Kristina M. W. Mitchell, "It's a Dangerous Business, Being a Professor," *The Chronicle of Higher Education*, June 15, 2017, https://www.chronicle.com /article/It-s-a-Dangerous-Business/240336/.

50. Lara Bazelon, "What It Takes to Be a Trial Lawyer If You're Not a Man," *The Atlantic*, September, 2018, https://www.theatlantic.com/magazine /archive/2018/09/female-lawyers-sexism-courtroom/565778/.

51. Yoonji Han, "From 'Vanilla' Skirt Suits to 'Too-Tight' Shirts: Female Lawyers Describe How It's Impossible to Win When It Comes to Professional Dress Codes," Business Insider, June 22, 2021, https://www.business insider.com/female-lawyers-dress-codes-law-firm-court-discrimination-sexism -2021-6.

52. Lacey Rose, "Oprah Talks Apple Plans, '60 Minutes' Exit, 'Leaving Neverland' Backlash and Mayor Pete 'Buttabeep, Buttaboop,'" *The Hollywood Reporter*, April 30, 2019, https://www.hollywoodreporter.com/features/oprah -winfrey-talks-apple-plans-60-minutes-split-2020-election-1205311.

53. Alan Pergament, "In Buffalo, Norah O'Donnell Is Less 'Game-Changer' and More 'Channel-Changer,'" *The Buffalo News*, August 6, 2019, https:// buffalonews.com/2019/08/06/in-buffalo-odonnell-is-less-game-changer-and -more-channel-changer/.

54. Erica Gonzales, "25 Celebrity Women on Gender Inequality in Holly- wood," *Harper's Bazaar*, March 8, 2017, https://www.harpersbazaar.com /culture/a12666/sexism-in-hollywood/.

55. "What Are the Biggest Challenges You've Faced as a Female Leader?," *Chronicle of Higher Education*, November 25, 2018, A8, https://www.chronicle .com/article/What-Are-the-Biggest/245151.

56. Ersilia M. DeFilippis, "Putting the 'She' in Doctor," *JAMA Internal Medicine* 178, no. 3 (2018): 323–24, https.//doi.org/10.1001/jamainternmed .2017.8362.

57. Bazelon, "What It Takes to Be a Trial Lawyer If You're Not a Man."

58. Lara Devgan, "The Problem with the Way Women Speak," The Doctor Weighs In, October 10, 2018, https://thedoctorweighsin.com/problem-with-the-way-women-speak/.

59. Devgan, "The Problem with the Way Women Speak."

60. Tina Tallon, "A Century of 'Shrill': How Bias in Technology Hurts Women's Voices," *The New Yorker*, September 3, 2019, https://www.new yorker.com/culture/cultural-comment/a-century-of-shrill-how-bias-in-tech nology-has-hurt-womens-voices.

61. Leanne M. Dzubinski, *Playing by the Rules: How Women Lead in Evangelical Mission Organizations*, vol. 52 (Eugene, OR: Pickwick Publications, 2021), 137.

62. Amy B. Diehl and Leanne M. Dzubinski, "Making the Invisible Visible: A Cross-Sector Analysis of Gender-Based Leadership Barriers," *Human Resource Development Quarterly* 27, no. 2 (2016): 185, https://doi.org/10.1002/hrdq.21248.

63. Emily Crockett, "The Amazing Tool That Women in the White House Used to Fight Gender Bias," Vox, September 14, 2016, https://www.vox.com/2016/9/14/12914370/white-house-obama-women-gender-bias-amplification.

CHAPTER 3

1. Rachel Donadio, "The Coming Setback for Women in the Workplace," *The Atlantic*, May 28, 2020, https://www.theatlantic.com/international/archive/2020/05/france-women-workplace-coronavirus-pandemic/612136/.

2. Gladys Lopez-Acevedo et al., "How Decline in Demand for Apparel Affects Poor Women in Bangladesh," *World Bank Blogs*, May 13, 2020, https://blogs.worldbank.org/endpovertyinsouthasia/how-decline-demand-apparel-affects-poor-women-bangladesh; Emily Stewart, "Women Are Burned Out at Work and at Home," Vox, May 18, 2020, https://www.vox.com/policy-and-politics/2020/5/18/21260209/facebook-sheryl-sandberg-interview-lean-in-women-coronavirus.

3. Colleen Flaherty, "No Room of One's Own," *Inside Higher Ed*, April 21, 2020, https://www.insidehighered.com/news/2020/04/21/early-journal-submission-data-suggest-covid-19-tanking-womens-research-productivity.

4. Misty L. Heggeness and Jason M. Fields, "Working Moms Bear Brunt of Home Schooling While Working during COVID-19," U.S. Census Bureau,

August 18, 2020, https://www.census.gov/library/stories/2020/08/parents
-juggle-work-and-child-care-during-pandemic.html.

5. Jens Peter Andersen et al., "COVID-19 Medical Papers Have Fewer
Women First Authors Than Expected," *eLife* 9 (2020): 1, 3, https://doi.org
/10.7554/eLife.58807.

6. R. Waismel-Manor, V. Wasserman, and O. Shamir-Balderman, "No
Room of Her Own: Married Couples' Negotiation of Workspace at Home
during COVID-19," *Sex Roles* 85 (2021): 636, https://doi.org/10.1007/s11199
-021-01246-1.

7. Virginia Woolfe, *A Room of One's Own* (London, UK: Hogarth Press,
1935 [1929]), 5.

8. Flaherty, "No Room of One's Own."

9. Julie Kashen, Sarah Jane Glynn, and Amanda Novello, *How COVID-19
Sent Women's Workforce Progress Backward* (Washington, DC: Center for American Progress, October 30, 2020), 1–2, https://www.americanprogress.org
/issues/women/reports/2020/10/30/492582/covid-19-sent-womens-work
force-progress-backward/; Andrea Hsu, Kathryn Anne Edwards, and Farida
Mercedes, "Why the Pandemic Is Forcing So Many Women to Leave Their
Jobs," interview by Michel Martin, *All Things Considered*, November 14, 2020,
https://www.npr.org/2020/11/14/935018298/why-the-pandemic-is-forcing
-so-many-women-to-leave-their-jobs.

10. Hsu, Edwards, and Mercedes interview by Michel Martin, *All Things
Considered*.

11. Jessica Calarco, "'Other Countries Have Social Safety Nets. The U.S.
Has Women,'" interview by Anne Helen Petersen, *Culture Study*, November 11, 2020, https://annehelen.substack.com/p/other-countries-have-social
-safety.

12. U.S. Department of Labor, "Table 3. Time Spent in Selected Primary
Activities, by Selected Characteristics, Averages for May to December, 2019 and
2020, last modified July 22, 2021, https://www.bls.gov/news.release/archives
/atus_07222021.htm; U.S. Department of Labor, "Table 7. Time Adults Spent
Caring for Household Children as a Primary Activity, by Sex of Childcare
Provider and Age of Youngest Child, Averages for May to December, 2019
and 2020," last modified July 22, 2021, https://www.bls.gov/news.release
/archives/atus_07222021.htm.

13. Ainsley Harris, "Why 'Flexibility' May Be the Least Helpful Thing
Companies Can Offer Working Parents Right Now," *Fast Company*, December 4, 2020, https://www.fastcompany.com/90581275/why-flexibility-may-be
-the-least-helpful-thing-a-company-could-offer-a-working-parent-right-now.

14. Anneken Tappe, "A Shocking Number of Women Dropped Out of the Workforce Last Month," CNN Business, October 8, 2020, https://www.cnn.com/2020/10/07/economy/women-workforce-coronavirus/index.html.

15. Andrea Hsu, "'This Is Too Much': Working Moms Are Reaching the Breaking Point during the Pandemic," NPR, September 29, 2020, https://www.npr.org/2020/09/29/918127776/this-is-too-much-working-moms-are-reaching-the-breaking-point-during-the-pandemi.

16. Hsu, "'This Is Too Much': Working Moms Are Reaching the Breaking Point during the Pandemic."

17. Hsu, "'This Is Too Much': Working Moms Are Reaching the Breaking Point during the Pandemic."

18. Benjamin Hansen, Joseph J. Sabia, and Jessamyn Schaller, "Schools, Job Flexibility, and Married Women's Labor Supply: Evidence from the COVID-19 Pandemic," *National Bureau of Economic Research Working Paper Series* No. 29660 (2022): 15, https://doi.org/10.3386/w29660.

19. Raymond A. Noe, "Women and Mentoring: A Review and Research Agenda," *Academy of Management Review* 13, no. 1 (1988): 65, https://doi.org/10.2307/258355.

20. Herminia Ibarra, "A Lack of Sponsorship Is Keeping Women from Advancing into Leadership," *Harvard Business Review*, August 19, 2019, https://hbr.org/2019/08/a-lack-of-sponsorship-is-keeping-women-from-advancing-into-leadership.

21. Heather Foust-Cummings, Sarah Dinolfo, and Jennifer Kohler, *Sponsoring Women to Success* (New York, NY: Catalyst, April 17, 2011), 3–6, https://www.catalyst.org/research/sponsoring-women-to-success/.

22. Foust-Cummings, Dinolfo, and Kohler, *Sponsoring Women to Success*, 1.

23. McKinsey & Company, "Women in the Workplace 2019," 2019, https://womenintheworkplace.com/Women_in_the_Workplace_2019.pdf.

24. Amy B. Diehl and Leanne M. Dzubinski, "An Overview of Gender-Based Leadership Barriers," in *Handbook of Research on Gender and Leadership*, ed. Susan R. Madsen (Northampton, MA: Edward Elgar Publishing, 2017), 277.

25. David Walker, "Sexism in the Photo Industry: Can't We Do Better?" *Photo District News*, September 4, 2017, https://www.pdnonline.com/features/industry-updates/sexism-photo-industry-cant-better.

26. Jessica Wragg, "How I Fight Sexism as One of the Few Female Butchers in a Male-Dominated Industry," *Good Morning America*, August 15, 2019, https://www.goodmorningamerica.com/living/story/fight-sexism-female-butchers-male-dominated-industry-64782954.

27. Amber L. Stephenson et al., "An Exploration of Gender Bias Affecting Women in Medicine," in *The Contributions of Health Care Management to Grand*

Health Care Challenges (Advances in Health Care Management, Vol. 20), ed. Jennifer L. Hefner and Ingrid Nembhard (Bingley, UK: Emerald Publishing Limited, 2021), 88.

28. Elizabeth A. Edwardsen, "First Person: An EM Career Marked by Ingrained Gender Bias," *Emergency Medicine News* 41, no. 11 (2019): 30, https://journals.lww.com/em-news/Fulltext/2019/11000/First_Person__An_EM_Career_Marked_by_Ingrained.24.aspx.

29. Tsedale M. Melaku, "Why Women and People of Color in Law Still Hear 'You Don't Look Like a Lawyer,'" *Harvard Business Review*, August 7, 2019, https://hbr.org/2019/08/why-women-and-people-of-color-in-law-still-hear-you-dont-look-like-a-lawyer.

30. Association for Psychological Science, "Workplace Ostracism More Distressing than Harassment," June 13, 2014, https://www.psychologicalscience.org/news/minds-business/workplace-ostracism-more-distressing-than-harassment.html.

31. Diehl and Dzubinski, "An Overview of Gender-Based Leadership Barriers," 276.

32. Leanne M. Dzubinski, M. Elizabeth Lewis Hall, and Richard L. Starcher, "The Stained-Glass Partition: Cross-Sex Collegial Relationships in Christian Academia," *Christian Higher Education* 20, no. 3 (2021): 184, https://doi.org/10.1080/15363759.2020.1756532.

33. Alice Silverberg, "Changing Places," *Alice's Adventures in Numberland* (blog), September 18, 2017, https://numberlandadventures.blogspot.com/2017/09/changing-places.html.

34. Roma Torre, "I Was the Face of NYC News for 27 Years. Now I'm Being Pushed Aside Because I'm a 61-Year-Old Woman," *Fast Company*, July 1, 2019, https://www.fastcompany.com/90370405/i-was-the-face-of-nyc-news-for-27-years-now-im-being-pushed-aside-because-im-a-61-year-old-woman.

35. Melena Ryzik, "How Saying #MeToo Changed Their Lives," *The New York Times*, June 28, 2018, https://www.nytimes.com/interactive/2018/06/28/arts/metoo-movement-stories.html.

36. Susan Chira and Catrin Einhorn, "How Tough Is It to Change a Culture of Harassment? Ask Women at Ford," *The New York Times*, December 19, 2017, https://www.nytimes.com/interactive/2017/12/19/us/ford-chicago-sexual-harassment.html.

37. Chira and Einhorn, "How Tough Is It to Change a Culture of Harassment? Ask Women at Ford."

38. Sarah Green Carmichael, "Boston Has Eliminated Sexism in the Workplace. Right?," *Boston*, July 23, 2017, https://www.bostonmagazine.com/news/2017/07/23/sexism-workplace/.

39. Walker, "Sexism in the Photo Industry: Can't We Do Better?"
40. Adapted from Stephenson et al., "An Exploration of Gender Bias Affecting Women in Medicine," 91.

CHAPTER 4

1. Ali Montag, "Here's What Oprah Did When She Found Out Her Male Co-Worker Was Making More Money Than Her," CNBC, August 28, 2018, https://www.cnbc.com/2018/06/01/what-oprah-winfrey-did-when-her-male-co-worker-was-making-more-money.html.
2. Joan C. Williams, "Stop Asking Women of Color to Do Unpaid Diversity Work," Bloomberg, April 14, 2022, https://www.bloomberg.com/opinion/articles/2022-04-14/women-of-color-in-tech-get-saddled-with-more-office-housework.
3. Madeline E. Heilman and Julie J. Chen, "Same Behavior, Different Consequences: Reactions to Men's and Women's Altruistic Citizenship Behavior," *Journal of Applied Psychology* 90, no. 3 (2005): 431, https://doi.org/10.1037/0021-9010.90.3.431.
4. Joan C. Williams and Marina Multhaup, "For Women and Minorities to Get Ahead, Managers Must Assign Work Fairly," *Harvard Business Review*, March 5, 2018, https://hbr.org/2018/03/for-women-and-minorities-to-get-ahead-managers-must-assign-work-fairly.
5. Ruchika Tulshyan, "Women of Color Get Asked to Do More 'Office Housework.' Here's How They Can Say No," *Harvard Business Review*, April 6, 2018, https://hbr.org/2018/04/women-of-color-get-asked-to-do-more-office-housework-heres-how-they-can-say-no.
6. Williams and Multhaup, "For Women and Minorities to Get Ahead, Managers Must Assign Work Fairly."
7. Sheryl Sandberg and Adam Grant, "Madam C.E.O., Get Me a Coffee," *New York Times*, February 8, 2015, https://www.nytimes.com/2015/02/08/opinion/sunday/sheryl-sandberg-and-adam-grant-on-women-doing-office-housework.html.
8. Amy B. Diehl and Leanne M. Dzubinski, "We Need to Talk about Using Pet Names for Women at Work," *Fast Company*, October 29, 2020, https://www.fastcompany.com/90569439/we-need-to-talk-about-using-pet-names-for-women-at-work.
9. Diehl and Dzubinski, "We Need to Talk about Using Pet Names for Women at Work."

10. Marta B. Calás and Linda Smirich, "Dangerous Liaisons: The 'Feminine-in-Management' Meets 'Globalization,'" *Business Horizons* 36, no. 2 (1993): 73, https://doi.org/10.1016/S0007-6813(05)80041-2. The researchers were drawing from material written in the 1930s and arguing that the pattern from the 1930s was present in the 1990s. Our work shows that the same pattern has continued with some aspects subtler now than in 1930.

11. Diehl and Dzubinski, "We Need to Talk about Using Pet Names for Women at Work."

12. Alexandria Ocasio Cortez (@aoc), "In Washington, I usually know my questions of power are getting somewhere when the powerful stop referring to me as 'Congresswoman' and start referring to me as "young lady" instead." Twitter, September 12, 2021, https://twitter.com/AOC/status/1437225 839989510151.

13. Amy B. Diehl and Leanne M. Dzubinski, "We Need to Stop 'Untitling' and 'Uncredentialing' Professional Women," *Fast Company*, January 22, 2021, https://www.fastcompany.com/90596628/we-need-to-stop-untitling-and-un credentialing-professional-women.

14. Jennifer Lycette, "Doctor Title and Gender. The Doctor is In; The Mrs. is Out: Forms of Address toward Female Physicians," *JL Lycette* (blog), June 25, 2017, https://jenniferlycette.com/doctor-title-gender/.

15. Anu Kathiresan, "It's Dr., Not Mrs.," KevinMD.com, July 15, 2019, https://www.kevinmd.com/2019/07/its-dr-not-mrs.html.

16. Caroline Kitchener, "A Female Historian Wrote a Book. Two Male Historians Went on NPR to Talk about It. They Never Mentioned Her Name. It's Sarah Milov," The Lily, July 14, 2019, https://www.thelily.com/a-female -historian-wrote-a-book-two-male-historians-went-on-npr-to-talk-about-it -they-never-mentioned-her-name/.

17. Silke-Maria Weineck, "All Things Ill-Considered: NPR's Sexist Blunder," *The Chronicle of Higher Education*, 2018, https://www.chronicle.com /article/All-Things-Ill-Considered-/243865. NPR later updated the web post about this segment with a correction that listed Dr. Silke-Maria Weineck as the book's coauthor.

18. Amy B. Diehl, Leanne M. Dzubinski, and Amber L. Stephenson, "Never Quite Right: Identity Factors Contributing to Bias and Discrimination Experienced by Women Leaders" (manuscript submitted for publication, December 26, 2022), 25.

19. Madeleine Kim, "11 Things Never to Do in an Interview, According to HR Professionals," M.M.LaFleur: The M Dash, accessed July 3, 2022, https:// mdash.mmlafleur.com/job-interview-dealbreakers.

20. Suzannah Weiss, "16 Women in Tech on Their Experiences with Workplace Sexism," *Bustle*, January 8, 2019, https://www.bustle.com/p/16-women-in-tech-on-their-experiences-with-workplace-sexism-15568057.

21. Weiss, "16 Women in Tech on Their Experiences with Workplace Sexism."

22. Rachel Gutman, "The Origins of Diversity Data in Tech," *The Atlantic*, February 3, 2018, https://www.theatlantic.com/technology/archive/2018/02/the-origins-of-diversity-data-in-tech/552155/.

23. Tracy Chou, "'I Had So Many Advantages, and I Barely Made It': Pinterest Engineer on Silicon Valley Sexism," Quartz, April 12, 2016, https://qz.com/659196/i-had-so-many-advantages-and-i-barely-made-it-pinterests-tracy-chou-on-sexism-in-tech/.

24. Weiss, "16 Women in Tech on Their Experiences with Workplace Sexism."

25. Cammy Pedroja, "Celebs Who Have Spoken Out Publicly about Sexism in Hollywood," The List, 2019, accessed September 8, 2019, https://www.thelist.com/79855/celebs-spoken-publicly-sexism-hollywood/.

26. Lydia Price, "Serena Williams, Jennifer Lawrence and 22 More Stars Share Powerful Stories about Sexism in Hollywood," *People*, September 10, 2018, https://people.com/celebrity/sexism-in-hollywood-10-powerful-stories/.

27. Diehl, Dzubinski, and Stephenson, "Never Quite Right: Identity Factors Contributing to Bias and Discrimination Experienced by Women Leaders," 9.

28. Beth Moore, "A Letter to My Brothers," *The LPM Blog*, May 3, 2018, https://blog.lproof.org/2018/05/a-letter-to-my-brothers.html.

29. Moore, Jessica, "Who Are You Wearing? Celebrity Styles on the Red Carpet." *Hollywood Branded* (blog), May 2, 2022, https://blog.hollywoodbranded.com/who-are-you-wearing-celebrity-styles-on-the-red-carpet.

30. Pedroja, "Celebs Who Have Spoken Out Publicly about Sexism in Hollywood."

31. Jessica Wragg, "How I Fight Sexism as One of the Few Female Butchers in a Male-Dominated Industry," Good Morning America, August 15, 2019, https://www.goodmorningamerica.com/living/story/fight-sexism-female-butchers-male-dominated-industry-64782954.

32. David Walker, "Sexism in the Photo Industry: Can't We Do Better?" *Photo District News*, September 4, 2017, https://www.pdnonline.com/features/industry-updates/sexism-photo-industry-cant-better.

33. Walker, "Sexism in the Photo Industry: Can't We Do Better?"

34. Wharton School of the University of Pennsylvania, "How Gender and Racial Biases Are Hurting Economics," *Knowledge @ Wharton*, March 28, 2019, http://knowledge.wharton.upenn.edu/article/women-economists-bias.

35. Kate Conger, "Exclusive: Here's the Full 10-Page Anti-Diversity Screed Circulating Internally at Google," Gizmodo, August 5, 2017, https://gizmodo .com/exclusive-heres-the-full-10-page-anti-diversity-screed-1797564320.

36. Susan Wojcicki, "Read YouTube CEO Susan Wojcicki's Response to the Controversial Google Anti-Diversity Memo," *Fortune*, August 9, 2017, https://fortune.com/2017/08/09/google-diversity-memo-wojcicki.

37. Nina Totenberg, "Justice Ruth Bader Ginsburg Reflects on the #MeToo Movement: 'It's About Time,'" *Morning Edition*, January 22, 2018, https://www.npr.org/2018/01/22/579595727/justice-ginsburg-shares-her -own-metoo-story-and-says-it-s-about-time.

38. Charlotte Triggs and Stephanie Petit, "Hoda Kotb Says She's 'Not Making Matt Lauer Money' as Today Co-Anchor," *People*, January 3, 2018, https:// people.com/tv/hoda-kotb-not-making-matt-lauer-salary-today-co-anchor/.

39. Demi Moore, *Inside Out* (New York, NY: Harper, 2019), 168.

40. Madeline Berg, "The Highest-Paid Actors 2020," *Forbes*, August 11, 2020, https://www.forbes.com/sites/maddieberg/2020/08/11/the-highest -paid-actors-of-2020-dwayne-johnson-ryan-reynolds/. Madeline Berg, "The Highest-Paid Actresses 2020: Small Screen Stars Like Sofia Vergara, Ellen Pompeo and Elisabeth Moss Shine," *Forbes*, October 2, 2020, https://www.forbes.com /sites/maddieberg/2020/10/02/the-highest-paid-actresses-2020-small-screen -stars-like-sofia-vergara-ellen-pompeo-and-elisabeth-moss-shine/.

41. Berg, "The Highest-Paid Actresses 2020: Small Screen Stars Like Sofia Vergara, Ellen Pompeo and Elisabeth Moss Shine."

42. Erin Donnelly, "Is This Why Jennifer Lawrence Got Paid Less for American Hustle?" Refinery29, 2015, https://www.refinery29.com/en-us /2015/10/95960/jennifer-lawrence-american-hustle-pay-gap.

43. Robin Bleiweis, Jocelyn Frye, and Rose Khattar, "Women of Color and the Wage Gap," Center for American Progress, November 17, 2021, https:// www.americanprogress.org/article/women-of-color-and-the-wage-gap/.

44. U.S. Census Bureau, *Table P-8. Age--People by Median Income and Sex* (Washington, DC: U.S. Census Bureau, November 9, 2021), https://www2 .census.gov/programs-surveys/cps/tables/time-series/historical-income-people /p08ar.xlsx.

45. U.S. Department of Labor, "Labor Force Statistics from the Current Population Survey: 39. Median Weekly Earnings of Full-Time Wage and Salary Workers by Detailed Occupation and Sex," U.S. Bureau of Labor Statistics, last modified January 20, 2022, https://www.bls.gov/cps/cpsaat39.htm.

46. Ann Crittenden, *The Price of Motherhood: Why the Most Important Job in the World Is Still the Least Valued* (New York, NY: Metropolitan Books, 2001), 65; Rebecca Gale, "Should Unpaid Labor Like Childcare Be Part of the GDP? One Group Is Trying to Make It Happen," *Fortune*, April 28, 2022, https://fortune .com/2022/04/28/eve-rodsky-unpaid-labor-part-of-gdp-by-2030/.

47. Kaiser Family Foundation, "Nonelderly Adult Poverty Rate by Gender," 2021, accessed January 29, 2023, https://www.kff.org/other/state -indicator/adult-poverty-rate-by-gender.

48. Isis Gaddis and Kathleen Beegle, "#10 How Are the Incomes of Women and Men Affected by COVID-19 (Coronavirus)?," May 6, 2020, https://www .jobsanddevelopment.org/how-are-the-incomes-of-women-and-men-affected -by-covid-19-coronavirus/; Caitlyn Collins et al., "COVID-19 and the Gender Gap in Work Hours," *Gender, Work & Organization* 28, no. S1 (2020): 101, https://doi.org/10.1111/gwao.12506. Using data from the U.S. Current Population Study, the Collins et al., study showed that mothers of young children reduced their working hours four to five times more than fathers from February to April 2020.

49. Jasmine Tucker, *Men Have Now Recouped Their Pandemic-Related Labor Force Losses While Women Lag Behind* (Washington, DC: National Women's Law Center, February 2022), 1, https://nwlc.org/wp-content/uploads/2022/02 /January-Jobs-Day-updated.pdf.

50. The World Bank, "Gender and COVID-19 (Coronavirus)," April 10, 2020, https://www.worldbank.org/en/topic/gender/brief/gender-and-covid -19-coronavirus; United Nations, "UN Report Finds COVID-19 Is Reversing Decades of Progress on Poverty, Healthcare and Education," July 7, 2020, https://www.un.org/development/desa/en/news/sustainable/sustainable -development-goals-report-2020.html.

51. United Nations, *The World's Women 2015* (New York, NY: Department of Economic and Social Affairs United Nations, Statistics Division, 2015), 23, https://unstats.un.org/unsd/gender/downloads/worldswomen2015_report.pdf.

52. U.S. Census Bureau, "National Poverty in America Awareness Month: January 2022," last modified January 21, 2022, https://www.census.gov/news room/stories/poverty-awareness-month.html.

53. Oxfam International, "Why the Majority of the World's Poor Are Women," 2021, accessed February 17, 2022, https://www.oxfam.org/en/even -it/why-majority-worlds-poor-are-women.

54. AARP and National Alliance for Caregiving, *Caregiving in the United States 2020* (Washington, DC: AARP, May 2020), 10, https://doi.org/10.26419 /ppi.00103.001; Karren J. Pope-Onwukwe, "Economic Challenges Facing Caregivers," March 30, 2022, https://www.americanbar.org/groups/senior

_lawyers/publications/voice_of_experience/2022/march-2022/economic-challenges-facing-caregivers/.

55. Social Security Administration, *What Every Woman Should Know* (Washington, DC: Social Security Administration, January 2021), 1, https://www.ssa.gov/pubs/EN-05-10127.pdf.

56. Social Security Administration, *Fast Facts and Figures about Social Security, 2021* (Washington, DC: Social Security Administration, September 2021), 20, https://www.ssa.gov/policy/docs/chartbooks/fast_facts/2021/fast_facts21.pdf.

57. Nicholas Fandos, Erin Schaff, and Emily Cochrane, "'Senate Being Locked Down': Inside a Harrowing Day at the Capitol," *The New York Times*, January 7, 2021, https://www.nytimes.com/2021/01/07/us/politics/capitol-lockdown.html.

58. American-Israeli Cooperative Enterprise, "Jewish Virtual Library: Witness," 2008, accessed February 17, 2022, https://www.jewishvirtuallibrary.org/witness.

59. T. Christian Miller and Ken Armstrong, "An Unbelievable Story of Rape," ProPublica, December 16, 2015, https://www.propublica.org/article/false-rape-accusations-an-unbelievable-story; A. Thomas Morris, "The Empirical, Historical and Legal Case against the Cautionary Instruction: A Call for Legislative Reform," *Duke Law Journal* 1988, no. 1 (1988): 155, https://doi.org/10.2307/1372549.

60. Miranda Fricker, *Epistemic Injustice Power and the Ethics of Knowing* (New York, NY: Oxford University Press, 2007), 9–17.

61. Liza Mundy, "I Rewatched Anita Hill's Testimony. So Much Has Changed. So Much Hasn't," *Politico*, September 23, 2018, https://www.politico.com/magazine/story/2018/09/23/rewatched-anita-hill-testimony-kavanaugh-metoo-220526.

62. Emily Tillet, Grace Segers, and Kathryn Watson, "Christine Blasey Ford, Brett Kavanaugh Hearing: The Top Takeaways," CBS News, September 27, 2018, https://www.cbsnews.com/news/christine-blasey-ford-brett-kavanaugh-hearing-sexual-assault-allegations-top-takeaways/.

63. Donald J. Trump (@realDonaldTrump), "I have no doubt that, if the attack on Dr. Ford was as bad as she says, charges would have been immediately filed with local Law Enforcement Authorities by either her or her loving parents. I ask that she bring those filings forward so that we can learn date, time, and place!" Twitter, September 21, 2018, https://twitter.com/realDonaldTrump/status/1043126336473055235.

64. Donald J. Trump (@realDonaldTrump), "Judge Kavanaugh showed America exactly why I nominated him His testimony was powerful, honest, and riveting. Democrats' search and destroy strategy is disgraceful and this

process has been a total sham and effort to delay, obstruct, and resist. The Senate must vote!" Twitter, September 27, 2018, https://twitter.com/realDonald Trump/status/1045444544068812800.

65. Tim Mak, "Kavanaugh Accuser Christine Blasey Ford Continues Receiving Threats, Lawyers Say," NPR, November 8, 2018, https://www.npr.org /2018/11/08/665407589/kavanaugh-accuser-christine-blasey-ford-continues -receiving-threats-lawyers-say.

66. Yoree Koh, "Silicon Valley Scandals Open Dialogue between Male VCs and Female Founders," *Wall Street Journal*, August 24, 2017, https://www .wsj.com/articles/sexual-harassment-scandals-lead-to-tough-conversations-in -silicon-valley-1503567006.

67. Arghavan Salles, "Gender Bias Narratives in Medicine," *Physician's Weekly*, July 23, 2019, https://www.physiciansweekly.com/gender-bias-narratives -in-medicine/.

68. Some diminishment strategies adapted from Diehl and Dzubinski, "We Need to Talk about Using Pet Names for Women at Work"; Diehl and Dzubinski, "We Need to Stop 'Untitling' and 'Uncredentialing' Professional Women."

CHAPTER 5

1. Amber L. Stephenson, Leanne M. Dzubinski, and Amy B. Diehl, "A Cross-Industry Comparison of How Women Leaders Experience Gender Bias," *Personnel Review* (2022): 13, https://doi.org/10.1108/PR-02-2021-0091.

2. Susan J. Fowler, "Reflecting on One Very, Very Strange Year at Uber," *Susan Fowler* (blog), February 19, 2017, https://www.susanjfowler.com/blog /2017/2/19/reflecting-on-one-very-strange-year-at-uber.

3. Fowler, "Reflecting on One Very, Very Strange Year at Uber."

4. Susan Fowler, "I Spoke Out Against Sexual Harassment at Uber. The Aftermath Was More Terrifying than Anything I Faced Before," *Time*, February 17, 2020, https://time.com/5784464/susan-fowler-book-uber-sexual -harassment/.

5. Fowler, "I Spoke Out Against Sexual Harassment at Uber. The Aftermath Was More Terrifying than Anything I Faced Before."

6. Mark Harris, "Meredith Vieira's Feud with '60 Minutes,'" *Entertainment Weekly*, March 15, 1991, https://ew.com/article/1991/03/15/meredith -vieiras-feud-60-minutes/.

7. Alexia Fernández Campbell, "They Did Everything Right—and Still Hit the Glass Ceiling. Now, These Women Are Suing America's Top Companies

for Equal Pay," Vox, December 10, 2019, https://www.vox.com/the-high
light/2019/12/3/20948425/equal-pay-lawsuits-pay-gap-glass-ceiling.

8. Equal Rights Advocates, "Know Your Rights at Work: Gender Discrimination at Work," 2019, accessed May 18, 2022, https://www.equalrights
.org/issue/economic-workplace-equality/discrimination-at-work/.

9. Elise Gould, "8 Years of the Lilly Ledbetter Fair Pay Act," Working
Economics Blog, Economic Policy Institute, April 26, 2017, https://www.epi
.org/blog/8-years-of-the-lilly-ledbetter-fair-pay-act/.

10. Campbell, "They Did Everything Right—and Still Hit the Glass Ceiling.
Now, These Women Are Suing America's Top Companies for Equal Pay."

11. Leena Rao, "Kleiner Perkins on the Past, Present and Future,"
TechCrunch, October 13, 2012, https://techcrunch.com/2012/10/13/kleiner
-perkins-on-the-past-present-and-future/.

12. Connie Loizos, "Ellen Pao: I Won't Appeal My Case against Kleiner Perkins," TechCrunch, September 10, 2015, https://techcrunch.com/2015/09/10
/ellen-pao-i-wont-appeal-my-case-against-kleiner-perkins/.

13. Chris Isidore, "Ellen Pao Ordered to Pay Kleiner Perkins $276,000 in Le-
gal Costs," CNN Business, June 19, 2015, https://money.cnn.com/2015/06/18
/technology/ellen-pao-kleiner-perkins-legal-costs/index.html.

14. Loizos, "Ellen Pao: I Won't Appeal My Case against Kleiner Perkins."
Kleiner Perkins waived the requirement for Pao to pay their legal fees but only
after she dropped the appeal. Terry Collins, "Done Deal: Ellen Pao Doesn't
Have to Pay Kleiner Perkins' Legal Fees," CNET, September 23, 2015, https://
www.cnet.com/tech/tech-industry/done-deal-ellen-pao-doesnt-have-to-pay
-kleiner-perkins/.

15. Patrick Dorrian and Paige Smith, "Walmart Women Must Pursue Pay,
Promotion Bias Suits Solo," Bloomberg Law, October 28, 2019, https://news
.bloomberglaw.com/daily-labor-report/walmart-women-must-pursue-pay
-promotion-bias-suits-individually.

16. Jonathan D. Silver, "Jury Awards Woman More than $13 Million in
Work Discrimination Case," *Pittsburgh Post-Gazette*, April 20, 2015, https://
www.post-gazette.com/business/career-workplace/2015/04/20/Jury-awards
-woman-more-than-13M-in-employment-bias-case-pittsburgh/stories
/201504200130.

17. Brooks Barnes, "A Suit against Disney Claims Unequal Pay for Women,"
The New York Times, April 2, 2019, https://www.nytimes.com/2019/04/02
/business/media/disney-gender-discrimination-lawsuit.html.

18. Brooks Barnes, "Pay Discrimination Suit against Disney Adds Pay Secrecy Claim," *The New York Times*, March 18, 2021, https://www.nytimes.com
/2021/03/18/business/media/disney-pay-discrimination-lawsuit.html.

19. American Association of University Women, "Freyd V. University of Oregon," September 2019, https://www.aauw.org/resources/legal/laf/current-cases/freyd-v-university-of-oregon/.

20. Meerah Powell, "Retired Professor and University of Oregon Settle Longstanding Lawsuit," Oregon Public Broadcasting, July 17, 2021, https://opb.org/article/2021/07/17/university-oregon-professor-settle-equal-pay-lawsuit/.

21. Emily Peck, "Staffers Say Sexism Runs Deep at the *Washington Post*," HuffPost, February 3, 2020, https://www.huffpost.com/entry/women-washington-post-sexism-culture_n_5e34b8a3c5b611ac94d4aa89.

22. Barbara Rodriguez, "Athletes Don't Have Pregnancy Protections. Here's Why That Could Finally Change," The 19th, November 17, 2021, https://19thnews.org/2021/11/athletes-pregnancy-protections-contract/.

23. Adam Goucher, "It's Time for Me to Use My Voice," *Kara Goucher* (blog), August 25, 2019, http://www.karagoucher.com/guest-blogger/.

24. Amy B. Diehl and Leanne M. Dzubinski, "Making the Invisible Visible: A Cross-Sector Analysis of Gender-Based Leadership Barriers," *Human Resource Development Quarterly* 27, no. 2 (2016): 189, https://doi.org/10.1002/hrdq.21248.

25. Roma Torre, "I Was the Face of NYC News for 27 Years. Now I'm Being Pushed Aside Because I'm a 61-Year-Old Woman," *Fast Company*, July 1, 2019, https://www.fastcompany.com/90370405/i-was-the-face-of-nyc-news-for-27-years-now-im-being-pushed-aside-because-im-a-61-year-old-woman.

26. Michael M. Grynbaum, "5 Anchorwomen to Leave NY1 after Settling Discrimination Suit," *The New York Times*, December 31, 2020, https://www.nytimes.com/2020/12/31/business/media/ny1-age-gender-lawsuit.html.

27. Alice Silverberg, "The Meritocracy," *Alice's Adventures in Numberland* (blog), August 11, 2017, https://numberlandadventures.blogspot.com/2017/08/the-meritocracy.html.

28. Kimberle Crenshaw, "Demarginalizing the Intersection of Race and Sex: A Black Feminist Critique of Antidiscrimination Doctrine, Feminist Theory and Antiracist Politics," *University of Chicago Legal Forum* 1989, no. 1 (1989): 142, https://chicagounbound.uchicago.edu/uclf/vol1989/iss1/8/.

29. Brenda Lloyd-Jones, "Implications of Race and Gender in Higher Education Administration: An African American Woman's Perspective," *Advances in Developing Human Resources* 11, no. 5 (2009): 609, https://doi.org/10.1177/1523422309351820.

30. U.S. Equal Employment Opportunity Commission, "Harassment," accessed May 18, 2022, https://www.eeoc.gov/laws/types/harassment.cfm.

31. Chia R. Feldblum and Victoria A. Lipnic, *Select Task Force on the Study of Harassment in the Workplace* (Washington, DC: U.S. Equal Employment Op-

portunity Commission, June 2016), https://www.eeoc.gov/select-task-force
-study-harassment-workplace.

32. L. M. Cortina and V. J. Magley, "Raising Voice, Risking Retaliation:
Events Following Interpersonal Mistreatment in the Workplace," *Journal of Occupational Health Psychology* 8, no. 4 (2003): 255, https://doi.org/10.1037/1076
-8998.8.4.247.

33. Tara Golshan, "Study Finds 75 Percent of Workplace Harassment Victims Experienced Retaliation When They Spoke Up," Vox, October 15, 2017,
https://www.vox.com/identities/2017/10/15/16438750/weinstein-sexual
-harassment-facts.

34. Feldblum and Lipnic, *Select Task Force on the Study of Harassment in the
Workplace.*

35. Jennifer L. Berdahl, "Harassment Based on Sex: Protecting Social Status
in the Context of Gender Hierarchy," *Academy of Management Review* 32, no. 2
(2007): 641, 44, 46, https://doi.org/10.5465/amr.2007.24351879.

36. Susan Chira, "Why Women Aren't C.E.O.s, According to Women
Who Almost Were," *The New York Times*, July 21, 2017, https://www.nytimes
.com/2017/07/21/sunday-review/women-ceos-glass-ceiling.html.

37. Lara Bazelon, "What It Takes to Be a Trial Lawyer If You're Not a
Man," *The Atlantic*, September, 2018, https://www.theatlantic.com/magazine
archive/2018/09/female-lawyers-sexism-courtroom/565778/.

38. Project Include, *Remote Work since Covid-19 Is Exacerbating Harm: What
Companies Need to Know and Do* (March 2021), 4, 6, 9, https://projectinclude
.org/assets/pdf/Project-Include-Harassment-Report-0321-F3.pdf.

39. Project Include, *Remote Work since Covid-19 Is Exacerbating Harm: Sum-
mary*, 1, accessed August 21, 2022, https://projectinclude.org/assets/pdf/Project
_Include_Executive_Summary_0321_R4.pdf.

40. Berdahl, "Harassment Based on Sex: Protecting Social Status in the Context of Gender Hierarchy," 641.

41. Julie Carpenter, "How Anita Hill Forever Changed the Way We Talk
about Sexual Harassment," CNN Money, November 9, 2017, https://money
.cnn.com/2017/10/30/pf/anita-hill-sexual-harassment/index.html.

42. U.S. Equal Employment Opportunity Commission, "Laws and Guidance," accessed September 4, 2020, https://www.eeoc.gov/laws-guidance-0;
Liza Mundy, "I Rewatched Anita Hill's Testimony. So Much Has Changed.
So Much Hasn't," Politico, September 23, 2018, https://www.politico.com
/magazine/story/2018/09/23/rewatched-anita-hill-testimony-kavanaugh
-metoo-220526.

43. Carpenter, "How Anita Hill Forever Changed the Way We Talk about
Sexual Harassment."

44. U.S. Equal Employment Opportunity Commission, "Charges Alleging Sex-Based Harassment (Charges Filed with EEOC) FY 2010–FY 2020," accessed February 18, 2022, https://www.eeoc.gov/statistics/charges-alleging-sex-based-harassment-charges-filed-eeoc-fy-2010-fy-2020. Sexual harassment claims fell in 2020 to 6,587 likely due to the COVID-19 pandemic lockdowns that resulted in many people working remotely.

45. Elena Nicolaou and Courtney E. Smith, "A #MeToo Timeline to Show How Far We've Come—and How Far We Need to Go," Refinery29, October 5, 2019, https://www.refinery29.com/en-us/2018/10/212801/me-too-movement-history-timeline-year-weinstein.

46. Catrin Einhorn and Rachel Adams, "The Tipping Equation," *The New York Times*, March 12, 2018, https://www.nytimes.com/interactive/2018/03/11/business/tipping-sexual-harassment.html.

47. Rebecca Ford, "Jennifer Lopez, Scarlett Johansson, Lupita Nyong'o and the Actress Roundtable," *The Hollywood Reporter*, November 13, 2019, https://www.hollywoodreporter.com/movies/movie-features/jennifer-lopez-scarlett-johansson-lupita-nyong-o-drama-actress-roundtable-1254056/.

48. Hadley Freeman, "Geena Davis: 'As Soon as I Hit 40, I Fell Off the Cliff. I Really Did,'" *The Guardian*, August 9, 2020, https://www.theguardian.com/culture/2020/aug/09/geena-davis-as-soon-i-hit-40-i-fell-off-the-cliff-i-really-did; Sara Andrade, "Sharon Stone Talks about Hollywood, #MeToo and Basic Instinct," *Vogue*, August 5, 2019, https://www.vogue.pt/sharon-stone-interview.

49. Andrade, "Sharon Stone Talks about Hollywood, #MeToo and Basic Instinct."

50. Freeman, "Geena Davis: 'As Soon as I Hit 40, I Fell Off the Cliff. I Really Did.'"

51. "When Women Run," FiveThirtyEight, January 29, 2020, https://fivethirtyeight.com/audio-features/when-women-run/.

52. Monica Lewinsky, "Shame and Survival," *Vanity Fair*, June, 2014, https://archive.vanityfair.com/article/2014/6/shame-and-survival; Molly Jong-Fast, "We All Owe Monica Lewinsky an Apology," *Vogue*, September 3, 2021, https://www.vogue.com/article/monica-lewinsky-owed-apology.

53. Lewinsky, "Shame and Survival."

54. Ramin Setoodeh, "Inside Matt Lauer's Secret Relationship with a 'Today' Production Assistant (Exclusive)," *Variety*, December 14, 2017, https://variety.com/2017/tv/news/matt-lauer-today-secret-relationship-production-assistant-1202641040/.

55. Setoodeh, "Inside Matt Lauer's Secret Relationship with a 'Today' Production Assistant (Exclusive)."

56. Hilarie Burton Morgan, *The Rural Diaries: Love, Livestock, and Big Life Lessons Down on Mischief Farm* (New York, NY: HarperOne, 2020), 76; Jackie Strause, "Ben Affleck Groping Claim Revived by Actress Hilarie Burton," *The Hollywood Reporter,* October 11, 2017, https://www.hollywoodreporter.com /news/ben-affleck-groping-claim-revived-by-actress-hilarie-burton-1047677.

57. Einhorn and Adams, "The Tipping Equation."

58. Her, "Women Are Sharing Their Horrible Stories of Sexual Harassment at Work," accessed May 18, 2022, https://www.her.ie/life/women-sharing -horrible-stories-sexual-harassment-work-306581.

59. Her, "Women Are Sharing Their Horrible Stories of Sexual Harassment at Work."

60. Jodie Kantor and Megan Twohey, "Harvey Weinstein Paid Off Sexual Harassment Accusers for Decades," *The New York Times,* October 5, 2017, https://www.nytimes.com/2017/10/05/us/harvey-weinstein-harassment-alle gations.html.

61. Ronan Farrow, "From Aggressive Overtures to Sexual Assault: Harvey Weinstein's Accusers Tell Their Stories," *The New Yorker,* October 10, 2017, https://www.newyorker.com/news/news-desk/from-aggressive-overtures-to -sexual-assault-harvey-weinsteins-accusers-tell-their-stories.

62. BBC News, "Harvey Weinstein Timeline: How the Scandal Unfolded," BBC News, February 24, 2020, https://www.bbc.com/news/entertainment -arts-41594672.

63. BBC News, "Harvey Weinstein Timeline: How the Scandal Unfolded."

64. Nancy Dillon, "Harvey Weinstein Trial Can Include 6 More Accusers, but Not Daryl Hannah or Rose McGowan," *Rolling Stone,* May 11, 2022, https://www.rollingstone.com/tv-movies/tv-movie-news/harvey-weinstein -rape-trial-six-more-accusers-not-daryl-hannah-1351581/.

65. Jodie Kantor and Megan Twohey, "Harvey Weinstein Paid Off Sexual Harassment Accusers for Decades."

66. Irin Carmon and Amelia Schonbek, "Was It Worth It?," The Cut, September 30, 2019, https://www.thecut.com/2019/09/coming-forward-about -sexual-assault-and-what-comes-after.html.

67. Gretchen Carlson, "Gretchen Carlson: Fox News, I Want My Voice Back," *The New York Times,* December 12, 2019, https://www.nytimes .com/2019/12/12/opinion/gretchen-carlson-bombshell-movie.html.

68. Amy B. Wang and Eugene Scott, "Biden Signs Bill Ending Forced Arbitration in Sexual Assault, Harassment Cases " *The Washington Post,* March 3, 2022, https://www.washingtonpost.com/politics/2022/03/03/biden-signs -new-law-ending-forced-arbitration-sex-assault-harassment/.

69. Guidepost Solutions, *The Southern Baptist Convention Executive Committee's Response to Sexual Abuse Allegations and an Audit of the Procedures and Actions of the Credentials Committee* (Washington, DC, May 15, 2022), 3–13, https://static1.squarespace.com/static/6108172d83d55d3c9db4dd67/t/628bfccb599a375bece1f66c/1653341391218/Guidepost+Solutions+Independent+Investigation+Report_.pdf.

70. Guidepost Solutions, *The Southern Baptist Convention Executive Committee's Response to Sexual Abuse Allegations and an Audit of the Procedures and Actions of the Credentials Committee*, 6, 92, 102, 42.

71. Guidepost Solutions, *The Southern Baptist Convention Executive Committee's Response to Sexual Abuse Allegations and an Audit of the Procedures and Actions of the Credentials Committee*, 6.

72. Guidepost Solutions, *The Southern Baptist Convention Executive Committee's Response to Sexual Abuse Allegations and an Audit of the Procedures and Actions of the Credentials Committee*, 148.

73. Rose Gamble, "Vatican Women's Magazine Condemns Sexual Abuse of Nuns by Priests," *The Tablet*, February 1, 2019, https://www.thetablet.co.uk/news/11319/vatican-women-s-magazine-condemns-sexual-abuse-of-nuns-by-priests.

74. Christopher Livesay, "Abused Nuns Reveal Stories of Rape, Forced Abortions," PBS News Hour, June 11, 2019, https://www.pbs.org/newshour/show/abused-nuns-reveal-stories-of-rape-forced-abortions.

75. "Pope Admits Clerical Abuse of Nuns Including Sexual Slavery," BBC News, February 6, 2019, https://www.bbc.com/news/world-europe-47134033.

76. Livesay, "Abused Nuns Reveal Stories of Rape, Forced Abortions."

77. Gamble, "Vatican Women's Magazine Condemns Sexual Abuse of Nuns by Priests."

78. Diehl and Dzubinski, "Making the Invisible Visible: A Cross-Sector Analysis of Gender-Based Leadership Barriers," 197.

79. Sharon Mavin, Gina Grandy, and Jannine Williams, "Theorizing Women Leaders' Negative Relations with Other Women," in *Handbook of Research on Gender and Leadership*, ed. Susan R. Madsen (Northampton, MA: Edward Elgar Publishing, 2017), 338.

80. Belle Derks, Colette Van Laar, and Naomi Ellemers, "The Queen Bee Phenomenon: Why Women Leaders Distance Themselves from Junior Women," *The Leadership Quarterly* 27, no. 3 (2016): 458, https://doi.org/10.1016/j.leaqua.2015.12.007.

81. Mavin, Grandy, and Williams, "Theorizing Women Leaders' Negative Relations with Other Women," 337–38.

82. Sharon Mavin, Gina Grandy, and Jannine Williams, "Experiences of Women Elite Leaders Doing Gender: Intra-Gender Micro-Violence between Women," *British Journal of Management* 25, no. 3 (2014): 452, https://doi.org/10.1111/1467-8551.12057.

83. Graham L. Staines, C. Tavris, and T. E. Jayaratne, "The Queen Bee Syndrome," *Psychology Today* 7, no. 8 (January 1974): 55, 57–58, https://doi.org/10.1037/e400562009-003.

84. Katie Couric, *Going There* (New York, NY: Little, Brown and Company, 2021), 260.

85. Suzannah Weiss, "16 Women in Tech on Their Experiences with Workplace Sexism," *Bustle*, January 8, 2019, https://www.bustle.com/p/16-women-in-tech-on-their-experiences-with-workplace-sexism-15568057.

86. Rosalind Wiseman, "Dealing with Grown-up 'Mean Girls,'" *The New York Times*, December 5, 2019, https://www.nytimes.com/2019/12/05/well/family/dealing-with-grown-up-mean-girls.html.

87. M. Teresa Cardador, Patrick L. Hill, and Arghavan Salles, "Unpacking the Status-Leveling Burden for Women in Male-Dominated Occupations," *Administrative Science Quarterly* 67, no. 1 (2021): 276, https://doi.org/10.1177/00018392211038505.

88. Cardador, Hill, and Salles, "Unpacking the Status-Leveling Burden for Women in Male-Dominated Occupations," 259.

89. Cardador, Hill, and Salles, "Unpacking the Status-Leveling Burden for Women in Male-Dominated Occupations," 269.

90. Cardador, Hill, and Salles, "Unpacking the Status-Leveling Burden for Women in Male-Dominated Occupations," 254–55.

91. Sharon Mavin, "Queen Bees, Wannabees and Afraid to Bees: No More 'Best Enemies' for Women in Management?" *British Journal of Management* 19, no. s1 (2008), https://doi.org/10.1111/j.1467-8551.2008.00573.x. While "Wannabee" was defined by Mavin as a lower-level woman who wants to move up, we define "wannabee" behavior as occurring when a status-equal but hierarchy-lower woman exhibits hostility toward women she perceives as competition.

92. Nolo, "Retaliation," 2020, accessed May 31, 2020, https://www.nolo.com/dictionary/retaliation-term.html.

93. Adapted from U.S. Department of Labor, "What Is Retaliation?" accessed May 31, 2020, https://www.whistleblowers.gov/know_your_rights; U.S. Equal Employment Opportunity Commission, "Retaliation—Making It Personal," https://www.eeoc.gov/retaliation-making-it-personal.

94. U.S. Equal Employment Opportunity Commission, "Questions and Answers: Enforcement Guidance on Retaliation and Related Issues," accessed

May 31, 2020, https://www.eeoc.gov/laws/guidance/questions-and-answers
-enforcement-guidance-retaliation-and-related-issues.

95. U.S. Equal Employment Opportunity Commission, "Charge Statistics (Charges Filed with EEOC) FY 1997 through FY 2021," accessed August 24, 2022, https://www.eeoc.gov/statistics/charge-statistics-charges-filed-eeoc-fy -1997-through-fy-2021.

96. Susan Chira, "We Asked Women in Blue-Collar Workplaces about Harassment. Here Are Their Stories," *The New York Times*, December 29, 2017, https://www.nytimes.com/2017/12/29/us/blue-collar-women-harassment .html.

97. Stephenson, Dzubinski, and Diehl, "A Cross-Industry Comparison of How Women Leaders Experience Gender Bias," 13.

98. Chira, "We Asked Women in Blue-Collar Workplaces about Harassment. Here Are Their Stories."

99. Farlex Partner Medical Dictionary, "Hostile Behavior," 2020, accessed September 5, 2020; Psychology Encyclopedia, "Hostility," 2020, accessed September 5, 2020, https://psychology.jrank.org/pages/312/Hostility.html.

100. Lily Zheng, "Do Your Employees Feel Safe Reporting Abuse and Discrimination?" *Harvard Business Review*, October 8, 2020, https://hbr.org /2020/10/do-your-employees-feel-safe-reporting-abuse-and-discrimination.

101. Zheng, "Do Your Employees Feel Safe Reporting Abuse and Discrimination?"

102. Amy Gallo, "How to Approach an Office Romance (and How Not to)," *Harvard Business Review*, February 14, 2019, https://hbr.org/2019/02 /how-to-approach-an-office-romance-and-how-not-to.

103. Gallo, "How to Approach an Office Romance (and How Not to)."

104. Gallo, "How to Approach an Office Romance (and How Not to)."

105. Adapted from Amber L. Stephenson et al., "An Exploration of Gender Bias Affecting Women in Medicine," in *The Contributions of Health Care Management to Grand Health Care Challenges (Advances in Health Care Management, Vol. 20)*, ed. Jennifer L. Hefner and Ingrid Nembhard (Bingley, UK: Emerald Publishing Limited, 2021), 91.

106. Zheng, "Do Your Employees Feel Safe Reporting Abuse and Discrimination?"

CHAPTER 6

1. Anna Coumou, "Seattle's Beer Industry Is Sexist," *The Stranger*, June 5, 2019, https://www.thestranger.com/features/2019/06/05/40390034/seattles -beer-industry-is-sexist.

2. Gail Pheterson, "Alliances between Women: Overcoming Internalized Oppression and Internalized Domination," *Signs* 12, no. 1 (1986): 148, https://doi.org/10.1086/494302.

3. Leanne M. Dzubinski, Amy B. Diehl, and Michelle O. Taylor, "Women's Ways of Leading: The Environmental Effect," *Gender in Management: An International Journal* 34, no. 3 (2019): 236, https://doi.org/10.1108/GM-11-2017-0150.

4. Jillian Kramer, "Women in Science May Suffer Lasting Career Damage from COVID-19," *Scientific American*, August 12, 2020, https://www.scientificamerican.com/article/women-in-science-may-suffer-lasting-career-damage-from-covid-19/.

5. Todd Butler, "Beyond Tenure Clock Management," *Inside Higher Ed*, January 19, 2021, https://www.insidehighered.com/advice/2021/01/19/tenure-clock-extensions-arent-enough-help-support-researchers-and-their-work.

6. Heather Antecol, Kelly Bedard, and Jenna Stearns, "Equal but Inequitable: Who Benefits from Gender-Neutral Tenure Clock Stopping Policies?" *American Economic Review* 108, no. 9 (2018): 2425, https://doi.org/10.1257/aer.20160613.

7. Kramer, "Women in Science May Suffer Lasting Career Damage from COVID-19."

8. Lynn Hulsey, "'I Couldn't Find the Balance.' Impact of Women Leaving Workforce Will Ripple through Economy," *Dayton Daily News*, December 13, 2020, https://www.daytondailynews.com/news/i-couldnt-find-the-balance-impact-of-women-leaving-workforce-will-ripple-through-economy/BQYXTA4GV5GVRMZVZ7PX6JJ2MM/.

9. Manisha Aggarwal-Schifellite, "Women Mostly Stayed in Workforce as Pandemic Unfolded, Defying Forecasts," *The Harvard Gazette*, May 17, 2022, https://news.harvard.edu/gazette/story/2022/05/women-mostly-stayed-in-workforce-after-pandemic-hit/.

10. Claudia Goldin, "Understanding the Economic Impact of COVID-19 on Women," Working Paper, *National Bureau of Economic Research Working Paper Series* No. 29974 (2022): 25, https://doi.org/10.3386/w29974.

11. Amy B. Diehl, Leanne M. Dzubinski, and Amber L. Stephenson, "Never Quite Right: Identity Factors Contributing to Bias and Discrimination Experienced by Women Leaders" (Manuscript submitted for publication, December 26, 2022), 13.

12. Julianna Goldman, "It's Almost Impossible to Be a Mom in Television News," *The Atlantic*, December 4, 2018, https://www.theatlantic.com/family/archive/2018/12/motherhood-television-news-difficult/576913/.

13. Goldman, "It's Almost Impossible to Be a Mom in Television News."

14. Goldman, "It's Almost Impossible to Be a Mom in Television News."

15. Ellen K. Pao, "Ellen Pao: This Is How Sexism Works in Silicon Valley," *New York Magazine*, August 20, 2017, https://www.thecut.com/2017/08/ellen-pao-silicon-valley-sexism-reset-excerpt.html.

16. Gretchen Livingston and Deja Thomas, "Among 41 Countries, Only U.S. Lacks Paid Parental Leave," Pew Research Center, December 16, 2019, https://www.pewresearch.org/fact-tank/2019/12/16/u-s-lacks-mandated-paid-parental-leave/. Miranda Bryant, "Maternity Leave: U.S. Policy Is Worst on List of the World's Richest Countries," *The Guardian*, January 27, 2020, https://www.theguardian.com/us-news/2020/jan/27/maternity-leave-us-policy-worst-worlds-richest-countries. While the United States mandates twelve weeks of unpaid family leave through the Family and Medical Leave Act, only 60 percent of workers are eligible. As of May 2022, only ten U.S. states plus the District of Columbia have passed their own paid family leave laws.

17. "When Women Run," FiveThirtyEight, January 29, 2020, https://fivethirtyeight.com/audio-features/when-women-run/.

18. Katherine Goldstein, "I Was a Sheryl Sandberg Superfan. Then Her 'Lean in' Advice Failed Me," Vox, December 8, 2018, https://www.vox.com/first-person/2018/12/6/18128838/michelle-obama-lean-in-sheryl-sandberg.

19. Goldman, "It's Almost Impossible to Be a Mom in Television News."

20. U.S. Department of Labor, "Family and Medical Leave Act," accessed August 26, 2022, https://www.dol.gov/agencies/whd/fmla; Goldman, "It's Almost Impossible to Be a Mom in Television News."

21. Goldman, "It's Almost Impossible to Be a Mom in Television News."

22. Joanna Syrda, "Gendered Housework: Spousal Relative Income, Parenthood and Traditional Gender Identity Norms," *Work, Employment & Society* (2022): 8, https://doi.org/10.1177/09500170211069780; Soo Youn, "When Moms Out-Earn Their Husbands, They Gain More Housework, Study Says," *The Washington Post*, May 2, 2022, https://www.washingtonpost.com/lifestyle/2022/05/02/housework-divide-working-parents/.

23. Amy Chai, "Choose: Medicine or Family. I Almost Had Both," *Op-Med*, April 19, 2022, https://opmed.doximity.com/articles/choose-medicine-or-family-i-almost-had-both.

24. Michelle Obama, *Becoming* (New York, NY: Crown Publishing Group, 2018), 192.

25. Obama, *Becoming*, 192–93.

26. Liza Mundy, "I Rewatched Anita Hill's Testimony. So Much Has Changed. So Much Hasn't," Politico, September 23, 2018, https://www.politico.com/magazine/story/2018/09/23/rewatched-anita-hill-testimony-kavanaugh-metoo-220526.

27. Chia R. Feldblum and Victoria A. Lipnic, *Select Task Force on the Study of Harassment in the Workplace* (Washington, DC: US Equal Employment Opportunity Commission, June 2016), https://www.eeoc.gov/select-task-force-study-harassment-workplace.

28. Mundy, "I Rewatched Anita Hill's Testimony. So Much Has Changed. So Much Hasn't."; U.S. Equal Employment Opportunity Commission, "Harassment," accessed May 18, 2022, https://www.eeoc.gov/laws/types/harassment.cfm.

29. Jennie Steinberg, "Why Sexual Assault Survivors Blame Themselves," *Jennie Steinberg through the Woods Therapy* (blog), October 27, 2017, https://www.throughthewoodstherapy.com/sexual-assault-survivors-blame/.

30. Ashlie J. Siefkes-Andrew and Cassandra Alexopoulos, "Framing Blame in Sexual Assault: An Analysis of Attribution in News Stories About Sexual Assault on College Campuses," *Violence Against Women* 25, no. 6 (2018): 754–55, https://doi.org/10.1177/1077801218801111.

31. Amy B. Diehl and Leanne M. Dzubinski, "An Overview of Gender-Based Leadership Barriers," in *Handbook of Research on Gender and Leadership*, ed. Susan R. Madsen (Northampton, MA: Edward Elgar Publishing, 2017), 281.

32. Nicholas Rice, "Debra Messing Says She Was 'Way Too Skinny' on *Will & Grace*: 'I Couldn't Be Healthy and Size 2,'" *People*, August 8, 2020, https://people.com/health/debra-messing-was-too-skinny-while-on-will-and-grace/.

33. Leanne M. Dzubinski, *Playing by the Rules: How Women Lead in Evangelical Mission Organizations*, vol. 52 (Eugene, OR: Pickwick Publications, 2021), 189; Diehl and Dzubinski, "An Overview of Gender-Based Leadership Barriers," 281.

34. Dzubinski, *Playing by the Rules: How Women Lead in Evangelical Mission Organizations*, 52, 190.

35. Sarah Green Carmichael, "Boston Has Eliminated Sexism in the Workplace. Right?" *Boston*, July 23, 2017, https://www.bostonmagazine.com/news/2017/07/23/sexism-workplace/.

36. Carmichael, "Boston Has Eliminated Sexism in the Workplace. Right?"

37. Goldstein, "I Was a Sheryl Sandberg Superfan. Then Her 'Lean in' Advice Failed Me."

38. Suzannah Weiss, "16 Women in Tech on Their Experiences with Workplace Sexism," *Bustle*, January 8, 2019, https://www.bustle.com/p/16-women-in-tech-on-their-experiences-with-workplace-sexism-15568057.

39. Caroline Kitchener, "It's Not Just Sarah Milov. Female Academics Aren't Credited in Media 'All the Time,'" The Lily, July 20, 2019, https://www.thelily.com/its-not-just-sarah-milov-female-academics-arent-credited-in-media-all-the-time/.

40. Kitchener, "It's Not Just Sarah Milov. Female Academics Aren't Credited in Media 'All the Time.'"

41. David Walker, "Sexism in the Photo Industry: Can't We Do Better?" *Photo District News*, September 4, 2017, https://www.pdnonline.com/features/industry-updates/sexism-photo-industry-cant-better.

42. Walker, "Sexism in the Photo Industry: Can't We Do Better?"

43. Ersilia M. DeFilippis, "Putting the 'She' in Doctor," *JAMA Internal Medicine* 178, no. 3 (2018): 323–24, https://doi.org/10.1001/jamainternmed.2017.8362.

44. Arghavan Salles, "Gender Bias Narratives in Medicine," *Physician's Weekly*, July 23, 2019, https://www.physiciansweekly.com/gender-bias-narratives-in-medicine/.

45. Susan Chira, "We Asked Women in Blue-Collar Workplaces about Harassment. Here Are Their Stories," *The New York Times*, December 29, 2017, https://www.nytimes.com/2017/12/29/us/blue-collar-women-harassment.html.

46. Chira, "We Asked Women in Blue-Collar Workplaces about Harassment. Here Are Their Stories."

47. Chira, "We Asked Women in Blue-Collar Workplaces about Harassment. Here Are Their Stories."

48. Society of Professional Journalists, "SPJ Code of Ethics," last modified September 6, 2014, http://www.spj.org/ethicscode.asp.

49. Brigid Schulte, "How Myths about Sexual Harassment Keep Us in the Dark," CNN Opinion, October 9, 2018, https://www.cnn.com/2018/10/09/opinions/kavanaugh-spotlights-sexual-harassment-myths-new-america-schulte/index.html.

50. Lydia Price, "Serena Williams, Jennifer Lawrence and 22 More Stars Share Powerful Stories about Sexism in Hollywood," *People*, September 10, 2018, https://people.com/celebrity/sexism-in-hollywood-10-powerful-stories/.

51. Laura Brown, "Oprah Winfrey on Her Presidential Prospects, Aging Philosophy ('Take No Shit'), and Who Her Oprah Is," *InStyle*, January 25, 2018, https://www.yahoo.com/lifestyle/oprah-winfrey-her-presidential-prospects-133000053.html.

52. Pauline Rose Clance and Suzanne Ament Imes, "The Imposter Phenomenon in High Achieving Women: Dynamics and Therapeutic Intervention," *Psychotherapy: Theory, Research & Practice* 15, no. 3 (1978): 241, https://doi.org/10.1037/h0086006.

53. Irin Carmon and Amelia Schonbek, "Was It Worth It?" The Cut, September 30, 2019, https://www.thecut.com/2019/09/coming-forward-about-sexual-assault-and-what-comes-after.html.

54. Diehl and Dzubinski, "An Overview of Gender-Based Leadership Barriers," 281.

55. Heidi Schlumpf, "Called to Lead: Women Seminary Leaders Talk about Their Experience at the Top," *In Trust*, Autumn 2018, https://www.intrust.org/Magazine/Issues/Autumn-2018/Called-to-lead.

56. Susan Chira, "Why Women Aren't C.E.O.s, According to Women Who Almost Were," *The New York Times*, July 21, 2017, https://www.nytimes.com/2017/07/21/sunday-review/women-ceos-glass-ceiling.html.

CHAPTER 7

1. Francoise Brougher, "The Pinterest Paradox: Cupcakes and Toxicity," Medium, 2020, https://medium.com/digital-diplomacy/the-pinterest-paradox-cupcakes-and-toxicity-57ed6bd76960. Kate Duffy, "Pinterest Has Paid $22.5 Million to Settle a Gender Discrimination Suit from Former Executive Francoise Brougher, Who Claimed She Was Fired after Speaking Up," Business Insider, December 15, 2020, https://www.businessinsider.com/pinterest-francoise-brougher-gender-discrimination-suit-coo-2020-12. Brougher filed a gender discrimination lawsuit, which Pinterest settled for $22.5 million in 2020.

2. Brougher, "The Pinterest Paradox: Cupcakes and Toxicity."

3. Susan Wojcicki, "Read YouTube CEO Susan Wojcicki's Response to the Controversial Google Anti-Diversity Memo," *Fortune*, August 9, 2017, https://fortune.com/2017/08/09/google-diversity-memo-wojcicki.

4. "Gender Bias in the Workplace Is Alive and Well," *The Detroit Jewish News*, August 27, 2019, https://thejewishnews.com/2019/08/27/gender-bias-in-the-workplace-is-alive-and-well/.

5. Victoria Gregory, Elisabeth Harding, and Joel Steinberg, "Self-Employment Grows during COVID-19 Pandemic," *On the Economy, Federal Reserve Bank of St. Louis*, July 5, 2022, https://www.stlouisfed.org/on-the-economy/2022/jul/self-employment-returns-growth-path-pandemic.

6. Guy D. Fernando, Shalini Sarin Jain, and Arindam Tripathy, "This Cloud Has a Silver Lining: Gender Diversity, Managerial Ability, and Firm Performance," *Journal of Business Research* 117 (2020): 492, https://doi.org/10.1016/j.jbusres.2020.05.042.

7. Marcus Noland, Tyler Moran, and Barbara Kotschwar, "Is Gender Diversity Profitable? Evidence from a Global Survey," *Peterson Institute for Inter-*

national Economics Working Paper No. 16-3 (February, 2016): 8, https://doi.org /10.2139/ssrn.2729348.

8. Noland, Moran, and Kotschwar, "Is Gender Diversity Profitable? Evidence from a Global Survey," 16.

9. F. Arnaboldi et al., "Gender Diversity and Bank Misconduct," *Journal of Corporate Finance* 71 (2021): 17, https://doi.org/10.1016/j.jcorpfin.2020.101834.

10. Simona Galletta et al., "Gender Diversity and Sustainability Performance in the Banking Industry," *Corporate Social Responsibility and Environmental Management* 29, no. 1 (2022): 171, https://doi.org/10.1002/csr.2191.

11. Christopher J. D. Wallis et al., "Comparison of Postoperative Outcomes among Patients Treated by Male and Female Surgeons: A Population Based Matched Cohort Study," *BMJ* 359 (2017), https://doi.org/10.1136/bmj.j4366; Christopher J. D. Wallis et al., "Association of Surgeon-Patient Sex Concordance with Postoperative Outcomes," *JAMA Surgery* 157, no. 2 (2022): 146, https://doi.org/10.1001/jamasurg.2021.6339.

12. Elsie Boskamp, "Average Cost Per Hire [2022]: All Cost of Hiring Statistics," Zippia, January 5, 2022, https://www.zippia.com/advice/cost-of-hiring -statistics-average-cost-per-hire/.

13. Eduardo Vasconcellos, "What Does It Cost to Hire an Employee?" Business News Daily, June 29, 2022, https://www.businessnewsdaily.com/16562 -cost-of-hiring-an-employee.html.

14. Natalie Gontcharova, "And So I Quit: Tired of the Grind, Parents Are Creating New Work-Life Balance for Themselves," *Parents*, July 5, 2022, https://www.parents.com/parenting/work/how-parents-are-reshaping-their -work-life-balance/.

15. Amy B. Diehl, Amber L. Stephenson, and Leanne M. Dzubinski, "Research: How Bias against Women Persists in Female-Dominated Workplaces," *Harvard Business Review*, March 2, 2022, https://hbr.org/2022/03/research -how-bias-against-women-persists-in-female-dominated-workplaces.

16. Letian Zhang, "An Institutional Approach to Gender Diversity and Firm Performance," *Organization Science* 31, no. 2 (2020): 439, https://doi.org /10.1287/orsc.2019.1297.

17. M. S. Rao, "The Global Companies That Failed to Adapt to Change," *Training*, November 1, 2018, https://trainingmag.com/the-global-companies -that-failed-to-adapt-to-change/; Businessballs, "Dr Ichak Adizes—Ten Stages Corporate Life Cycle Model," accessed August 21, 2022, https://www .businessballs.com/organisational-culture/adizes-ten-stages-corporate-life -cycle-model/.

18. City for All Women Initiative, *Advancing Equity and Inclusion: A Guide for Municipalities* (Ottawa, ON: CAWI, June 2015), 17-18, https://www.cawi-ivtf.org/sites/default/files/publications/advancing-equity-inclusion-web_0.pdf.

19. Adapted from USAID, "Gender Equality Roadmap Organizational Phase Assessment," last modified May 27, 2022, https://www.usaid.gov/en gendering-industries/accelerated-program/roadmap-organizational-assessment. The explanation of the levels and suggested strategies are inspired from USAID's assessment document.

20. Catalyst, "The Great Reimagining: Equity for Women, Equity for All," 2022, accessed June 5, 2022, https://www.catalyst.org/the-great-reimagining/; USAID, "Gender Equality and Women's Empowerment," 2022, accessed June 5, 2022, https://www.usaid.gov/what-we-do/gender-equality-and-womens -empowerment; *Harvard Business Review*, "Gender," 2022, accessed June 5, 2022, https://hbr.org/topic/gender; *Harvard Business Review*, "Women at Work," 2022, accessed June 5, 2022, https://hbr.org/2018/01/podcast-women -at-work. Global nonprofit Catalyst offers a wealth of information and studies on building workplaces that work for women. *Harvard Business Review* has a "Women at Work" podcast and many helpful articles related to workplace gender diversity. USAID also offers resources on gender equality and women's empowerment.

21. Deborah M. Kolb et al., "Making Change: A Framework for Promoting Gender Equity in Organizations," in *Reader in Gender, Work, and Organization*, ed. Robin J. Ely, Erica G. Foldy, and Maureen A. Scully (Malden, MA: Blackwell Publishing, 2003), 13.

22. Mark Feffer, "How Small-Business Owners Successfully Delegate HR," Society for Human Resource Management, April 26, 2018, https://www .shrm.org/resourcesandtools/hr-topics/employee-relations/pages/how-small -business-owners-successfully-delegate-hr-.aspx.

23. USAID, "Gender Equity Executive Leadership Program," last modified May 20, 2022, https://www.usaid.gov/engendering-industries/leadership -program; Harvard Division of Continuing Education, "Inclusive Leadership for a Diverse Workplace," 2022, accessed June 17, 2022, https://professional.dce .harvard.edu/programs/inclusive-leadership-for-a-diverse-workplace/. These are just two examples of gender equity and inclusive leadership professional development programs.

24. City for All Women Initiative, *Advancing Equity and Inclusion: A Guide for Municipalities*, 23.

25. Noland, Moran, and Kotschwar, "Is Gender Diversity Profitable? Evidence from a Global Survey," 14.

26. Noland, Moran, and Kotschwar, "Is Gender Diversity Profitable? Evidence from a Global Survey," 15.

27. Amy B. Diehl et al., "Measuring the Invisible: Development and Multi-Industry Validation of the Gender Bias Scale for Women Leaders," *Human Resource Development Quarterly* 31, no. 3 (2020): 268, 70-71, https://doi.org/10.1002/hrdq.21389.

28. Kolb et al., "Making Change: A Framework for Promoting Gender Equity in Organizations," 14.

29. City for All Women Initiative, *Advancing Equity and Inclusion: A Guide for Municipalities*, 29.

30. Noland, Moran, and Kotschwar, "Is Gender Diversity Profitable? Evidence from a Global Survey," 13.

31. Diehl, Stephenson, and Dzubinski, "Research: How Bias against Women Persists in Female-Dominated Workplaces."

32. Noland, Moran, and Kotschwar, "Is Gender Diversity Profitable? Evidence from a Global Survey," 3.

33. Noland, Moran, and Kotschwar, "Is Gender Diversity Profitable? Evidence from a Global Survey," 16.

34. Diehl, Stephenson, and Dzubinski, "Research: How Bias against Women Persists in Female-Dominated Workplaces."

35. Oriane Georgeac and Aneeta Rattan, "Stop Making the Business Case for Diversity," *Harvard Business Review*, June 15, 2022, https://hbr.org/2022/06/stop-making-the-business-case-for-diversity.

36. Noland, Moran, and Kotschwar, "Is Gender Diversity Profitable? Evidence from a Global Survey," 15.

37. City for All Women Initiative, *Advancing Equity and Inclusion: A Guide for Municipalities*, 30.

CHAPTER 8

1. Amy B. Diehl, "Approaches of Women in Higher Education Leadership: Navigating Adversity, Barriers and Obstacles," in *Women and Leadership in Higher Education*, ed. Karen A. Longman and Susan R. Madsen (Charlotte, NC: Information Age, 2014), 135–51.

2. Diehl, "Approaches of Women in Higher Education Leadership: Navigating Adversity, Barriers and Obstacles," 142.

3. Diehl, "Approaches of Women in Higher Education Leadership: Navigating Adversity, Barriers and Obstacles," 143.

4. Ella F. Washington, "Recognizing and Responding to Microaggressions at Work," *Harvard Business Review*, May 10, 2022, https://hbr.org/2022/05/recognizing-and-responding-to-microaggressions-at-work.

5. Diehl, "Approaches of Women in Higher Education Leadership: Navigating Adversity, Barriers and Obstacles," 144.

6. Leanne M. Dzubinski, M. Elizabeth Lewis Hall, and Richard L. Starcher, "The Stained-Glass Partition: Cross-Sex Collegial Relationships in Christian Academia," *Christian Higher Education* 20, no. 3 (2021): 202, https://doi.org/10.1080/15363759.2020.1756532.

7. Leanne M. Dzubinski, *Playing by the Rules: How Women Lead in Evangelical Mission Organizations*, vol. 52 (Eugene, OR: Pickwick Publications, 2021), 209.

BIBLIOGRAPHY

Andersen, Jens Peter, Mathias Wullum Nielsen, Nicole L. Simone, Resa E. Lewiss, and Reshma Jagsi. "COVID-19 Medical Papers Have Fewer Women First Authors than Expected." *eLife* 9 (2020): e58807. https://doi.org /10.7554/eLife.58807.

Andersen, Margaret L., and Patricia Hill Collins, eds. *Race, Class, and Gender: An Anthology.* 6th ed. Belmont, CA: Thomson Wadsworth, 2007.

Andersen, Margaret L., and Dana Hysock. *Thinking about Women: Sociological Perspectives on Race and Gender.* 8th ed. Boston, MA: Pearson, 2009.

Antecol, Heather, Kelly Bedard, and Jenna Stearns. "Equal but Inequitable: Who Benefits from Gender-Neutral Tenure Clock Stopping Policies?" *American Economic Review* 108, no. 9 (2018): 2420–41. https://doi.org/10.1257 /aer.20160613.

Arnaboldi, F., B. Casu, A. Gallo, E. Kalotychou, and A. Sarkisyan. "Gender Diversity and Bank Misconduct." *Journal of Corporate Finance* 71 (2021): 1–30. https://doi.org/10.1016/j.jcorpfin.2020.101834.

Association for Psychological Science. "Workplace Ostracism More Distressing than Harassment." June 13, 2014. https://www.psychologicalscience.org /news/minds-business/workplace-ostracism-more-distressing-than-harass ment.html.

Beck, Julie. "The Concept Creep of 'Emotional Labor.'" *The Atlantic,* November 26, 2018. https://www.theatlantic.com/family/archive/2018/11/arlie -hochschild-housework-isnt-emotional-labor/576637/.

Berdahl, Jennifer L. "Harassment Based on Sex: Protecting Social Status in the Context of Gender Hierarchy." *Academy of Management Review* 32, no. 2 (2007): 641–58. https://doi.org/10.5465/amr.2007.24351879.

Bierema, Laura L. "Critiquing Human Resource Development's Dominant Masculine Rationality and Evaluating Its Impact." *Human Resource Development Review* 8, no. 1 (2009): 68–96. https://doi.org/10.1177/1534484308330020.

Borchers, Callum. "Your Office Is Open and the Liquor Is Flowing." *The Wall Street Journal*, April 14, 2022. https://www.wsj.com/articles/your-office-is-open-and-the-liquor-is-flowing-hybrid-work-beer-wine-booze-11649871713.

Calás, Marta B., and Linda Smircich. "Dangerous Liaisons: The 'Feminine-in-Management' Meets 'Globalization.'" *Business Horizons* 36, no. 2 (1993): 71–81. https://doi.org/10.1016/S0007-6813(05)80041-2.

Callahan, Molly. "Is There Implicit Gender Bias in the Field of Economics?" *Phys.org*, January 15, 2020. https://phys.org/news/2020-01-implicit-gender-bias-field-economics.html.

Cardador, M. Teresa, Patrick L. Hill, and Arghavan Salles. "Unpacking the Status-Leveling Burden for Women in Male-Dominated Occupations." *Administrative Science Quarterly* 67, no. 1 (2021): 237–84. https://doi.org/10.1177/00018392211038505.

Cartei, Valentina, Jane Oakhill, Alan Garnham, Robin Banerjee, and David Reby. "'This Is What a Mechanic Sounds Like': Children's Vocal Control Reveals Implicit Occupational Stereotypes." *Psychological Science* 31, no. 8 (2020): 957–67. https://doi.org/10.1177/0956797620929297.

City for All Women Initiative. *Advancing Equity and Inclusion: A Guide for Municipalities*. Ottawa, ON: CAWI, June 2015. https://www.cawi-ivtf.org/sites/default/files/publications/advancing-equity-inclusion-web_0.pdf.

Clance, Pauline Rose, and Suzanne Ament Imes. "The Imposter Phenomenon in High Achieving Women: Dynamics and Therapeutic Intervention." *Psychotherapy: Theory, Research & Practice* 15, no. 3 (1978): 241–47. https://doi.org/10.1037/h0086006.

Collins, Caitlyn, Liana Christin Landivar, Leah Ruppanner, and William J. Scarborough. "COVID-19 and the Gender Gap in Work Hours." *Gender, Work & Organization* 28, no. S1 (2020): 101–12. https://doi.org/10.1111/gwao.12506.

Cortina, L. M., and V. J. Magley. "Raising Voice, Risking Retaliation: Events Following Interpersonal Mistreatment in the Workplace." *Journal of Occupational Health Psychology* 8, no. 4 (2003): 247–65. https://doi.org/10.1037/1076-8998.8.4.247.

Crenshaw, Kimberle. "Demarginalizing the Intersection of Race and Sex: A Black Feminist Critique of Antidiscrimination Doctrine, Feminist Theory and Antiracist Politics." *University of Chicago Legal Forum* 1989, no. 1 (1989): 139–67. https://chicagounbound.uchicago.edu/uclf/vol1989/iss1/8/.

Crittenden, Ann. *The Price of Motherhood: Why the Most Important Job in the World Is Still the Least Valued*. New York, NY: Metropolitan Books, 2001.

Derks, Belle, Colette Van Laar, and Naomi Ellemers. "The Queen Bee Phenomenon: Why Women Leaders Distance Themselves from Junior Women." *The Leadership Quarterly* 27, no. 3 (2016): 456–69. https://doi.org/10.1016/j.leaqua.2015.12.007.

Diehl, Amy B. "Approaches of Women in Higher Education Leadership: Navigating Adversity, Barriers and Obstacles." In *Women and Leadership in Higher Education*, edited by Karen A. Longman and Susan R. Madsen, 135–51. Charlotte, NC: Information Age, 2014.

———. "'Guys' Is Not Gender-Neutral—Let's Stop Using It Like It Is." *Fast Company*, April 27, 2021. https://www.fastcompany.com/90629391/guys-is-not-gender-neutral-lets-stop-using-it-like-it-is.

———. "How Gender Bias Inhibits Progress and What Leaders Can Do About It." *Ms. Magazine*, August 18, 2021. https://msmagazine.com/2021/08/18/gender-bias-covid-vaccine-katalin-kariko/.

———. "Making Meaning of Adversity: Experiences of Women Leaders in Higher Education." PhD diss., Indiana University of Pennsylvania, 2013. Proquest (3589972).

Diehl, Amy B., and Leanne M. Dzubinski. "Making the Invisible Visible: A Cross-Sector Analysis of Gender-Based Leadership Barriers." *Human Resource Development Quarterly* 27, no. 2 (2016): 181–206. https://doi.org/10.1002/hrdq.21248.

———. "An Overview of Gender-Based Leadership Barriers." In *Handbook of Research on Gender and Leadership*, edited by Susan R. Madsen, 271–86. Northampton, MA: Edward Elgar Publishing, 2017.

———. "We Need to Stop 'Untitling' and 'Uncredentialing' Professional Women." *Fast Company*, January 22, 2021. https://www.fastcompany.com/90596628/we-need-to-stop-untitling-and-uncredentialing-professional-women.

———. "We Need to Talk about Using Pet Names for Women at Work." *Fast Company*, October 29, 2020. https://www.fastcompany.com/90569439/we-need-to-talk-about-using-pet-names-for-women-at-work.

———. "When People Assume You're Not in Charge Because You're a Woman." *Harvard Business Review*, December 22, 2021. https://hbr.org/2021/12/when-people-assume-youre-not-in-charge-because-youre-a-woman.

Diehl, Amy B., Amber L. Stephenson, and Leanne M. Dzubinski. "Research: How Bias against Women Persists in Female-Dominated Workplaces." *Harvard Business Review*, March 2, 2022. https://hbr.org/2022/03/research-how-bias-against-women-persists-in-female-dominated-workplaces.

Diehl, Amy B., Amber L. Stephenson, Leanne M. Dzubinski, and David C. Wang. "Measuring the Invisible: Development and Multi-Industry Validation of the Gender Bias Scale for Women Leaders." *Human Resource Development Quarterly* 31, no. 3 (2020): 249–80. https://doi.org/10.1002/hrdq.21389.

Dzubinski, Leanne M. *Playing by the Rules: How Women Lead in Evangelical Mission Organizations.* Vol. 52, Eugene, OR: Pickwick Publications, 2021.

———. "Playing by the Rules: How Women Lead in Evangelical Mission Organizations." PhD diss., University of Georgia, 2013. http://getd.libs.uga.edu/pdfs/dzubinski_leanne_b_201305_phd.pdf.

Dzubinski, Leanne M., Amy B. Diehl, and Michelle O. Taylor. "Women's Ways of Leading: The Environmental Effect." *Gender in Management: An International Journal* 34, no. 3 (2019): 233–50. https://doi.org/10.1108/GM-11-2017-0150.

Dzubinski, Leanne M., M. Elizabeth Lewis Hall, and Richard L. Starcher. "The Stained-Glass Partition: Cross-Sex Collegial Relationships in Christian Academia." *Christian Higher Education* 20, no. 3 (2021): 184–208. https://doi.org/10.1080/15363759.2020.1756532.

Elsesser, Kim, and Letitia Anne Peplau. "The Glass Partition: Obstacles to Cross-Sex Friendships at Work." *Human Relations* 59, no. 8 (2006): 1077–100. https://doi.org/10.1177/0018726706068783.

Feldblum, Chia R., and Victoria A. Lipnic. *Select Task Force on the Study of Harassment in the Workplace.* Washington, DC: US Equal Employment Opportunity Commission, June 2016. https://www.eeoc.gov/select-task-force-study-harassment-workplace.

Fernando, Guy D., Shalini Sarin Jain, and Arindam Tripathy. "This Cloud Has a Silver Lining: Gender Diversity, Managerial Ability, and Firm Performance." *Journal of Business Research* 117 (2020): 484–96. https://doi.org/10.1016/j.jbusres.2020.05.042.

Flaherty, Colleen. "No Room of One's Own." *Inside Higher Ed*, April 21, 2020. https://www.insidehighered.com/news/2020/04/21/early-journal-submission-data-suggest-covid-19-tanking-womens-research-productivity.

Foust-Cummings, Heather, Sarah Dinolfo, and Jennifer Kohler. *Sponsoring Women to Success.* New York, NY: Catalyst, April 17, 2011. https://www.catalyst.org/research/sponsoring-women-to-success/.

Fricker, Miranda. *Epistemic Injustice Power and the Ethics of Knowing.* New York, NY: Oxford University Press, 2007.

Gale, Rebecca. "Should Unpaid Labor Like Childcare Be Part of the GDP? One Group Is Trying to Make It Happen." *Fortune*, April 28, 2022. https://fortune.com/2022/04/28/eve-rodsky-unpaid-labor-part-of-gdp-by-2030/.

Galletta, Simona, Sebastiano Mazzù, Valeria Naciti, and Carlo Vermiglio. "Gender Diversity and Sustainability Performance in the Banking Industry."

Corporate Social Responsibility and Environmental Management 29, no. 1 (2022): 161–74. https://doi.org/10.1002/csr.2191.

Gallo, Amy. "How to Approach an Office Romance (and How Not to)." *Harvard Business Review*, February 14, 2019. https://hbr.org/2019/02/how-to-approach-an-office-romance-and-how-not-to.

Gaucher, Danielle, Justin Friesen, and Aaron C. Key. "Evidence That Gendered Wording in Job Advertisements Exists and Sustains Gender Inequality." *Journal of Personality and Social Psychology* 101, no. 1 (2011): 109–28. https://doi.org/10.1037/a0022530.

Glass, Christy, and Alison Cook. "Leading at the Top: Understanding Women's Challenges above the Glass Ceiling." *The Leadership Quarterly* 27, no. 1 (2016): 51–63. https://doi.org/10.1016/j.leaqua.2015.09.003.

Goldin, Claudia. "Understanding the Economic Impact of COVID-19 on Women." Working Paper. *National Bureau of Economic Research Working Paper Series* No. 29974 (2022). https://doi.org/10.3386/w29974.

Grandis, Jennifer R. "Fishing, Strip Clubs and Golf: How Male-Focused Networking in Medicine Blocks Female Colleagues from Top Jobs." *The Conversation*, April 8, 2022. https://theconversation.com/fishing-strip-clubs-and-golf-how-male-focused-networking-in-medicine-blocks-female-colleagues-from-top-jobs-179931.

Hall, M. Elizabeth Lewis, Brad Christerson, and Shelly Cunningham. "Sanctified Sexism: Religious Beliefs and the Gender Harassment of Academic Women." *Psychology of Women Quarterly* 34, no. 2 (2010): 181–85. https://doi.org/10.1111/j.1471-6402.2010.01560.x.

Hansen, Benjamin, Joseph J. Sabia, and Jessamyn Schaller. "Schools, Job Flexibility, and Married Women's Labor Supply: Evidence from the COVID-19 Pandemic." *National Bureau of Economic Research Working Paper Series* No. 29660 (2022). https://doi.org/10.3386/w29660.

Harris, Ainsley. "Why 'Flexibility' May Be the Least Helpful Thing Companies Can Offer Working Parents Right Now." *Fast Company*, December 4, 2020. https://www.fastcompany.com/90581275/why-flexibility-may-be-the-least-helpful-thing-a-company-could-offer-a-working-parent-right-now.

Heilman, Madeline E., and Julie J. Chen. "Same Behavior, Different Consequences: Reactions to Men's and Women's Altruistic Citizenship Behavior." *Journal of Applied Psychology* 90, no. 3 (2005): 431–44. https://doi.org/10.1037/0021-9010.90.3.431.

Hsu, Andrea. "'This Is Too Much': Working Moms Are Reaching the Breaking Point during the Pandemic." NPR, September 29, 2020. https://www.npr.org/2020/09/29/918127776/this-is-too-much-working-moms-are-reaching-the-breaking-point-during-the-pandemi.

Hsu, Andrea, Kathryn Anne Edwards, and Farida Mercedes. "Why the Pandemic Is Forcing So Many Women to Leave Their Jobs." By Michel Martin. *All Things Considered.* National Public Radio. November 14, 2020. https://www.npr.org/2020/11/14/935018298/why-the-pandemic-is-forcing-so-many-women-to-leave-their-jobs.

Ibarra, Herminia. "A Lack of Sponsorship Is Keeping Women from Advancing into Leadership." *Harvard Business Review*, August 19, 2019. https://hbr.org/2019/08/a-lack-of-sponsorship-is-keeping-women-from-advancing-into-leadership.

Kanter, Rosabeth Moss. *Men and Women of the Corporation.* New York, NY: Basic Books, 1977.

Kashen, Julie, Sarah Jane Glynn, and Amanda Novello. *How COVID-19 Sent Women's Workforce Progress Backward.* Washington, DC: Center for American Progress, October 30, 2020. https://www.americanprogress.org/issues/women/reports/2020/10/30/492582/covid-19-sent-womens-workforce-progress-backward/.

Kolb, Deborah M., Joyce K. Fletcher, Debra. E. Meyerson, Deborah Merrill-Sands, and Robin J. Ely. "Making Change: A Framework for Promoting Gender Equity in Organizations." In *Reader in Gender, Work, and Organization*, edited by Robin J. Ely, Erica G. Foldy, and Maureen A. Scully, 10–15. Malden, MA: Blackwell Publishing, 2003.

Korzec, Rebecca. "The Glass Ceiling in Law Firms: A Form of Sex-Based Discrimination." *Journal of Employment Discrimination Law* 2, no. 3 (2000): 251–63. https://ssrn.com/abstract=1418046.

Lloyd-Jones, Brenda. "Implications of Race and Gender in Higher Education Administration: An African American Woman's Perspective." *Advances in Developing Human Resources* 11, no. 5 (2009): 606–18. https://doi.org/10.1177/1523422309351820.

Mavin, Sharon. "Queen Bees, Wannabees and Afraid to Bees: No More 'Best Enemies' for Women in Management?" *British Journal of Management* 19, no. s1 (2008): S75–S84. https://doi.org/10.1111/j.1467-8551.2008.00573.x.

Mavin, Sharon, Gina Grandy, and Jannine Williams. "Experiences of Women Elite Leaders Doing Gender: Intra-Gender Micro-Violence between Women." *British Journal of Management* 25, no. 3 (2014): 439–55. https://doi.org/10.1111/1467-8551.12057.

———. "Theorizing Women Leaders' Negative Relations with Other Women." In *Handbook of Research on Gender and Leadership*, edited by Susan R. Madsen, 328–43. Northampton, MA: Edward Elgar Publishing, 2017.

Miller, Michael G., and Joseph L. Sutherland. "The Effect of Gender on Interruptions at Congressional Hearings." *American Political Science Review* (2022): 1–19. https://doi.org/10.1017/S0003055422000260.

Mohr, Tara Sophia. "Why Women Don't Apply for Jobs Unless They're 100% Qualified." *Harvard Business Review*, August 25, 2014. https://hbr.org/2014/08/why-women-dont-apply-for-jobs-unless-theyre-100-qualified.

Noe, Raymond A. "Women and Mentoring: A Review and Research Agenda." *Academy of Management Review* 13, no. 1 (1988): 65–78. https://doi.org/10.2307/258355.

Noland, Marcus, Tyler Moran, and Barbara Kotschwar. "Is Gender Diversity Profitable? Evidence from a Global Survey." *Peterson Institute for International Economics Working Paper No. 16-3.* (February 2016). https://doi.org/10.2139/ssrn.2729348.

Obama, Michelle. *Becoming.* New York, NY: Crown Publishing Group, 2018.

Pao, Ellen K. *Reset: My Fight for Inclusion and Lasting Change.* New York, NY: Spiegel & Grau, 2017.

Papanek, Hanna. "Men, Women, and Work: Reflections on the Two-Person Career." *American Journal of Sociology* 78, no. 4 (1973): 852–72. https://doi.org/10.1086/225406.

Parker, Patsy. "The Historical Role of Women in Higher Education." *Administrative Issues Journal* 5, no. 1 (2015): 3–14. https://doi.org/10.5929/2015.5.1.1.

Pheterson, Gail. "Alliances between Women: Overcoming Internalized Oppression and Internalized Domination." *Signs* 12, no. 1 (1986): 146–60. https://doi.org/10.1086/494302.

Sadker, Myra, and David Miller Sadker. *Failing at Fairness: How America's Schools Cheat Girls.* New York, NY: Scribner, 2010.

Siefkes-Andrew, Ashlie J., and Cassandra Alexopoulos. "Framing Blame in Sexual Assault: An Analysis of Attribution in News Stories about Sexual Assault on College Campuses." *Violence Against Women* 25, no. 6 (2018): 743–62. https://doi.org/10.1177/1077801218801111.

Solomon, Barbara Miller. *In the Company of Educated Women: A History of Women and Higher Education in America.* New Haven, CT: Yale University Press, 1985.

Staines, Graham L., C. Tavris, and T. E. Jayaratne. "The Queen Bee Syndrome." *Psychology Today* 7, no. 8 (January 1974): 55–60. https://doi.org/10.1037/e400562009-003.

Stephenson, Amber L., Amy B. Diehl, Leanne M. Dzubinski, Mara McErlean, John Huppertz, and Mandeep Sidhu. "An Exploration of Gender Bias affecting Women in Medicine." In *The Contributions of Health Care Management to Grand Health Care Challenges (Advances in Health Care Management, Vol. 20),* edited by Jennifer L. Hefner and Ingrid Nembhard, 77–95. Bingley, UK: Emerald Publishing Limited, 2021.

Stephenson, Amber L., Leanne M. Dzubinski, and Amy B. Diehl. "A Cross-Industry Comparison of How Women Leaders Experience Gender Bias." *Personnel Review* (2022). https://doi.org/10.1108/PR-02-2021-0091.

Stewart, Emily. "Women Are Burned Out at Work and at Home." Vox, May 18, 2020. https://www.vox.com/policy-and-politics/2020/5/18/21260209 /facebook-sheryl-sandberg-interview-lean-in-women-coronavirus.

Stout, Jane G., and Nilanjana Dasgupta. "When He Doesn't Mean You: Gender-Exclusive Language as Ostracism." *Personality and Social Psychology Bulletin* 37, no. 6 (2011): 757–69. https://doi.org/10.1177/0146167211406434.

Syrda, Joanna. "Gendered Housework: Spousal Relative Income, Parenthood and Traditional Gender Identity Norms." *Work, Employment & Society* (2022). https://doi.org/10.1177/09500170211069780.

Tallon, Tina. "A Century of 'Shrill': How Bias in Technology Hurts Women's Voices." *The New Yorker*, September 3, 2019. https://www.newyorker.com /culture/cultural-comment/a-century-of-shrill-how-bias-in-technology -has-hurt-womens-voices.

Tulshyan, Ruchika. "Women of Color Get Asked to Do More 'Office Housework.' Here's How They Can Say No." *Harvard Business Review*, April 6, 2018. https://hbr.org/2018/04/women-of-color-get-asked-to-do-more -office-housework-heres-how-they-can-say-no.

University of Sussex. "Jobs for the Boys: How Children Give Voice to Gender Stereotyped Job Roles." *Phys.org*, July 27, 2020. https://phys.org /news/2020-07-jobs-boys-children-voice-gender.html.

USAID. "Gender Equality Roadmap Organizational Phase Assessment." Last modified May 27, 2022. https://www.usaid.gov/engendering-industries /accelerated-program/roadmap-organizational-assessment.

Waismel-Manor, R., V. Wasserman, and O. Shamir-Balderman. "No Room of Her Own: Married Couples' Negotiation of Workspace at Home During COVID-19." *Sex Roles* 85 (2021): 636–49. https://doi.org/10.1007/s11199 -021-01246-1.

Wallis, Christopher J. D., Angela Jerath, Natalie Coburn, Zachary Klaassen, Amy N. Luckenbaugh, Diana E. Magee, Amanda E. Hird, et al. "Association of Surgeon-Patient Sex Concordance with Postoperative Outcomes." *JAMA Surgery* 157, no. 2 (2022): 146–56. https://doi.org/10.1001/jama surg.2021.6339.

Wallis, Christopher J. D., Bheeshma Ravi, Natalie Coburn, Robert K. Nam, Allan S. Detsky, and Raj Satkunasivam. "Comparison of Postoperative Outcomes among Patients Treated by Male and Female Surgeons: A Population Based

Matched Cohort Study." *BMJ* 359 (2017): j4366. https://doi.org/10.1136/bmj.j4366.

Washington, Ella F. "Recognizing and Responding to Microaggressions at Work." *Harvard Business Review*, May 10, 2022. https://hbr.org/2022/05/recognizing-and-responding-to-microaggressions-at-work.

Williams, Joan C. "Stop Asking Women of Color to Do Unpaid Diversity Work." Bloomberg, April 14, 2022. https://www.bloomberg.com/opinion/articles/2022-04-14/women-of-color-in-tech-get-saddled-with-more-office-housework.

Williams, Joan C., and Marina Multhaup. "For Women and Minorities to Get Ahead, Managers Must Assign Work Fairly." *Harvard Business Review*, March 5, 2018. https://hbr.org/2018/03/for-women-and-minorities-to-get-ahead-managers-must-assign-work-fairly.

Woolfe, Virginia. *A Room of One's Own*. London, UK: Hogarth Press, 1935 [1929].

Youn, Soo. "When Moms Out-Earn Their Husbands, They Gain More Housework, Study Says." *The Washington Post*, May 2, 2022. https://www.washingtonpost.com/lifestyle/2022/05/02/housework-divide-working-parents/.

Zhang, Letian. "An Institutional Approach to Gender Diversity and Firm Performance." *Organization Science* 31, no. 2 (2020): 439–57. https://doi.org/10.1287/orsc.2019.1297.

Zheng, Lily. "Do Your Employees Feel Safe Reporting Abuse and Discrimination?" *Harvard Business Review*, October 8, 2020. https://hbr.org/2020/10/do-your-employees-feel-safe-reporting-abuse-and-discrimination.

INDEX

ability:
   discriminatory factor, 135, 154;
   women's, 105, 135, 138, 177,
   208
Abramson, Jill, 31–33
abuse:
   institutional, 8, 146–47;
   physical, 151.
      See also retaliatory actions
   reporting, 155, 157, 160, 173,
   181;
   sexual, 145–46
accusations:
   false, 151.
      See also retaliatory actions
   rape, 117, 145
acknowledgement:
   lack of, 86.
      See also invisible
   contributions
   for sponsors, 90
acquiescence, 6–7, 50, 161–83,
   186–87, 198;
   shattering, 178–83
actions:
   legal, 129, 133;
   negative job, 151, 197.
      See also retaliation
   strategic, 197;

taking notes of discriminatory,
   154
Adams, Amy, 113
"add women and stir," 192
administrative work, 95.
   See also office housework
adversity, 7, 83, 203, 209
affirmation, 86, 103, 171
Affleck, Ben, 144
African American women, 46, 80, 104.
   See also Black women
age, discriminatory factor, 129–30,
   154, 193
age discrimination, 134–35, 151
Age Discrimination in Employment
   Act, 151
agency, women's, 42, 210
agentic leadership style, 33
aggressive, 53.
   See also derogatory labels for
   women
Ailes, Roger, 145
alcohol-centered events, 13–14, 27,
   36, 81, 169
allies:
   finding, 206;
   strategies for, 35–43, 67–70, 89,
   91 93, 121–23, 125–26, 154, 156,
   158–59, 179, 181–83, 204

ABOUT THE AUTHORS

Amy Diehl, PhD, is an award-winning information technology leader and gender equity researcher who has authored numerous scholarly journal articles and book chapters. Her writing has also appeared in *Harvard Business Review*, *Fast Company*, and *Ms. Magazine*. *Glass Walls* is her first book. She is also a sought-after speaker, consultant, and lawsuit expert witness. She resides in a small town in Pennsylvania. You can visit her online at amy-diehl.com.

Leanne M. Dzubinski, PhD, is acting dean and associate professor of intercultural education in the Cook School of Intercultural Studies at Biola University in California. She is the author of *Women in the Mission of the Church: Their Opportunities and Obstacles throughout Christian History* and *Playing by the Rules: How Women Lead in Evangelical Mission Organizations*. She has written many scholarly articles related to gender bias, and her work has been published in *Harvard Business Review* and *Fast Company*. Prior to moving to California, she worked in western Europe for many years.